A Community Social Worker's Handbook

Bob MacLaren

A
Community
Social
Worker's
Handbook

ROGER HADLEY
MIKE COOPER
PETER DALE and
GRAHAM STACY

TAVISTOCK PUBLICATIONS
London and New York

First published in 1987 by
Tavistock Publications Ltd
11 New Fetter Lane, London EC4P 4EE

© 1987 Roger Hadley, Mike Cooper, Peter Dale, and Graham Stacy

Photoset by Mayhew Typesetting, Bristol, England
Printed in Great Britain by Richard Clay Ltd,
Bungay, Suffolk

British Library Cataloguing in Publication Data

A Community social worker's handbook.
  1. Social group work — Great Britain
  2. Community development — Great Britain
  I. Hadley, Roger
  361.8'0941   HV245
ISBN 0-422-60430-5
ISBN 0-422-60440-2 Pbk

Contents

Contributors

Contributors' positions are those at the time they prepared material for this book. Current positions, where different, are given in brackets.

Jan Cocks, Social Worker — Honor Oak Team, London Borough of Lewisham

Mike Cooper, Area Officer (Assistant Director, Wakefield) — Normanton Team, Wakefield

Eleni Diakou, Team Leader (Neighbourhood Officer, Islington) — Docklands Team, London Borough of Newham

Chris Sevink, Team Manager (Foremost Project, East Sussex) — Whitehawk Team, East Sussex

Graham Stacy, Team Leader — Longbenton Team, North Tyneside

Stuart Watts, Social Worker (Senior Social Worker, Grampian) — Area 3, London Borough of Newham (Docklands Team)

Roger Wearing, Area Controller — Huntly Team, Grampian

Neil Weatherall, Team Manager — Rye Team, East Sussex

Gary Westwater, Area Officer (Assistant District Manager, Strathclyde) — Easterhouse, Strathclyde (Lochend Team)

Preface and acknowledgements

At those times when practice reaches impatiently ahead of established theory and teaching, a gap in knowledge and understanding is often created between the pioneers of change and the rest of us. Such gaps can readily widen to the point where they impede the sharing and evaluation of the experience of the innovators. The recent development of community social work provides an example of this dilemma. Over the last decade an increasing number of local-authority social services teams have begun to test out more localized and community-orientated methods of working. Many of the practitioners involved have reported significant gains from these changes. Yet most of the teaching and writing about social work continues to be based on traditional models of client-centred work in which the social worker operates with individual users in one-to-one relationships and with little regard to contexts wider than those of the immediate family.

The problem arises in part from the caution with which many people greet new or relatively untried methods. It can also be linked to resistance from the vested interests of the professions and others involved, and to the fact that most social work teachers gained their own field experience in earlier systems. In the longer run, perhaps, as more research is undertaken and there is greater understanding of the processes involved, the social work establishment may begin to respond more effectively to these changes. In the meantime, however, in the field moves towards more community-orientated methods continue and the practitioners and others directly and indirectly involved need to share their experiences and learn from each other if each new venture is not to be forced to discover the wheel afresh. Indeed, anyone taking part in meetings or training programmes on community social work can hardly fail to be struck by the lively awareness of this need, whether on the part of practitioners, students, or teachers. The more experienced workers are bombarded with questions: what do you do if . . . ?, what do you do when . . . ?

It is as a means of extending and systematizing such sharing of experience that we have written this handbook. We make no claims to offer an academic treatise, in the sense of evaluative research. But in bringing together the experience of several well-established community-orientated teams within a common analytical framework, we believe the book goes well beyond being merely anecdotal and can help in coping with the common challenges posed by the introduction and development of community social work.

The book, like community social work itself, has been a collaborative effort. The raw material from which it has been constructed has been provided principally by the team managers and/or leaders of eight social services teams in different parts of Britain. Two of these, Mike Cooper and Graham Stacy, are co-authors of the study, and the framework used was first tested out on their experience. Subsequently, the scheme developed was applied to the other six teams. Systematic and detailed information on team experience was prepared within this framework by the contributors in these teams (representing their own and not their employers' views). To these contributors for sharing their experience and wisdom, and for their patient and thoughtful responses to our questioning, we owe our greatest debt of thanks. Without their contributions the book could not have been written. The four authors have shared in analysing and systematizing these contributions, and they alone are responsible for the final shape of the book and the guidelines it proposes for practitioners. Roger Hadley was responsible for co-ordinating the work of the authors and the final editing of the manuscript. In all other senses the book is their collective work.

We should like to thank the following for permission to reproduce material from their work: Jerôme Guay (*Table 1*, pp. 8–9); Paul Henderson and David Thomas (*Table 3*, p. 58); Charles Froland, Diane Pancoast, Nancy Chapman, and Priscilla Kimboko (*Table 5*, pp. 110–13); Rosalind Seyd, Alan Tennant, Michael Bayley, and Paul Parker (*Figure 9*, p. 148).

We gratefully acknowledge the helpful comments made on the first draft by Glenys Jones, Professor Jerôme Guay, John Sampson, and Rosie Stacy. We owe a particular debt to Dr Clare Wenger for her detailed comments on the final draft. We have made several changes as a result of these observations, but, of course, must ourselves take the ultimate responsibility for such shortcomings as may remain. Finally, we would like to thank Angela Fortune for her help in typing the manuscript.

Abbreviations

ASW .... Approved Social Worker
BASW......... British Association of Social Workers
BJSW.......... British Journal of Social Work
CQSW .... Certificate of Qualification in Social Work
CSS............. Certificate of Social Service
CSV .... community services volunteer
CSW........... community social work
CVS .... Council of Voluntary Service
DHSS.......... Department of Health and Social Security)
                (often used to mean the local office where
                supplementary benefit payments are made)
EMI............. elderly mentally infirm
EPH .... elderly people's home
EWO .... Educational Welfare Officer
GP .... General Practitioner
IT................ intermediate treatment
ITO .... Intermediate Treatment Officer
MD .... metropolitan district
MSC........... Manpower Services Commission
NACRO ...... National Association for the Care and Resettle-
                ment of Offenders
NAI............. non-accidental injury
NALGO...... National Association of Local Government
                Officers
NHS........... National Health Service
NISW .... National Institute for Social Work
OT .... occupational therapist
PADE .... Practice and Development Exchange (organized
                by NISW)
PASS.......... Programme Analysis of Service Systems (see
                Wolfensberger and Glenn 1975)
PSS .... personal social services
SB............... supplementary benefit
SSD............ social services department

SSO .... Social Services Officer
WRVS......... Women's Royal Voluntary Service

On how to use this book

Before you switch on, read this!

1. This book is designed both as a systematic review of the issues involved in putting community social work into practice and as a reference book or manual.
2. To get the most out of it, for either purpose, you will need to understand the principles on which it is structured.
3. *Chapter 1* explains the purposes and rationale of the book. *Chapter 2* describes the background and organization of the eight community social work teams on whose experience the book is primarily based
4. *Chapters 3–6* contain the core of the book. They are organized around four main themes: localization, integration, methods and roles, and management and development.

    Each of these chapters follows the same plan and contains separate sections on:

    Issues (prefixed A)

    Team experience (prefixed B)

    Practice guidelines (prefixed C for teams and D for senior management). Each guideline is marked thus ■ and subsections of guidelines are marked thus ● and indented.
5. *Chapter 7* examines some of the issues raised in the book and considers the future development of community social work.
6. Given that this book aims to be a reference manual as well as an analysis of a method of working, there is some overlap between sections and the same topics are sometimes addressed from different perspectives in the different chapters. Use the extensive index to locate all references to a particular topic.
7. A fuller account of the structuring of this book is given in Chapter 1, pp. 15–17 below.

1 *Purposes and rationale*

This handbook is a response to the movement towards the decentralization of social services and the increasing development of community-orientated methods in social work. As the pace of these changes has quickened, more and more social workers and other staff are faced with new demands and challenges in their work but find that in their past training and experience there is little to help them shape relevant responses. The purpose of our handbook is to help meet the needs of such workers by distilling the practice of a group of eight social services teams that have adopted community social work approaches ahead of the field and between them have accumulated many years of experience.

The handbook is constructed on a common philosophy of community social work, which we found to underlie the approach of the teams. It can be read from beginning to end as a systematic review of the issues involved in putting such a perspective into practice. In this form it will be particularly useful to teams about to adopt a community-based approach, to existing community-based teams reviewing their methods of work, and to all students of social work.

Alternatively, the handbook can be used simply as a reference book by those wanting to explore views and experience on specific aspects of community social work. To help in this we have cross-referenced major items and included a comprehensive index. Given the dual purpose of the book we make no apology for the fact that there is some overlap and repetition in the core chapters when the same themes are approached from different perspectives.

Community social work

The term *community social work* only gained common currency in the British social services following the publication of the Barclay Report in 1982. However, the ideas which it encompasses are considerably older. Social work in the nineteenth century was often conceived in terms of a much broader setting than casework. The settlement movement, for example, was initially focused on the educational and recreational needs of the communities served, and later expanded into many other activities such as housing and legal advice (Seed 1973: 32–40). Work with young people was also developed through clubs and other forms of what might now be called 'group work' (see, for example, Young and Ashton 1956: 235–58). Casework, however, has been important throughout the development of the profession. In post-war years, partly as a result of the growing influence of psychiatry and psychoanalysis, partly in response to the opportunities opening up in the new welfare bureaucracies, this emphasis became even stronger. With the development of genericism in social work training (Young-husband 1978: II, 32) basic courses included some exposure to the ideas of group and community work, but the focus on individual clients remained central.

The return to a broader perspective in Britain can be seen as part of a widely based trend in social policy in the 1960s and early 1970s in which the achievements of the post-war welfare legislation were critically reassessed and in which new kinds of collective intervention were explored. There was growing awareness that major inequalities still existed in Britain and that much social and economic deprivation remained in spite of the welfare state. The limits of universalist policies to tackle these problems became increasingly recognized. It seemed to many critics that there might be greater gains from adopting a more selective approach in which additional resources were concentrated on the worst off communities. Further, it was argued that the paternalistic style of intervention that had characterized state-run services had discouraged popular interest and involvement, and that more participative methods of managing services should be encouraged.

These changes in approach were manifested in the introduction of priority funding and development in education and housing, in the Home Office Community Development Project, and in the Urban Aid and inner-city initiatives. They were paralleled by, and sometimes combined with, policies aimed at increasing citizen participation, as in tenants' involvement in the management of some local-authority housing estates and in local-authority planning exercises, as well as increasing support for voluntary organizations and volunteering (Hadley and McGrath 1980: 7–9).

The report of the Seebohm Committee in 1968, recommending the integration of the previously separate children's, welfare, and health departments of the local authority into unified social services departments also reflected these developments. While proposing the creation of integrated and often, in consequence, large-scale departments, the report supported the decentralization of services within these organizations and the development of close collaboration with community networks (Seebohm 1968: Chapters 16 and 19).

Client-centred social work

In spite of these developments and the introduction of integrated social services departments in England and Wales in 1971 (and social work departments in Scotland in 1970), the predominant method of social work in the UK within statutory social services continued, and continues today, in the traditional mould of one-to-one work. In this approach, intervention tends to be centred on the problems of individuals, or individuals and their families.

Most social workers' daily work is concerned with a 'caseload' of such clients, usually referred from a relatively large geographical area. Social workers operating in this way seldom have the opportunity or motivation to acquire detailed knowledge of the wider worlds of their clients – for example, networks of extended family, neighbours, friends, the institutions of the locality, and so on. Their referrals are spread far too widely for them to acquire this kind of knowledge on a systematic basis. Even if they had it, it is doubtful if they would regard it as relevant. Their proper focus, as they see it, like that of other 'caring' professionals, is the individual. They are, in Martin Davies's metaphor, the 'mechanics of modern society' (Davies 1984), concerned with the malfunctioning of parts of the engine, not with restructuring the machine itself. This focus on the individual user to the exclusion of his or her world and the common features of users' problems would seem to be underpinned by a combination of factors:

1. Community networks of family, friends, and neighbours in contemporary society are perceived by many social workers

as relatively weak, especially in the case of the kinds of people referred as clients to social services departments. It is therefore only realistic to concentrate intervention primarily on the individual or the individual and his or her family.

2. This focus is also consistent with the practice of other workers in the 'people' professions from doctors to teachers, and has the sanction of status and precedent.

3. Social legislation affecting the personal social services has generally been framed in terms of individuals rather than groups or communities.

4. Social services organizations tend to emphasize the individual client as the unit of work in the way they describe the jobs of staff and in the systems of work which they establish from referral and allocation to treatment.

CRITIQUE

As the social services departments became consolidated and it became possible to establish a picture of their operation and performance, criticisms began to accumulate of the still predominant traditional methods of social work practice as not sufficiently relevant. These criticisms dealt principally with the ineffectiveness of social work itself but included organizational and policy issues as well. They included the following points.

Casework, even when well-resourced, seldom seems to achieve more than marginal gains in the problem areas referred. Research published in the 1970s showed depressingly poor results in a wide range of interventions (e.g. Mullen, Dumpson, and Associates 1972; Fischer 1976; Briar 1976).

Social work in the SSDs tends to be mainly reactive. Referrals are often not made until the users' problems have reached crisis point. At this stage successful intervention is usually much more difficult.

Workers have difficulty in establishing a detailed view of the context of cases and, in particular, the nature of the informal networks of those concerned. They are also likely to find it difficult to build close relationships with staff from other agencies involved locally, given the wide geographical spread of users and the speed with which they may often have to take decisions about intervention.

In these circumstances social workers are likely to be ignorant of local resources which might help users, or unable to assess accurately their true potential when they do find them. As a result they are likely to have to rely more heavily on their own output and such other sources of direct aid as they may be able to call on from within their departments.

Such practices taken together are likely to overemphasize the professional–user relationship, to undervalue alternative lines of response, and to foster dependence on the social worker.

Following from the methods described above, social work emerges as highly labour intensive, a characteristic which makes improvements in intervention expensive and means services are particularly vulnerable to cuts in staffing.

Although social workers and other social services department staff are closely involved in their daily work in dealing with users whose problems may have many elements in common, the individualized nature of their intervention is likely to inhibit the development of an understanding of these common features and to impede the ability of the agency to plan coherent strategies which reach beyond the level of casework.

Emerging alternatives

A number of factors have combined together to encourage the development of alternative methods of working and organization which emphasize a strong orientation towards the community. These factors include:

a growing awareness of the deficiencies of traditional client-centred methods and the frustrations they can entail;

increasing knowledge and understanding of the nature of informal caring systems and other forms of voluntary action in our society and the potential for interweaving statutory services with such systems;

the influence of the pioneers in community-based teams and the evidence that their work offers of alternative methods;

the impact of cut-backs in local-government spending which have compelled the serious consideration of alternatives;

political changes on both the right and left which for different reasons have favoured the introduction of policies of decentralization. On the right these tend to be founded on policies of self-help and local responsibility (Jenkin 1983). On the left they are likely to derive from 'local socialism' which seeks to revitalize relations between representatives and electorate founded on the local delivery and control of services (Barnes 1984; Gyford 1985)

THE SHAPING OF ALTERNATIVE PRACTICE

Dissatisfaction with traditional models of social work and social services has not been confined to armchair criticism. Increasingly since the mid-1970s social services teams have begun to test and introduce alternative approaches which have aimed to break away from the dominant structures and methods of client-centred work.

In some cases this has been mainly confined to changes at the margins of team activity. Client-centred methods have remained the core work but some time is set aside for establishing groups or for community projects. Or perhaps a sub-office is opened to make access to the team easier, or a worker is seconded to a local general practice. In other teams more thorough-going change has been attempted involving the orientation of the team as a whole. In these, major emphasis has been placed on localizing services, on identifying and working with informal networks and voluntary organizations, and on closer collaboration with other local statutory agencies.

Until 1980 such developments were confined to individual teams, operating either on their own initiative or as pilot or priority area teams set up by SSDs. In that year it was possible to identify forty such teams operating in different parts of the country (Hadley and McGrath 1980). However, in 1981, East Sussex SSD, the first local authority to adopt a decentralized approach on a comprehensive basis, more than doubled that number by creating forty-five local or 'patch' teams (Hadley, Dale, and Sills 1984: 13–15). Since then several other local authorities have moved in the same direction (Hadley and Cooper 1984) and today probably more than one in five teams in the country are decentralized or in the process of decentralization, and still further authorities are actively considering the adoption of similar strategies.

The move towards more community-orientated methods in social work and social services gained substantial support from the report of the Barclay Committee on the role and tasks of social workers. The committee was set up by the National Institute for Social Work in 1980 with the support of the Secretary of State for Social Services. Its report, published in

1982, recognized clearly that most social care in our society is provided by informal carers (principally kin) and recommended that social work should be much more directly concerned with the support of such carers than it traditionally had been. To this end social workers need to understand the context of users' lives and in particular their social networks, their strengths and weaknesses. This approach the committee defined as 'community social work':

> 'By this we mean formal social work which, starting from problems affecting an individual or group and the responsibilities and resources of social services departments and voluntary organisations, seeks to tap into, support, enable and underpin the local networks of formal and informal relationships which constitute our basic definition of community, and also the strengths of a client's communities of interest.'
>
> (Barclay 1982: xvii)

The committee stressed that this kind of social work required decentralized services, much greater flexibility in the roles of social workers, and greater autonomy for the managers of front-line teams (Barclay 1982: Chapter 13). However, there was disagreement in the committee on how far the process of restructuring needed to go to achieve these ends. In particular the issue centred on the notion of community and its implications for CSW. The majority believed that CSW could be built on *either* communities of interests *or* locality.

Communities of interest are defined as relationships between people based on common concerns which may exist outside a geographical community. For example, people 'may share a particular social disadvantage or handicap, or a common interest based on work, leisure activities, or attendance at the same doctor, surgery, or hospital out patients' (Barclay 1982: xiii). Similarly, they may have interests or beliefs that link them to people all over the country and abroad. CSW focusing on communities of interest might be based, for instance, on a general practice, a family centre, or a hospital. It could be practised by a team that remains relatively centralized and serves quite large populations.

Community as locality refers to the small areas or neighbourhoods in which people live. Such neighbourhoods may or may not be communities in the sense of shared interests and values.

Table 1 *A comparison of traditional and community-orientated approaches to social work*

Characteristics of traditional approach	Characteristics of community approach	Changes required for community approach
Reactive Practitioner reacts to demands for service made when the situation has deteriorated and the user's network can no longer cope.	*Preventive/proactive* Practitioner intervenes before a service is demanded and before the situation has deteriorated and the user's network can no longer cope.	1. Reduction of reactive responses, replaced by proactive intervention. 2. Reduction of case-by-case approach based on work of individual professional. 3. Close interaction with the local community.
Services at arm's length Professional practice is influenced by bureaucratic and institutional norms, is often predefined by departmental programmes, and is completely monopolized by numerous and pressing demands of individual clients.	*Services close to the community* Professional practice is defined by the living conditions and environmental situation of users and their social surroundings.	1. Variability and flexibility in the method of conceiving, realizing, and evaluating local programmes. 2. Individuals are considered in the round, not compartmentalized by programme. 3. Recognize importance of informal networks. 4. Sharing of professional responsibilities.

Based on professional responsibility	*Based on shared responsibility*	
The practitioner is entirely and exclusively responsible for the solution to the user's problems.	The practitioner shares responsibility with citizens and/or natural helpers.	Practitioners replace, in part, their direct responsibilities by activities supporting others who assume part of these responsibilities.
Centred on the individual client	*Centred on the social network*	
The only target of intervention is the individual client. Evaluation is directed mainly at his/her internal problems and the degree of pathology.	The target of intervention is the social network, including the client's. Evaluation centres on the distribution of responsibility and capacities to adapt.	The practitioner needs to develop skills to evaluate the weight of responsibility experienced by the principal carers, to support them and to identify and elicit the support of potential users and non-users.

Translated and adapted from training documents prepared by Professor Jerôme Guay, Université Laval, Quebec.

Those who are independent and mobile and belong to active communities of interest may not be particularly concerned about the quality of relations in their home neighbourhood. But the resources of the locality can be of the first importance to the most dependent people whose needs fall within the remit of the personal social services. These, particularly the frail elderly, and the mentally and physically ill and handicapped living in the community, 'are tied because of frailty, illness, fear, handicap, low income or habit to their local area' (Brown, Hadley, and White 1982: 220).

If the more dependent people of this kind are to continue to live any sort of fulfilled existence in their own homes, the types of action required are likely to involve practical help, advice, friendship, emotional support, and some kind of monitoring. Ideally, such help will come from family, friends, and neighbours. In practice, it is not always available, or may be available in part but require reinforcement if it is to continue. In these circumstances, it should be the responsibility of social services to provide such reinforcement or to help arrange a substitute network of support. Given the need for frequent, reliable, practical, and flexible contact, such a system must have a strong local component.

This logic, taken together with the case for easy access to services, lies at the heart of the argument for a locally based, community-orientated service, advanced by the dissenting minority in the Barclay Report (Brown, Hadley, and White 1982). It in no way precludes other approaches such as work with communities of interest or the provision of specialist advice and support for some categories of clients. But it does firmly identify the locality or neighbourhood as the front line of community social work.

A useful diagram summarizing and contrasting the characteristics of the traditional, client-centred approach to social work and the community-orientated approach has been developed by Professor Jerôme Guay of Laval University. It is reproduced in adapted form in *Table 1*. It also identifies the nature of the changes required in practice to move from the former to the latter approach. It is particularly interesting to compare the features of community-orientated community social work identified in Professor Guay's model on the basis of work in North America with those underlying the organization and practice of CSW in Britain.

Common features underlying the organization and practice of CSW

Familiarity with the aims and practice of a considerable number of locally based teams attempting to practise community social work suggests that there are sufficient similarities in their approaches and experience to provide useful guidelines for other teams setting out on this road. The basis of this book is the practice of eight well-established CSW teams located in different parts of the country, chosen to represent something of the wide range of areas served and different structures adopted. Their experience has been analysed and presented under four main headings relating to common themes in their organization and practice: localization, integration, methods, and management. Each of these themes, briefly summarized below, forms the basis for a separate chapter in the handbook. First, however, it is important to indicate something of the nature of the common values shared by members of the teams and other CSW teams with which we are familiar.

VALUES

While the teams who contributed to this book serve authorities of differing political complexion, and the personal outlook of the members we got to know varied considerably, on certain fundamental tenets of CSW there appeared to be a substantial measure of agreement. In particular there was awareness of the risk that social work may prove a *disabling* activity (Illich *et al.* 1977) and strong support for the contrary notions of enabling and empowerment. Expression of similar aims can sometimes be found in discussions on the goals of traditional one-to-one work. The difference in CSW, however, is the emphasis on the community rather than the individual, on mutual aid rather than self-help, on modifying or changing the system rather than simply adapting to it.

None of the contributing teams claims to have been able to move over to methods of working which are comprehensively based on CSW principles. All would agree that change towards CSW is a slow and difficult process. They are at various stages on a long road. Nevertheless, all believe that they have acquired space to make at least some progress and to extend the proportion of their time which is devoted to CSW.

ORGANIZATIONAL THEMES

Localization

Community social work teams are typically deployed to cover much smaller areas than traditionally organized teams. Populations served by such teams – or subsections of such teams – tend to be of the order of 5,000 to 10,000, and few are over 20,000, compared with 25,000 to 100,000 or more served by traditional teams. Localization is regarded as essential in order to make access to the team easy for users and other local agencies, to gain knowledge of informal caring networks, to devise and apply relevant supportive methods of working in collaboration with informal carers and other agencies, and to open the services to the views, influence, and involvement of the community.

Integration

Community social work teams are likely to seek to establish more integrated approaches in a number of different spheres. *Within the social services department* varying degrees of integration are likely to be possible according to which staff and what resources have been devolved to team level. Some teams control no more than one or two grades of staff, as for example social workers and social work assistants. Others may also include domiciliary staff. A few now manage all main services, including residential and day-care institutions. But whatever the range, the teams are characterized by methods of operation which bring the staff concerned into close working partnerships in their day-to-day routines, sharing information and making joint plans.

Integration with individuals and agencies outside the department is also the aim of community social work teams in the sense of establishing common approaches and practice. However, given that the parties involved belong to different social groupings or organizations, the problems of achieving close working links are often likely to be more complex, and the resulting relationships might be more accurately described as collaborative rather than integrative.

Methods and roles

The aims of early intervention and of integrative or collaborative strategies call for the development of a wide range of skills amongst the staff of community social work teams and a readiness to switch flexibly between methods and roles as particular circumstances demand.

Management and development

Community social work, because it involves staff in wide-ranging responsibilities and requires them to respond rapidly and flexibly to varying local conditions, calls for substantial team autonomy and for participative methods of leadership within the team. Similarly, given the emphasis on maximizing resources of the team and the community it serves, rather than on the rationing of fixed packages of service, developmental or entrepreneurial styles of management characterize the successful community social work team.

Teams contributing to this book

Teams using community social work methods have arrived at their new structures by a number of different routes. The nature of the road taken may well affect the scope of the team's work. Three routes to community social work are particularly common: *team-level initiatives*, when a conventionally organized area team decides to adopt a community social work approach; *pilot- or priority-area initiatives*, when senior management introduces community social work methods in a few select areas to test out the approach or to meet special needs; *department-wide changes*, when community social work is introduced across the board by senior management or as a result of councillors' decisions.

The teams contributing their experience to this book include representatives of each of these three categories. They also cover a wide range of different geographical and social and economic settings, from the densely populated inner city to sparsely peopled countryside.

Three teams adopted community social work methods on their own initiative: Normanton (in Wakefield MD), Longbenton (North Tyneside MD), and Huntly (Grampian Region). Two were established in priority areas: Honor Oak (in the London Borough of Lewisham) and Lochend (in the Easterhouse area of Glasgow, Strathclyde Region). One was set up as a pilot for changes which might be adopted in the authority as a whole: Docklands (London Borough of Newham). The remaining two were initiated as part of a department-wide decentralization programme: Whitehawk (in Brighton, East Sussex) and Rye (East Sussex). Of these eight teams, half serve areas which have the demographic and economic characteristics of inner-city areas whether they are physically located in the central part of the cities concerned or on peripheral estates: Honor Oak, Docklands, Lochend, and Whitehawk. Normanton and Long-benton are in other urban areas and Huntly and Rye serve thinly populated rural areas.

Method of preparing this handbook

As noted in the Preface, the framework used to systematize the experience of the contributing teams was prepared by the authors and tested out in teams which were led by two of them, Mike Cooper and Graham Stacy, in Normanton and Long-benton. An amended version was then circulated to the contri-butors in the remaining six teams. Data supplied by the teams within this framework were analysed by the authors and form the main basis for our suggested guidelines for practice. However, in formulating the guidelines we also drew where relevant on other sources including, in particular, the growing literature on community social work and the contacts of the individual authors with practice in a number of other teams.

Two caveats should be entered concerning the particular perspectives resulting from the method adopted in compiling this book. The first concerns the composition of the contributing teams. CSW is essentially an integrative approach and ideally the principles involved apply equally to the whole range of social services activities including field, domiciliary, residential, and day-care work. However, in practice so far CSW has been developed principally in field teams, and has been restricted to social workers and in some cases domiciliary workers. Only recently have some departments adopted fully integrated teams which also cover residential and day-care services. It should be noted that the material on which this book has been based reflects this weighting of CSW experience towards field and domiciliary work and that only two of the contributing teams, Rye and Whitehawk, had responsibility for the full range of services.

Secondly, it should also be emphasized that the perspective of this book is essentially that of the practitioner. We would have liked to have been able to complement this approach with the views of the users of CSW. Unfortunately, in common with most SSDs, the departments within which the contributing teams were located did not carry out systematic evaluations of users' views in the areas served on which we could draw. Nor did we have the resources to mount our own consumer studies. It would seem particularly important in the further development of CSW, with its emphasis on responsiveness and accountability to the community, that ways should be sought to bring users firmly into the assessment process.

A guide to the use of this book

We have stressed that community social work is being carried out in a wide variety of different contexts and that there can be no blueprints for structures and methods in an approach which emphasizes flexibility, adaptation, and creativity. Further, the reader will need to keep in mind that the experiences brought together in this book are drawn from teams at different stages in their development, dealing with different patterns of need. While there is solid evidence of common operating principles, there is also evidence of differences in emphasis, priorities, and styles of working. The new practitioners, too, must fashion their own appropriate strategies, learning from others but relating this experience to the particular needs and resources of the communities they serve and the potentialities of the organizations within which they work.

As we have already noted, this book is intended to be both a systematic exploration of how community social work can be put into practice and a reference work which can be used for consultation on specific issues.

Readers who want to use the book mainly as a reference work will find an extensive index at the end of the book. The method of cross-referencing within the book is described below, in the section on the structure of Chapters 3–6. *Readers planning to work right though the book* and those who want a *guide to informed skipping* within the text may find it helpful to read the following brief summary account of the contents of Chapters 2–7.

Chapter 2, 'The teams in context' describes the setting, organization, and management of each of the eight contributing teams.

Chapters 3–6 examine the experience of the contributing teams, using the four organizing themes of localization, integration, methods, and management.

Chapter 3, 'Localization': the identification of neighbourhoods and the drawing of team boundaries are discussed. The chapter goes on to consider reception, referrals, the employment of local staff and volunteers, and the issue of confidentiality.

Chapter 4, 'Integration': the integration of social services is reviewed, beginning with relationships with informal networks in the community, then integral integration within the SSD, and finally integration with other agencies.

Chapter 5, 'Methods and roles': this chapter gets to the heart of the CSW approach. It focuses on the changes in methods and roles which CSW implies in the day-to-day activities of social workers. It deals in turn with the skills of CSW, specialization, and role flexibility.

Chapter 6, 'Management and development': here we examine the crucial role of management in the development of CSW. The main focus is on team management but additional guidelines are added to highlight the implications of CSW for senior management. There are four main sections dealing in turn with management within the team, management and the wider organization, evaluation, and change and development.

Chapter 7, 'Review and future directions': the concluding chapter of the book reviews issues and criticisms set out at the end of Chaper 1 in the light of the material presented in the intervening chapters. It ends with a brief discussion of the future development of CSW.

ISSUES, TEAM EXPERIENCE, AND PRACTICE GUIDELINES

Each of the four chapters analysing the contributing teams' experiences of CSW (Chapters 3–6) is subdivided within the different topics discussed into three sections:

Issues: emerging as the central questions in the topic concerned. These are numbered and prefixed with the letter A, e.g. A.1; A.2; etc.

Team experience: of the eight contributing teams, summarized under the headings identified in the Issues section and prefixed by the letter B, e.g. B.1; B.2, etc.

Practice guidelines: practical suggestions for team managers, leaders, and members based on team experience and other material, prefixed by the letter C, e.g. C.1; C.2; etc. Suggestions aimed specifically at departmental management, contained in the last sections of Chapters 4 and 5 and in Chapter 6, are prefixed by the letter D. Each principal guideline is marked thus ▉, each subsection thus ●. These guidelines have generally been cast in a prescriptive form, not to imply that they represent the *only* way to proceed, but to convey their rule-of-thumb nature: this is the kind of practical advice offered by other practitioners who have tried to tackle the same kinds of problem.

Issues and objections

The move towards CSW has led to a lively debate both about its practical feasibility as a strategy for organization and practice, and about its wider political and social implications. It is not the purpose of this book to extend this debate by exploring in detail the various arguments that have been deployed. However, the material presented here inevitably touches on many of the points involved and it may be of interest to readers to have a guide to the most relevant sections of the text. To this end we set out below a number of the principal criticisms levelled at CSW, listing after each the chapters and sections which relate to them. In the concluding chapter we will return to consider briefly the weight of the criticisms in the light of this material. In addition, we have added a short discussion of four issues not dealt with directly at any length in the following chapters: industrial relations, gender, race, and public participation.

1. *Community assumptions.* (a) Many localities do not have strong informal caring systems, nor can they readily be created in such areas by SSDs. (b) Some local communities may be strong but their strength may be used to stigmatize

and exclude less 'popular' service users. (c) CSW teams may be too intrusive, weaken natural sytems, and introduce a new colonialism at the local level (For (a) and (b), see Chapter 2, Area covered by the teams, pp. 27, 30, 33, 36, 38, 42; Chapter 3, Neighbourhoods and micro-neighbourhoods, pp. 53–9; Chapter 4, Integration with informal networks, pp. 96–114; Chapter 6, Links with the community, pp. 210–20.)

2. *Staff.* (a) CSW may work well when there are able and committed staff. But how widely available is such an élite? With inadequate, or uncommitted people the social services may be worse off with CSW teams than in a more controlled and limited operation of the conventional type. (See Chapter 4, Integration of aims and philosophy, pp. 115, 116, 120; Chapter 5, Acquiring skills and staff, pp. 138, 143, 162.) (b) The isolation of staff in small teams where there is little chance to discuss matters of common interest with fellow professionals is likely to undermine the skills of the worker; Chapter 6, Isolation, pp. 210, 213, 216.

3. *Relationships with users.* (a) Confidentiality may be much more difficult to ensure in a locally based team. (See Chapter 3, pp. 92–4; Chapter 4, pp. 106–07.) (b) Similarly, teams may find it difficult to accept that social work is about control as well as care. (See Chapter 5, An informal style of operation, pp. 138, 141, 151.)

4. *Equality.* The diversity of local areas and of the ability of different teams to respond to needs/strengths of the areas served may lead to greater inequities in the services available. (See Chapter 6, pp. 209, 211, 215, 218, 221–27.)

5. *Skills.* (a) The genericism required in CSW will lead to a loss of special skills and a general lowering of practice standards. (See Chapter 5, Specialization, pp. 163–81; Chapter 6, pp. 195, 200, 207, 209.) (b) The breadth of work required of community social workers is unrealistically large.

6. *Management.* The front-line skills required of management at integrated team level suggest that only particularly able people could succeed at the job. For others, there will be real risks of overload, burn-out, or just gross incompetence. (See Chapter 6, pp. 195, 200, 207, 209.)

OTHER ISSUES

Industrial relations

Trade unions see their primary task as the defence of their members' interests. CSW can be perceived as a threat to traditional unionism on two counts. First, it encourages maximum flexibility in jobs and fuzziness in the boundaries between different roles, and consequently clashes with the well-established trade union principle of the clear demarcation of jobs and their responsibilities, so as to prevent dilution and exploitation. Secondly, it involves the geographical dispersal of staff to relatively small teams. Trade unionists may perceive this as weakening their ability to consult and mobilize their forces when occasion demands. In some local authorities union concern about these issues has led to long delays in plans for decentralization and the introduction of community-orientated methods of work, in spite of a recognition that users are likely to benefit from the changes proposed.

There are no simple solutions to the problems involved. However, the experience of some of the authorities which have successfully moved towards decentralization offers a few pointers. In particular, greater role flexibility, which often brings with it important savings to the department, has been conceded in return for better conditions of work and terms of service. For example, the number of Level 3 social work posts may be increased, training programmes may be expanded, and hourly paid domiciliary staff may be transferred to salaried posts. The right of unions to meet with their members regularly, in spite of their geographical dispersion, can be negotiated as part of any package of changes of this kind.

In the longer run, however, it seems that the real challenge for trade unions will be to find ways of moving from a predominantly defensive stance towards a more creative and proactive approach. Community social work is likely to lead to increased staff participation in decision making and the development of more responsible and satisfying jobs. If unions are to remain relevant to their members they will need to become as interested and involved in promoting these aspects of their members' work lives as in ensuring their proper remuneration and protection. (See Chapter 4, pp. 115, 118, 121; Chapter 5, Union reactions, pp. 182, 187, 192.)

Gender

A second area of concern about CSW has been its potential impact on women. Some feminists have argued that it is likely to reinforce the processes locking women into the role of primary providers of care in the community (Finch 1984). Two factors, in particular, are stressed. First, the central place given to informal care in CSW. The largest proportion of informal care is currently provided by female relatives of the dependent person. CSW, by targeting informal care and developing strategies to support it, will underpin a status quo which is essentially inequitable. Secondly, CSW teams stress the importance of developing the roles of ancillary and domiciliary workers who are predominantly female and low-paid. Again, CSW is at risk of reinforcing exploitation and inequality.

Advocates of CSW, while acknowledging the role of women in both informal care and the formal provision of community services, believe that neither of these arguments stand up to serious examination. First, the strategy of supporting informal carers seeks, as its prime objective, to reduce the costs involved for them. It attempts to do this by entering into partnership with carers and reducing the load on them through the provision of services which can substitute for some, most, or all of the caring tasks. The notion of partnership is important because it involves the recognition of carers' wishes and a process of negotiation with them rather than an attempt to pin them down in the caring role.

When they are first encountered by CSW teams, carers are usually preoccupied with the practical aspects of their situation and it is obviously desirable as a first priority to provide the practical relief which they request and which can range from marginal support to complete substitution. It is recognized, however, that the set of values implied by a woman's felt need or duty to maintain the role of carer is likely to reflect the male-dominated values of our culture and the socialization process which women have undergone. The provision of practical help can release women from the demands of caring and allow them space and opportunity for themselves. In addition, approaches which put women in touch with carers' groups and other community organizations can directly create the opportunity for them to achieve a heightened consciousness of their situation and to mount a challenge to the status quo.

On the issue of the employment of women in ancillary and domiciliary roles, supporters of CSW point out that the more important roles given to such staff in CSW teams are likely to enhance the sense of satisfaction they gain from their jobs and can provide the basis for achieving improvements in their conditions of employment as, for example, in those authorities that have created the higher-grade posts of care workers to replace home helps and care assistants. Further, the emphasis placed by CSW on enabling and participation applies to staff as well as users. In so far as it increases women's self-confidence and capacity to act, it also helps towards their empowerment, rather than reinforcing their unequal status. (See Chapter 4, pp. 96, 99, 104, 106.)

Race

It has also been suggested that CSW, in encouraging a local focus in social services, can divert attention from the needs of racial minority groups by diluting the numbers covered by each team and undermining influence built up by their organizations at authority level (see, e.g., Shields and Webber 1986). On the other hand, CSW practitioners argue that the very localness of teams opens them to the influence of all categories of users. Further, where it is possible to encourage the direct employment of local people in CSW teams, there are good opportunities to bring members of such minorities into the team and through them to extend contacts with their communities and expose the team to their influence.

Public participation

CSW has been criticized because its main thrust has been concerned with organizational and professional issues rather than with the questions of popular accountability and control. This view has been expressed in particular by those who advocate the rapid development of local democracy so that it extends into neighbourhood involvement in the management and delivery of services (Beresford 1984; Beresford and Croft 1986).

In this view, with very few exceptions CSW has been developed as a managerial or professional tool. Services become localized but local people still have no say in their control. They may or may not be more effective in conventional terms but they have no way of reflecting local people's views. Further, by being in the community without being community-controlled, they are likely to breed disillusionment about the potential of local democracy.

Practitioners of CSW tend to support the notion of more effective representation of local opinion in social services. In a number of areas they have sought to establish local forums or have conducted consultation exercises to try to fill the vacuum left by our centralized political system. Most recognize such developments as little more than first steps on the road to real representation of users and potential users. They also recognize that the forces standing in the way of any major shift of power in this direction remain formidable. Even in the bold experiments in local socialism in such authorities as Islington and Hackney (London Borough of Islington 1986; Shields and Webber 1986), and in the province-wide decentralization of health and social services in Quebec (Godbout 1983), progress towards power sharing is at a very early stage. However, the practitioners do not see the absence of a formal system of neighbourhood democracy as grounds for delaying moves to establish CSW teams. First, their very creaction strengthens the case for more local systems of representation. If services are devolved to neighbourhood level, then the argument for the establishment of institutions for neighbourhood participation follows. Second, the introduction of CSW teams is likely over time to enhance significantly local people's understanding of the nature and purposes of contemporary social services. Such understanding, it can be argued, is a prerequisite of effective involvement. Finally, CSW opens social services to a wide range of informal influences by local groups and individuals. While such influences may be in no way comparable to the effects of representative participation or control through formal political institutions, it is at least a significant step towards more accountable services. (See Chapter 4, pp. 124, 126, 135; Chapter 6, Team management, the wider organization and the community, pp. 209–18.)

In writing this book, while recognizing the importance of these different issues, we have not set out to explore the detailed changes in social services which the development of the different perspectives involved might imply. Our principal aim is more modest. Starting from where people and services are *now*, rather than from where we might like them to be, we are concerned with creating the conditions for the development of a more community-orientated perspective in the organization and delivery of social services. We believe, however, that CSW where it is adopted not only allows but positively encourages social services teams to open themselves to such fundamental challenges to established perceptions. The major thrust of CSW away from individual situations and towards social analysis provides a context within which issues such as gender, race, and political power can be recognized and understood, and more informed pressures for changes in policy and practice can develop.

Developing the book

As far as we know, while there are now available a number of texts directly relevant to the practice of CSW (e g. Holman 1983; Guay 1984; Seyd *et al.* 1984; Payne 1986), this is the first attempt to provide a handbook on community social work in a country where there are statutory social services departments. Any new venture of this kind is itself a learning experience. While we believe the handbook in its present form can make a positive contribution to the development of community social work, we hope that there will be further editions in which we can include material from new developments in the field and incorporate improvements suggested by you, the reader. Please do write to us with your comments, ideas, and practical experiences.

2 The teams in context

In this chapter we provide an introductory sketch of each of the eight teams whose experience makes up the core of this handbook. In each case we describe the character of the area served, the origins of the team, the manner in which it relates to the department as a whole, and the organization and composition of the team at the time the material contributed to this book was prepared. We hope that these sketches will enable readers to place the individual examples of team experience which are described in Chapters 3–6 within their specific contexts.

The teams are presented according to the *method* by which community-orientated approaches were adopted and the principal purposes pursued. First, we consider the three teams which had adopted *local modifications* to conventional structures on the initiative of team members. These are followed by the three teams set up by senior management as *social priority* or *pilot* projects. The last section covers two teams established as part of a *department-wide* plan to introduce decentralized methods of operation.

Since demographic factors including population density, age distribution, family structure, occupation, and employment levels are likely to be particularly important in determining the nature and extent of demands on social services, it is also relevant to consider the *type of area* they serve. *Table 2* classifies the eight teams according to a number of factors which are intended to provide a simple framework which readers may find it helpful to use in comparing the contributing teams to other teams known to them. These factors are: the source of the initiative for their establishment; their position on an urban-rural continuum; population size; the staff groups comprising the team; and whether the area covered by the team is divided into smaller sections or sub-patches.

While, as *Figure 1* shows, the teams cover a wide geographical spread from Sussex (Whitehawk) in the south to Grampian (Huntly) in the north, with four located in large metropolitan

Table 2 *Summary of the characteristics of the contributing teams*

	population[1]	type of area	origin of team	staff groups	sub-patches?
Huntly (Grampian)	15,000	rural	local modification	fieldwork	No
Normanton (Wakefield)	20,000	small industrial town	local modification	fieldwork, domiciliary, clerical	Yes (3)
Longbenton (N. Tyneside)	16,000	suburban estate	local modification	fieldwork, clerical	No
Honor Oak (Lewisham)	2,000	suburban estate	social priority	fieldwork, clerical	No
Lochend (Strathclyde)	10,000	suburban estate	social priority	fieldwork, community work, clerical	No
Docklands (Newham)	15,000	inner city	pilot	fieldwork, community work, domiciliary, clerical	Yes (3)
Rye (E. Sussex)	20,000	rural	dept-wide	fieldwork, domiciliary, residential, clerical	No
Whitehawk (Brighton, E. Sussex)	10,000	suburban estate	dept-wide	fieldwork, domiciliary, residential, clerical	No

[1] To nearest 1,000

Figure 1 *Location of the contributing teams*

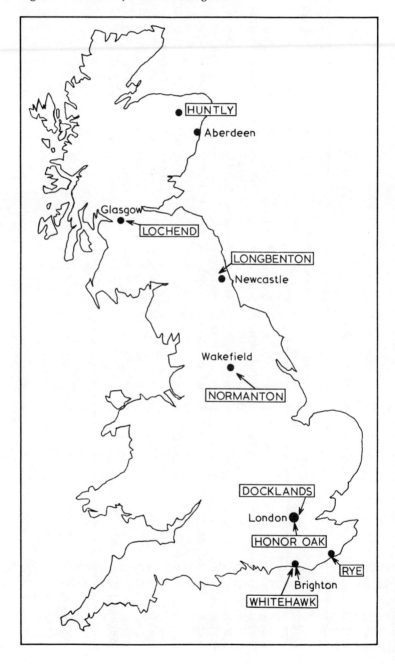

areas, two in other urban settings, and two in rural environments, they do not in any sense constitute a representative
sample of the areas served by social services departments across
the country as a whole. They over-represent people in working-
class occupations, the unemployed, the less well paid, and the
poor. We make no apologies for this bias in the selection. Such
areas generally make the highest demands on social services
departments, and community social work will be of little value
in the years to come if it cannot respond to the challenges
involved. Nevertheless, a minority of the teams serve more
representative populations (Rye and Huntly) and others include
substantial enclaves of this kind (Normanton, Docklands,
Longbenton).

Teams adopting a community orientation on their own initiative

Three of the contributing teams owe their adoption of community social work organization and methods to local managers and
other staff. In chronological order they are Huntly (1975),
Normanton (1976), and Longbenton (1978).

HUNTLY

Area covered by the team

The Huntly team cover a stretch of thinly populated country in
the Grampian Region of Scotland, lying 40 miles and more
north-west of the city of Aberdeen. The boundaries enclose 564
square miles and 25 parishes, with populations ranging from 88
to 4,275. The total population covered is about 15,000. The
largest concentrations of population are in the three small towns
of Huntly (4,275), Alford (1,175), and Insch (1,276).

The main occupations in the area are agriculture and forestry.
In addition there are some small factories in each of the three
towns, a number of craft workers, and a seasonal tourist trade.
Most of the area is outside the Aberdeen commuter belt and is
also outside the area which benefited directly from the development of North Sea oil. However, a small number of people are
employed as off-shore oil workers. Overall, unemployment is
not high by comparison with national figures although it is
above average for the region.

Until 1981 population in the three main towns remained static and declined in the rural hinterlands. Now, however, there is evidence that numbers are increasing throughout the area as more people choose to retire to the countryside and as others, especially young families, choose to move out of Aberdeen to live in rural properties.

Origins of the team

The development of a community-orientated approach to social work in the Huntly team evolved over a period of about ten years. The team's origins can be traced back to the early 1970s when a social work presence was established in Huntly in the person of an 'area officer'. The area officer in Grampian is a local-government official with a mix of duties. He acts as registrar for births, deaths, and marriages, carries out administrative functions for the education department, and gives about a third of his time to social work. Initially, the area officer in Huntly was supported by a part-time social worker based in Inverurie, 23 miles away.

In 1972 it was decided that Huntly needed its own full-time social worker and a separate office was opened in the town to serve its inhabitants and people living in the immediate hinterland. The first worker appointed followed a fairly traditional approach to his work and the department had a low profile in the town. However, three years later there was a change of worker and with this the beginnings of a change in philosophy. The new worker did not start with a clear-cut agenda for change but his previous experience had given him an orientation towards community social work. In his own words it seemed 'the only practical way of working in a rural area that was generally deprived of resources'. He adopted a high profile in Huntly, made wide-ranging contacts with the local community, and as a result referrals to the department increased substantially. The social worker joined the other local agencies in setting up a number of community projects. As this way of working developed, the social worker's methodology became more sophisticated and more explicit. What had started as a commonsense response to the problems of a rural area progressed into an approach that he felt would be valid in tackling social problems in whatever area they might occur, whether rural or urban, and whatever level of resources existed.

While the management of the Grampian Social Work Department as a whole did not share this philosophical stance, there was growing support in the local Gordon Division of the department for the wider application of community social work methods in the area. In 1983–84, after a lengthy period of discussion, it was decided to break the whole division into four patches, each with its own sub-team.

Organization of the department and team

The Grampian Region Social Work Department is organized in five divisions, with its headquarters in Aberdeen. The Gordon Divisional office is in the town of Inverurie, which lies between the Huntly patch and Aberdeen, about 23 miles to the southeast. The four patches are managed from Inverurie. They are grouped in two pairs, each led by a senior social worker. As illustrated in *Figure 2*, most domiciliary services are also deployed at this level and shared between the paired teams. Within the Huntly patch there are three local contact points: at Huntly, Alford, and Insch. In addition, users can make contact through the divisional office at Inverurie.

Figure 2 *The organization and staffing of the Huntly team*

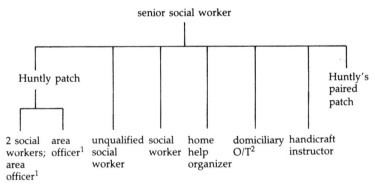

senior social worker

Huntly patch

Huntly's paired patch

2 social workers; area officer[1] area officer[1] (based at Huntly)

area officer[1] (based at Alford)

unqualified social worker

social worker

home help organizer

domiciliary O/T[2]

handicraft instructor

(based at regional office and serving both Huntly and its paired patch)

[1] area officer = local-government official with responsibilities of registrar, education administration, and social work (see page 28).
[2] O/T = Occupational Therapist.

Management

The Huntly team has a monthly meeting chaired by the senior social worker primarily to decide on future developments and to discuss common problems which may then be referred to the monthly divisional meetings. The day-to-day running of the Huntly patch is left very much to the locally based staff. The Huntly office team has a regular weekly allocation meeting where unallocated referrals received from various local contact points are assigned. This meeting also tends to review ongoing projects and discusses matters of immediate concern related to the whole patch.

NORMANTON

Area covered by the team

Normanton is a small industrial town in West Yorkshire. It lies about 5 miles east of the city of Wakefield and since 1974 has been part of the Wakefield Metropolitan District. The population of Normanton in 1981 was just over 18,000. The Normanton area team covers the whole of the town and also serves three small neighbouring villages with a combined population of 2,000.

Until the middle of the last century Normanton was a small farming village. Its rapid growth in the second half of the century was due first to the establishment of railway freight yards and workshops and subsequently to the sinking of several coal-mines in the surrounding area. Both industries have declined during the twentieth century: today the rail yards are closed and the local pits are exhausted. Coal-mining remains the largest single employer, however, as people commute to more distant pits. The National Coal Board still employs 30 per cent of men living in the town. Manufacturing in Wakefield and on a small industrial estate in Normanton has expanded to take up much of the slack created by the decline of the staple industries. Nevertheless, the town has shared in the country's economic problems and unemployment in the local area was 13.5 per cent in March, 1984.

The town has well above the national proportion of manual workers (75 per cent compared with 64 per cent). Approaching half the population (46 per cent) live in council housing. Other indicators suggest that the population characteristics of the town do not differ markedly from national patterns except for an above-average proportion of elderly people (19 per cent compared with 17 per cent).

Departmental organization and origins of the team

When the Wakefield Metropolitan District was created in 1974 area social services teams were based in all the population centres which had previously been urban district council areas. Today no team covers a population of more than 42,000 and six of the eleven areas contain fewer than 30,000 people. All teams have the same basic structure and include social workers, social work assistants, care workers, home-help organizers, street wardens, and administrative staff.

Area offices have full control of all generic fieldwork services, domiciliary services, and the admission of people to Part III establishments in the area. They have autonomy in making Section I payments and boarding-out payments, specifying home helps' hours, and organizing the reception and discharge of clients in care. All other functions of the department are controlled by the Central Office.

The potential for area teams to devise localized structures and working methods is considerable and all teams are now using some form of patch organization. The Normanton team was the first to develop and refine a patch approach, beginning in 1976 when the team moved from Pontefract to its base in the town. This initiative was instigated by the area officer as a result of his previous experience of community work. His aim was to put into practice the Seebohm Report's proposals for a community-based generic service which would be closer to the community and would provide a more responsive service for those in need (for a fuller account of the team, see Cooper 1980; Hadley and McGrath 1984).

Organization of the team

Normanton is one of Wakefield's smaller teams. It has a core staff of nineteen based in its town-centre office (see *Figure 3*). In addition there are home helps and street wardens. The town has been divided into three sub-areas or patches and each of these is served by a separate patch team under the leadership of a Level 3 social worker.

Figure 3 *The organization and staffing of the Normanton team*

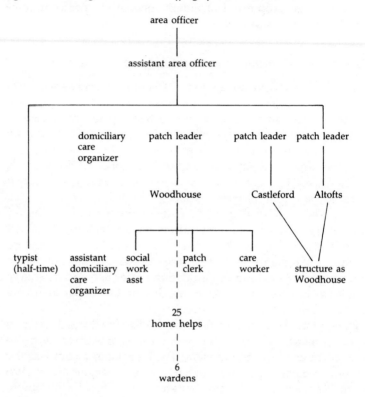

Team management

The area officer and assistant area officer have overall responsibility for the work of the team but day-to-day management in the area is a participatory process. The area officer is responsible for community development, voluntary-agency liaison, resource creation, and interdepartmental advocacy for the team. The assistant area officer takes formal responsibility for casework, supervision of patch leaders and case liaison with other agencies. In the patches, work allocation and supervision is the responsibility of the patch leaders. The domiciliary care organizer oversees the running of the home helps, wardens, meals on wheels, and luncheon clubs. Additionally, she specializes in liaison and committee work with local old people's organizations. Some overall functions such as control of Part III bed allocations, transport, the blind register, and so on, are taken on as extra responsibilities by individual team members.

Patch teams meet weekly on a formal basis to monitor their workloads, and routine work is recorded. The whole area team also meets weekly to receive general information, have discussions with representatives of outside agencies, debate team issues, and make decisions about changes and developments. Outside these set-piece meetings, various *ad hoc* groups of workers form from time to time to clarify practice, develop new methods of working, and undertake research.

LONGBENTON

Area covered by the team

The area covered by the Longbenton team falls into two distinct parts separated by 4 miles of open country and disused pits. Any community-based work carried out in one part has no spill-over into the other and the amount of work to be done is thus doubled.

The area which produces the highest number of referrals is the Longbenton estate. This was built in the late 1950s as Newcastle overspill and is situated on the very edge of the Newcastle conurbation. Where the estate stops the fields begin. The estate is made up entirely of council housing, the majority of which is three-storey blocks of two-bedroom flats with poor sound and heat insulation, insecure communal entries, and no enclosed play spaces. Around the central blocks of flats is a thin ring of family houses with gardens, some of which have been purchased under the right-to-buy legislation. In the middle of the estate are two thirteen-storey tower blocks which are popular with some residents due to their security and a lonely prison for others. The tower blocks are formally designated as hard to heat by the DHSS. The estate as a whole is designated as an 'Inner Area'. There is a programme of refurbishment of some of the blocks and the completed flats are very popular.

Wideopen is the team's collective name for the second half of the area. It includes four other localities, once separate villages: Hazelrigg, Brunswick Green, Woodlands Park, and Seaton Burn. Only the last of these, a mining village, retains its distinct boundaries. The other villages have been swallowed up in the spread of post-war speculative building which has created a

relatively affluent dormitory for Newcastle and a popular retire-
ment area for owner occupiers.

There are no sources of employment on the Longbenton estate
and in 1981, 19 per cent of the male population of working age
was unemployed. Today, evidence suggests that the total
unemployed is probably three times this level. According to the
Housing Department, over 80 per cent of households in the area
are in receipt of housing benefit. Wideopen is much more affluent. The total population of the area in 1981 was 15,633. This
was divided fairly equally between Longbenton and Wideopen.
Longbenton has more than the national average of over 65s and
considerably more of over 80s. Families with school-age children
are substantially under-represented and as a result some schools
have closed. In contrast, families with under school-age children
are over-represented. Wideopen has more than its fair share of
elderly people but otherwise a more average distribution of
population characteristics.

Crime, alcohol, and drug abuse are substantial problems in
Longbenton. These difficulties are compounded (and perhaps
partly caused) by the relative paucity of well-established
support networks. This is due in part to the rehousing on the
estate of people who have previously lived in the older parts of
the authority by the River Tyne. As a whole the population of
the estate is unsettled with many movements in and out each
week. It is difficult in these circumstances for the estate to settle
down and for networks to mature and take the place of old
allegiances.

In Wideopen the very respectability of the area gives rise to
problems in that more people are unwilling to ask their neighbours for help or to approach the social services department.
Council housing is scarce and it is difficult for children to obtain
tenancies near their parents. Elderly owner occupiers have
either moved into the area themselves after their children have
left or have seen their mobile children move away. An increasing number of problems concerning teenagers are beginning to
come the way of the team. The area is distant from relevant
resources such as IT units.

Origins of the team and the organization of the department

The team was established on a local footing in 1978 on the

initiative of the area manager. He wanted to find more effective ways of relating to professionals working with other agencies and to encourage the social work teams to respond more positively and effectively to local people and local problems. The team's decision to accelerate its adoption of a CSW approach dated from the appointment of the present team leader in 1981.

The department is organized into a central office and four autonomous areas, from which all services are managed including residential establishments, field social work, day care, and domiciliary care. Each area has an area manager, an assistant area manager, and a residential services controller. The assistant area manager manages the team leaders, the domiciliary care and home care organizers. The residential controller managers the residential and day care establishments. Each area except North Shields is subdivided on a geographical basis between three teams. North Shields area retains four social work teams organized along specialist lines.

Organization and management of the team

The structure of the Longbenton team is very simple. It consists of a team leader, two social workers (Level 3), three social workers (Level 2), two social services officers, and two team clerks, managed by the administration section but operating as part of the team. Two team meetings are held each week. Both function as allocation meetings but one is extended to allow for a regular information exchange. One meeting each month is also extended to enable the team to have a more extensive discussion of a particular issue. Individual supervision is scheduled for all team members on a fortnightly basis.

Social-priority and pilot teams

Two of the teams contributing to this book, in Lewisham (London) and Easterhouse (Glasgow), were established on the initiative of the management of their departments with the aim of improving services to areas of particularly high social deprivation. Another team, in Newham (London), was designed as a pilot experiment to test out a model of organization which might later be adopted by the social services department as a whole.

HONOR OAK

Area covered by the team

The Honor Oak team covers an inter-war housing estate in
Brockley, in the London Borough of Lewisham. The estate was
built by the local council to accommodate families from poor
housing in the Docklands area, and today is still predominantly
council-owned property. Most people are housed in large blocks
of flats. The demolition of some of the old blocks and the
modernization of others has resulted in some reduction in the
population of the estate in recent years. Today it houses just
over 2,000 people.

The Honor Oak estate is geographically isolated from neighbouring areas, being bounded on one side by a cemetery and on
two others by railway lines. The only access for vehicles is by a
single road which enters the estate under one of the railway
lines. Employment on the estate is limited to work in a few small
shops and most people work outside its boundaries in Lewisham and other parts of south London.

The population on the estate, which is predominantly working class, contains a lower than average proportion of retired
people but much higher proportions of one-parent families (25
per cent) and of people in ethnic minority groups (35 per cent),
nearly all of them West Indian (1981 Census).

Origins of the team

The team, known as the Honor Oak Advice and Information
Centre, was established in 1973 as a result of the initiative of the
local district officer in the social services department. The Housing Department provided accommodation in adjoining flats in
one of the blocks on the estate. It also agreed to second two of
its staff to work with the social services team.

The decision to establish the team grew out of the recognition
of the large volume of work generated by the estate, on account,
in particular, of the high level of family breakdown there and
the number of children being received into care. It was
estimated, for example, that in 1972–73, although only one-
tenth of the child population of the Western District Office in
Lewisham lived on the estate, more than one-third of the children received into care had Honor Oak addresses. The problem

of providing a good service was compounded by the lack of estate-based resources and the fact that the District Office was some distance away.

It was therefore decided to set up a small unit in the estate, on an experimental basis, consisting of social workers and community workers, in order to provide an accessible and responsive service through the provision of information of services, short-term casework, group work, and community work. It was hoped that involvement with groups of residents would make it easier to identify particular areas of need and to support efforts to mobilize resources to meet them.

Organization of the department

Social services in Lewisham are provided through six district offices, each managed by a district officer who has overall responsibility for the work of the district and direct control of community work activities. Each district office has a number of social work teams (covering all casework activities but not community work) which are managed by team leaders and responsible to the area team co-ordinator. Home helps are also organized at district level but all more specialized services such

Figure 4 *The organization and staffing of the Honor Oak team*

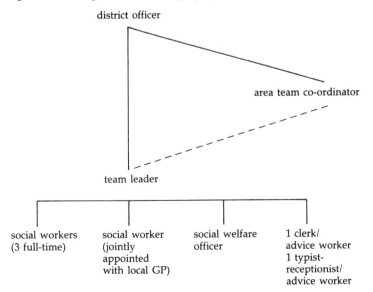

as teams for the mentally and visually handicapped are based at head office.

The structure of the Honor Oak team is set out in *Figure 4*. The team's social welfare officer deals mainly with elderly people. The clerk and typist in addition to their administrative duties are expected to become involved in advice work and other group and community activities undertaken by the team.

Management

The Honor Oak team leader is primarily responsible for his/her work to the district officer because the team's activities are seen as principally within his remit for community development. Any casework matters, however, continue to be the responsibility of the area team co-ordinator. The team leader is, in practice, given a very free hand by the district office which is only rarely involved in formal management meetings. Most internal management issues are settled by discussion at the team's weekly meetings. Individual cases are allocated at these meetings and all new projects are brought to them for approval. The team usually takes at least one day out every year when its members meet away from the office to carry out an overall review of their work.

LOCHEND

Area covered by the team

Easterhouse is a large post-war peripheral housing scheme on the east side of Glasgow, consisting mainly of three-storey tenement property, with some two-storey tenements and a small number of back- and front-door houses. All the houses are in the public sector, with Glasgow District Council as the landlord. A recent development has been the introduction of 'homesteading', the sale of difficult-to-let and often very dilapidated flats at very low prices to buyers who are then eligible for grants to rehabilitate them.

East One Area Social Work Team covers Easterhouse, Ballieston, and part of Garrowhill (a total population of about 45,000). The Lochend sub-team covers the Bishoploch, Lochend, Commonhead, and Rogerfield areas of Easterhouse (BLCR) with a total population of about 10,000. The area consists almost entirely of tenement property and has little homesteading.

Easterhouse has consistently suffered from very high unemployment. Although the statistics are not broken down into neighbourhoods, the BLCR area seems to have been particularly badly affected and local research indicates at least 80 to 90 per cent unemployment in some parts of the area. Entire streets are without individuals in any form of employment. Of those who do have jobs, the large majority are semi-skilled and unskilled manual workers. There is a predominance of single-parent families and families with children under 5. One recent study showed that 40 per cent of the population are under 16. The elderly population, in contrast, is relatively small.

Much of the BLCR is regarded as difficult to let and a large proportion of the inhabitants have been rehoused there by the homeless unit or from other parts of the city. Glasgow District Council's policy of letting houses to 16 to 18-year-olds has meant many young people housed with very little support and concomitant problems to themselves and their neighbours.

The results are very low levels of social cohesion, community identity, and participation in community life. To add to the difficulties of the area there is a high crime rate linked to a recent steep rise in the incidence of drug abuse. A further issue concerns gang boundaries which, while less of a problem than in the past, still means that young people are often reluctant to go to school or use youth provision if it means crossing into areas other than their own.

In spite of these difficulties, however, social work staff note that the people of the BLCR still have remarkable resilience and resourcefulness.

Origins of the sub-team

The sub-team was set up in 1981 to work in partnership with the BLCR Community Council. The initiative came from the area officer and team members, and stemmed from a commitment to introduce a community development perspective in the team's work. It is important to emphasize, however, that the sub-team was only one of the means used by the area to promote community development. Two years previously the Easterhouse Child Centred Project (ECCP) had been established with Urban Aid funding. Its main components were an intermediate treatment team and a day assessment centre. The focus of this project was on preventing the removal of children from the community. As a part of the project a study was done of the area and it was found that the BLCR had the highest concentration of single-parent families with children under 5 within Easterhouse.

Subsequently, extensive discussions took place in the area team and it was agreed that the establishment of a sub-team in the BLCR would:

1. make fieldwork services more accessible;
2. offer an understandable point of reference to other local agencies;
3. enable the team to broaden its community perspective so that a more balanced picture of the needs and resources in the area could be established;
4. highlight the opportunity for developing partnerships with local people in the planning and provision of social work services, particularly collaboration with the BLCR community council.

An added incentive to the initiative was the decision of the Housing Department to decentralize some of their functions and to set up a sub-office to cover the BLCR area.

Organization of the social work department

Strathclyde Region Social Work Department is the largest social services organization in the country and the scale of operations creates a number of problems for decentralized services. The region is divided into divisions of which Glasgow is the largest. Some specialist adviser posts are located at this level. The divisions in turn are divided into districts. There are six of these in Glasgow and occupational therapy, home-help, and specialist services for blind and mentally handicapped people are managed from their headquarters. Districts are subdivided into three or four area teams, each covering a population of between 50,000 and 70,000. The organization of individual teams varies but the general emphasis is on client-centred rather than community-centred approaches. Attempts to collaborate more closely with home helps and OTs are impeded by their location at district rather than area level.

East District serves a population of 150,000 and is divided into three area teams: East One, Two, and Three. Each includes urban-aided projects serving areas of particular social need.

Team organization

The East One team has an establishment of twenty social workers divided between intake, long-term, and Lochend sub-teams. It also has three school-based social workers and two health-centre based workers. Each sub-team is led by a senior social worker and the sub-teams are supported by two social work assistants and five homemakers.

Other local resources include the Easterhouse Child Centred Project, with an intermediate treatment unit and staff; a day assessment unit and staff; an eight-strong community development sub-team; a joint housing and social work project with four urban aid homemakers; a family centre and a day nursery.

Team management

The management team is made up of the area officer and the seniors leading each of the sub-teams. It meets fortnightly and is responsible for all the decisions affecting the area and sub-teams, including the Lochend team. All members of the team meet together weekly with the focus alternating between routine business and special topics.

Sub-team structure

The Lochend sub-team has inputs from four groups of workers: social workers, community workers, IT workers, and clerical workers. There are five social workers and a homemaker, all of whom are supervised by a senior social worker. There is a community work assistant who is supervised by a senior community worker. The team's two clerks are likewise supervised by a senior administrative officer outside the sub-team. There is also some input from an IT officer. *Figure 5* summarizes the team structure.

Sub-team management

Given these different lines of responsibility the coming together of different staff in weekly sub-team meetings is crucial. The meeting is divided between an allocation session and a

Figure 5 *The organization and staffing of the Lochend team*

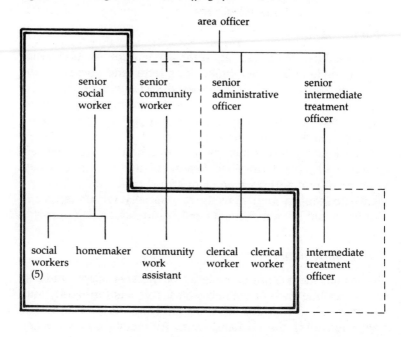

========== = full responsibility within the Lochend sub-team

– – – – – – – – – = partial responsibility within the Lochend sub-team

business session. The allocation session discusses and decides the formal allocation of cases, with ultimate responsibility for the decision resting with the senior social worker. The business session considers matters referred from the management team and issues coming up from within the BLCR. Responsibility for chairing the business session is rotated amongst the members of the sub-team.

DOCKLANDS

Area covered by the team

The team covers the section of the London Docklands area which falls within the London Borough of Newham. This is a strip of territory on the north bank of the River Thames covering just over 4 square miles. With the heavy bombing of the area in the Second World War, the decline of the docks in the post-war era, and the closure of the last dock some two decades ago, there was a considerable loss of population leaving large areas of derelict land. By 1979 there were only 11,000 people living in the Newham part of the Docklands. However, by that time the London Docklands Development Corporation (LDDC) had been set up, backed by central government funds, to regenerate the Docklands area. Since then modernization and rebuilding have led to some increase in population and there are now about 15,000 people living in the Newham Docklands. As yet, however, little new industry has been attracted and most of the working population are employed outside the Docklands.

Today much of the area can still be characterized by the words used by the originator of the Docklands social service team in the late 1970s as 'acres of wasteland interspersed with small communities of people living in run-down terraced Victorian houses and with the skyline marked by the occasional cluster of high rise flats' (Simpson 1980: 90). Three such communities house the majority of the inhabitants of Newham Docklands, each containing about 5,000 people. These are North Woolwich and Silverton, West Beckton, and East Beckton.

The social problems of the area differ to some extent between the three sub-areas or communities. Unemployment is generally high but is at its worst in more isolated North Woolwich and Silvertown. This community also has the highest proportion of elderly people. Problems associated with families and young people are more likely to be found in West Beckton which has the highest proportion of new, larger units of council housing. All parts of the area feel the effects of poor commercial and social services resources and all are affected by high crime rates. Nevertheless, the very isolation of the communities has tended to give them something of the feeling of village life and a common identity. This is strongest in North Woolwich and Silvertown and in the working-class parts of East Beckton. In both these areas informal networks remain very strong. The Docklands area has only one enclave of middle-class residents, in a new private estate established in East Beckton.

Origins of the team

The idea for setting up an experimental community-based team in the Docklands originated with the then assistant director of social services for Newham, Dennis Simpson, in 1979 (Simpson 1980: 81–95). Because of financial constraints and other difficulties the team did not become fully operational until 1982. The philosophy behind the establishment of the team can be summarized briefly as the belief that social services should be made easily accessible at a local level and should incorporate a community dimension. In this way they should become responsive to community needs rather than merely reactive to the demands made upon them. More specifically, the aims of the team were defined as:

(a) to ensure more democratic agency decision making;
(b) to increase the relevance of community self-determination;
(c) to reduce the alienation experienced by community groups;
(d) to attempt to de-label the helping process in the provision of services.

Proposals for the creation of the Docklands team included the following:

1. Inner-city partnership money should be used to fund new posts primarily to form the Docklands team;
2. The Docklands strategic plan boundaries should be used to define a new social services area to be serviced exclusively by the new team.
3. Staff should be located in three separate (patch) offices in the West Beckton, East Beckton, and North Woolwich areas.
4. Social workers, community workers, home helps, family aides, and clerical workers should be dispersed in mixed groups as social services (not social work) sub-teams in the three locally based offices.
5. A fundamental objective of the team should be to blur the boundaries between different professional groups and to move away from the conventional professional and organizational constraints in the way they operated.

Organization of the department

At the inception of the Docklands project the organization of Newham social services followed conventional lines. The department consisted of three functional divisions — fieldwork, residential, and administrative. Although all area teams had decided to move towards a patch-based approach they remained centrally organized and a considerable proportion of the field workers remained in specialist teams.

Organization of the team

The organization of the Docklands team is set out in *Figure 6*. It consists of 8 full-time staff and 9 part-time staff, together with 25 part-time home helps and a group of volunteers varying in numbers from 5 to 15. There are also vacancies for three community workers which have existed since the team was established owing to problems over their job descriptions and accountability.

Figure 6 *The organization and staffing of the Docklands team*

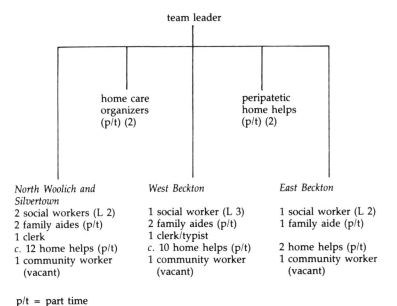

team leader

home care organizers (p/t) (2)

peripatetic home helps (p/t) (2)

North Woolich and Silvertown
2 social workers (L 2)
2 family aides (p/t)
1 clerk
c. 12 home helps (p/t)
1 community worker
(vacant)

West Beckton
1 social worker (L 3)
2 family aides (p/t)
1 clerk/typist
c. 10 home helps (p/t)
1 community worker
(vacant)

East Beckton
1 social worker (L 2)
1 family aide (p/t)
2 home helps (p/t)
1 community worker
(vacant)

p/t = part time
2 = level 2
3 = level 3

Management

All members of the team are accountable to the team leader for their day-to-day work. However, the home care organizers and administrative staff also have access to senior staff in their own field, outside the team, should they wish to seek their advice and support. The team leader directly supervises the social workers, the home care organizers, and administrative staff. Family aides are supervised by social workers in their patches and home helps by the home care organizers.

The main management processes of the team are handled in two kinds of meetings: those held weekly in each patch and the fortnightly meetings of the team as a whole. The *patch meetings* are chaired by the team leader and attended by all staff except the home helps. East Beckton has recently started to include its home helps but in the other two patches the larger numbers of staff involved have so far prevented a similar development. Patch meetings consider all new referrals to the team over the previous week and decide whether to leave cases with the workers who first received them or transfer them to other staff. The meetings also review and take decisions on existing and new project work. Matters which may affect the team as a whole are placed on the agenda of the main team meeting.

The *team meetings*, which involve all staff except the home helps, are chaired on a rotating basis by each member of the team. The meetings receive and discuss information about department-wide developments, consider issues raised by individual patches or special working groups, and make policy for the team as a whole.

In addition to the regular meetings there are occasional meetings of staff belonging to the same occupational group – for example social workers or family aides –to discuss issues of common interest. The team as a whole has also established the practice of holding an annual study day away from the office to review its policies and practice and to make plans for future developments.

Department-wide decentralization

A number of social services departments have embarked on the systematic decentralization of their local teams and have encouraged their staff to adopt a community social work orientation.

East Sussex was the first to undertake a radical change of this kind when in 1981 it moved from area to patch teams. Two of the contributors to this book were, at the time of writing, team managers in the new organization, one for the rural district served from the small town of Rye and the other for the city-edge council estate of Whitehawk in Brighton. The organization of the East Sussex department has been described at some length elsewhere (Hadley, Dale, and Sills 1984: 13–19; Young 1985) and our account in this book is restricted to a brief summary.

The county of East Sussex has a population of about 640,000. For the purposes of the new organization of the social services department it was divided into two divisions, west and east, and eleven area and forty-five patch teams. (Subsequent organizational changes have reduced the number of areas to eight and patch teams to forty-two.) Each patch team covers an average of about 14,000 people but there is in practice a considerable range in size between the smallest (about 5,000) and the largest (25,000). Except for two family and children's centres, hospital social work, and intermediate treatment, all social services facilities are managed at patch team level. Team managers are thus responsible for integrating field, domiciliary, day, and residential services.

ORGANIZATION OF THE RYE TEAM

Rye is one of the four patch teams serving the Rother Area and was based in the area office at Bexhill, 17 miles from Rye, for the first year of its life. At this distance it was difficult to begin to practise a more community-orientated approach but in 1983 the team moved on to the patch and began to develop the methods of community social work. The organization and staffing of the team are set out in *Figure 7*.

Management

Team meetings are held fortnightly and involve all the patch office-based staff except for one of the team clerks who looks after reception. Homes hold their own staff meetings which the team manager and some other staff attend occasionally. Home helps are divided into four groups on a geographical basis and receive supervision once a month.

Figure 7 *The organization and staffing of the Rye team*

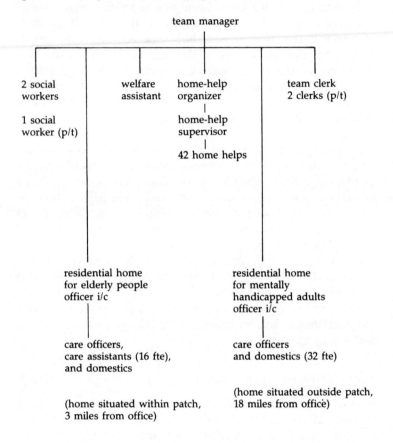

fte = full time equivalent, p/t = part-time

WHITEHAWK

Area covered by the team

The Whitehawk patch team area lies on the eastern edge of Brighton. The main part of the patch is conterminous with the Whitehawk Estate itself. This is a large post-war council-built development lying north of the Kemp Town seafront area of Brighton, covering an area about a mile north-south by half a mile east-west. In addition to the main Whitehawk Estate, the patch includes the adjoining Manor Farm Estate (also mainly council housing) and the nearby Roedean and Bristol Estates, which have large proportions of private accommodation. The population of the area covered by the patch was 10,231 in 1981 but has been growing rapidly since then and is expected to reach between 14,000 and 15,000 by 1988.

The patch has many inner-city problems, concentrated mainly in the Whitehawk and Manor Farm Estates. The area is one of the very few educational priority areas in East Sussex and is marked by high levels of unemployment and poverty, high incidence of mental handicap, mental illness, single-parent families, isolated families and illiteracy. In the early 1970s Whitehawk achieved national notoriety as the estate where Maria Colwell died. Barristers and solicitors in local courts have been heard pleading as mitigating circumstances that their clients have been brought up or live on the estate. Perhaps unsurprisingly the people living in the predominantly private housing of the Roedean and Bristol estates do not see themselves as part of Whitehawk and do their best to distance themselves from its reputation.

Origins of the team

The possibility of opening a sub-office in Whitehawk to provide a better service to this multi-problem estate was first mooted in 1974 by the then divisional director for Brighton. Difficulties, including the perceived threat to the area team which would lose part of its staff to the sub-team, impeded change. However, in 1976, with the added impetus of an increasingly overcrowded central office, it was finally agreed to open a Whitehawk office for a twelve-month experimental period. The project was renewed each year until 1980 when the team leader left. At this stage serious consideration was given to withdrawing the team to the central Brighton office but then the proposals for a general decentralization of services within the department was announced and it was decided to maintain the Whitehawk sub-team.

The new team leader appointed to manage the Whitehawk patch was a strong advocate of community social work and made his own recommendations for developing the organization and practice of the team in advance of the main departmental reorganization. Included in his plan was the introduction of new office management procedures at the local level and the full integration of all social services within the team boundaries: residential, day-care, domiciliary and field social work. His proposals, which turned out to be very much in tune with those emerging at senior management level in plans for a departmental reorganization, were finally accepted by divisional management and implemented at the end of 1980. Up to this time the Whitehawk sub-office had restricted its work to long-term cases: all initial referrals and short-term work continued to be handled by the area team. Under the new system, however, the team leader insisted that social work staff must be ready to take on generic workloads. In his view the claim that specialist intake workers were required was unfounded. Staff who had previously concentrated on long-term work could, given adequate support from colleagues, soon learn to handle initial assessments and short-term cases. One of the existing sub-office staff refused to adapt his role in this way and moved back to the central team but the others rapidly adapted to their new roles.

Files on all users living in Whitehawk were transferred to the patch office. It was interesting to note that as the team got to know these cases it became apparent that about 80 per cent had been given a much lower priority for service than the sub-team felt was justified. It was their strong impression that the centralized area team had been dealing with these cases not on the basis of the priority and needs of the client but of the priorities and needs of the social worker. In other words, most social workers had been avoiding difficult work in Whitehawk if they could.

The reorganization of the Whitehawk team was quickly followed by the general reorganization of the department. This brought with it an expansion of the staff of the sub-team to include an additional three social workers, two team clerks, and a home-help organizer. In spite of being given a high priority within the department, the building of the larger office premises needed by the expanded team took two years to complete and involved considerable upheaval for the team in the interim.

Figure 8 *The organization and staffing of the Whitehawk team*

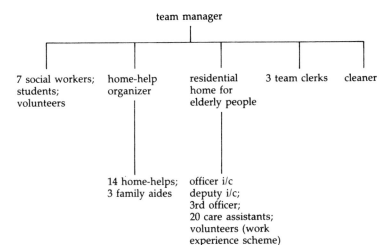

Organization and management of the team

The team structure and staffing are set out in *Figure 8*. The management of the team is based on team meetings, group meetings, and individual supervision. There is a once-a-week team meeting which considers clients and groups, and the allocation of work, in which information is exchanged and issues discussed.

Side by side with the line structure a functional structure is developing in which old professional boundaries are frequently crossed. For instance, integrated training combining care assistants, home heps, social workers, volunteers, and office staff has taken place. Similarly, group supervision has been introduced bringing together social workers, family aides, and team clerks. Again old boundaries are crossed or erased when home helps work in the elderly people's home on the patch, when social workers manage home help resources, or the officer in charge of the elderly people's home becomes directly involved in assessing potential residents in their own homes. The team has yearly plans which are dovetailed into area, divisional, and departmental policies. Team days out to review progress against such plans are a regular feature of team management. Supervision is agreed on an almost contractual basis between the team manager and staff, and regular yearly staff development reviews are undertaken.

Summary

In sum, the eight teams on which this handbook is based are located over the length of the land in a wide variety of settings from the densely settled city centre to thinly populated countryside, from areas with severe economic and social problems to areas with no more than an average share of either. The teams receive varying degrees of support from their departments in their attempts to develop CSW, include different categories of staff, are resourced at different levels, and are at various stages in the development of community-orientated working. Yet in spite of this diversity, they share, as the following chapters illustrate, a considerable amount of common ground in their conceptions of CSW and in the methods they are evolving to turn these conceptions into practice.

3 Localization

The localization of the principal front-line services is a fundamental precondition for the successful development of community social work (CSW). The underlying rationale of this view has been explored in Chapter 1. In the present chapter we review the practical issues raised by the application of a policy of localization in the light of the experience of the contributing teams. The chapter falls into three main parts. The first addresses questions concerning the identification of neighbourhoods and the establishment of team boundaries and office facilities. The second considers reception and referrals in locally based teams. The third examines the use of local staff and volunteers and the associated issues of confidentiality.

Neighbourhoods and micro-neighbourhoods

ISSUES

A.1 *The identification of neighbourhoods and micro-neighbourhoods*

The term 'neighbourhood' is used in this book in an objective sense, following Warren's definition: 'the social organisation of a population residing in a geographically proximate locale. This includes not only social bonds between members of the designated population but all of that group's links to non-neighbours as well' (Warren 1981: 62).

The boundaries of a neighbourhood may be defined by various features such as railway lines, main roads, rivers, and open spaces but the area covered will normally be a 'walking distance' one, perhaps not more than a mile square and often much smaller. Neighbourhoods defined in this way may or may not be communities in the sense that their inhabitants perceive the existence of common values and interests on the basis of their proximity. Within the neighbourhoods there are also many

micro-neighbourhoods defined in terms of a 'next-door neighbour, the person in the next apartment or the most immediate
set of adjacent households' (Warren 1981: 63).

Both neighbourhoods and micro-neighbourhoods are important to the community social worker because they are potentially
important to the citizen. The nature of social relationships at this
level may substantially influence the quality of everyday life.
More significantly from the point of view of the social services,
they are particularly likely to be important if a person is dependent on the support of others in order to remain living in his or
her home. The greater the level of dependence, the greater the
probability that help will be provided by people living locally
(Bayley, Seyd, and Tennant 1985: 65-6).

A.2 *The characterization of neighbourhoods*

Evidence from neighbourhood studies shows that their social
organization can vary considerably with major consequences for
the patterns of mutual aid at both informal and formal levels
(e.g. Froland *et al.* 1981; Warren 1981; Leat 1983; Yoder 1985;
Willmott 1986). Such variations are of the first importance for
CSW in that the potential for intervention and the type of intervention that is appropriate are likely to differ in different types
of neighbourhood. For example, in a neighbourhood with what
Warren has described as a *parochial* social organization, with
strong informal networks, the agency may be able to work with
the neighbourhood as a system and may need to rely less on the
networks of individual clients (Froland *et al.* 1981). In *anomic*
neighbourhoods, with weak or non-existent informal networks,
however, such strategies would be non-starters.

It is therefore important for CSW practitioners to be able both
to *identify* neighbourhoods and, where possible, the micro-
neighbourhoods within the areas they cover, and to become as
fully informed as they can of the *character* of the social organization of these neighbourhoods, especially in terms of those
features which are likely to affect present and potential levels
and quality of care (see also Chapter 4, p. 103).

TEAM EXPERIENCE

B.1 *The identification of neighbourhoods and micro-neighbourhoods*

All the teams felt able to divide their areas into a number of discrete neighbourhoods with the exception of Honor Oak where the small estate served was itself regarded as constituting a single neighbourhood. However, even in Honor Oak each block of flats was regarded as having its own character.

In Whitehawk four neighbourhoods were defined, each based on a separate housing estate. Of the two Longbenton neighbourhoods, similarly, one was synonymous with the Longbenton estate and the other with the separate conglomeration of villages to the north. In Normanton one neighbourhood was easily identifiable in the village of Altofts lying to the north of the town. Four other neighbourhoods could be distinguished, two being post-war housing developments, and two in surviving older housing. The Docklands team described three neighbourhoods in its area, each separated from the other by derelict land and unused docks.

In both Rye and Huntly each of the villages and small towns in the large rural areas served by the teams is recognized as a separate neighbourhood. The villages, however, give some kind of allegiance to the local towns, mainly on the basis of transport links.

Defining features
Most of the neighbourhood boundaries are readily defined. The areas covered are reasonably compact and certainly meet Warren's (1981) walking distance criterion. In many cases they are differentiated by clear geographical boundaries such as main roads, railways, parks and cemeteries, derelict land, and countryside. In Whitehawk another type of boundary can be identified where the one privately owned estate is marked off clearly from adjoining local-authority housing.

The origins or age of an area can also affect neighbourhood boundaries. Within Normanton, for example, one estate can be differentiated from nearby housing partly on the basis of the concentration of people who have formerly lived in the condemned housing demolished to make way for it.

Few of the teams indicated any systematic knowledge of

micro-neighbourhoods although it is clear from examples given just how important they can be in affecting people's perceptions and readiness to participate. In Longbenton, for instance, elderly people in a sheltered housing complex were unwilling to attend a regular social event unless it was organized in their own very local territory, within the complex itself.

B.2 *The characterization of neighbourhoods*

The nature of the neighbourhoods covered by the teams varies considerably. The more homogeneous and stable neighbourhoods (e.g. North Woolwich and Silvertown in Docklands, and Altofts in Normanton) seem to have the strongest informal networks; the more transitory neighbourhoods (e.g. Lochend) the weakest. However, the relationship between length of settlement and helping systems is not always as obvious. The Rye team notes marked variations in the levels of mutual aid in the villages it serves which cannot be explained in this way.

PRACTICE GUIDELINES

C.1 *The identification of neighbourhoods and micro-neighbourhoods*

■ **Given the significance of neighbourhoods as appropriate arenas for action in CSW, it is important for community-based teams to identify the neighbourhoods within their areas as soon as they can. To identify neighbourhoods:**

● establish probable geographical boundaries of neighbourhoods, using maps and study in the field, and plotting major physical boundaries;
● within these boundaries, establish if there are important differentiating factors, other than geography, which may create clear subdivisions of the area into two or more neighbourhoods, e.g. different phases in building, different categories of tenure;
● check this evidence against subjective evaluation of the neighbourhoods and their boundaries by: (a) residents, (b) others with relevant local knowledge such as shopkeepers, clergy, schoolteachers, etc.;
● draw up lists of neighbourhoods identified by this process;

● be alert to the possible need to redefine neighbourhood boundaries in the light of: (a) fuller information; (b) subsequent demographic shifts or other changes.

Micro-neighbourhoods will normally be so numerous within any one neighbourhood that systematic and comprehensive identification of them is scarcely likely to be possible for teams to achieve. However, knowledge of micro-neighbourhoods can be accumulated on an *ad hoc* basis through:

● work with individuals and families to establish their interaction with their micro-neighbourhoods;
● group and project work in particular parts of the neighbourhood;
● regular pooling of such information by members of the team and recording methods which assist the accumulation of such information

C.2 *The characterization of neighbourhoods*

■ **The more a team knows about relevant aspects of the social organization of the neighbourhoods it is serving, the better able it will be to plan both neighbourhood and area strategies of intervention.**

Henderson and Thomas have produced a useful summary of what neighbourhood workers need to know about their neighbourhoods and how they can find their data. Most of their suggestions are equally relevant to community social workers. They are summarized in *Table 3*, which offers a valuable and detailed method of getting to know a neighbourhood and could provide a useful programme for the newly established team. However, this method will be time-consuming to undertake and it may be that in the short run teams will find it more profitable to adopt a less elaborate and more focused characterization.

Warren's (1981: 67) typology of neighbourhoods also provides a helpful framework. He identifies six main types of neighbourhoods whose variations in help seeking and problem management can be largely explained in terms of three factors: (a) the extent of individual identification with the area; (b) the degree of social exchange within the neighbourhood; (c) the extent to which the area is explicitly linked to the larger community.

Table 3 *Data on the neighbourhood and how to collect it*

What does the neighbourhood worker need to know?
1. History.
2. Environment.
3. Residents: (a) basic information; (b) social welfare data;
   (c) perceptions of the area; (d) community networks; (e) values
   and traditions.
4. Organisations: (a) local and central government; (b) economic
   activities; (c) religious organisations; (d) associations; (e) voluntary
   organisations.
5. Communications.
6. Power and Leadership: (a) business and organised labour;
   (b) elective politics; (c) administrative politics; (d) civic politics;
   (e) community politics.

How to go about data collection
Planning:
Purpose, sources of information, methods, organisation and
personnel time, resources, putting data to use.

Four aspects of data collection

1. Looking for a neighbourhood – using the census and easily
   obtainable social indicators.
2. *Broad-angle scan of the chosen neighbourhood:* analysing the census,
   street work, scanning the newspapers, using the worker's own
   agency records, getting to know the authorities, getting to know
   community groups, finding out who serves the neighbourhood.
3. *Narrow-scope scan.* This is comprehensive and detailed; focused
   and selective; systematic and thorough in its methods.
4. Analysis, interpretation, and write-up.

Source: Henderson and Thomas (1980: 83)

The six main types of neighbourhood identified by Warren
(1981: 67–8) can be set on a continuum from the integral (high
levels of identification, exchange, and linkage with the wider
community) through the parochial, diffuse, stepping-stone, and
transitory, to the anomic neighbourhood (with low levels of all
three factors).

■ **Teams can use this approach to collect information at two
levels which will help them to establish what kind of neighbourhoods they are working with and to plan appropriate
intervention strategies:**

● *Gathering impressionistic evidence about neighbourhoods.* Members of the team can seek to obtain views on each of the three factors listed above from individual users, from other local people met in the course of the day's work, and from other agency staff working in the neighbourhood and in the larger community to which it is linked. The pooling of such impressions on a team basis may provide at least a rough and ready picture of the kinds of neighbourhoods the team is serving, in terms of the Warren typology.

● *Gathering systematic evidence.* Properly conducted survey work of a sample of individuals living in the neighbourhood should provide systematic and reliable evidence on all three factors. The snag with such an approach is that it is time consuming and requires at least some survey technique skills. For those without such skills there are several useful do-it-yourself manuals available (e.g. Phillips 1981). Alternatively or additionally, external help may be available from a department's research staff or from a local college. (See also Chapter 4, p. 106.)

Drawing team and sub-team boundaries

ISSUES

How small is beautiful? What is the most appropriate scale of operation for the team practising CSW? Some seem to hope to find a magic number, whether for the population to be served, the square miles to be covered, or the membership of the team. However, given the wide variety of areas served by teams in both demographic and geographical terms, and the considerable differences in the kinds of staff who compose the teams, it seems highly unlikely that any simple answers will be found which are capable of fitting all circumstances.

The most important issues which it would seem necessary to consider are:

A.1 interrelationships between team members, the effect of size on the ability of the team to function as a coherent whole;

A.2 accessibility of the team to its users and potential users (see also: Chapter 4, p. 97; Chapter 5, pp. 141, 151; Chapter 6, p. 211);

A.3 boundaries which may have relevance locally, e.g.,

neighbourhoods, shopping catchment systems;

A.4 need to build close relations with other local agencies such as the primary health care team, schools, voluntary agencies (see also: Chapter 4, p. 124; Chapter 6, p. 211);

A.5 whether or not it is intended to divide the area into sub-areas or patches.

Factors influencing management in defining team boundaries

Most of the team boundaries were determined before the teams were created and they have had little direct involvement in determining them. Their information on the factors used to determine boundaries is second-hand and in some cases speculative. Nevertheless it appears that a number of common factors were influential in several cases. These are briefly reviewed before discussion of the teams' experiences of the resulting boundaries.

Population
Although the population resident in each of the eight team areas ranges from 2,000 to 20,000, the majority of the teams cover populations in a much narrower band, between 10,000 and 15,000. In the case of the two East Sussex teams one factor in choosing this particular range was span of control, in other words the number of staff involved to be managed at this level. A related factor in Longbenton was the number of team leaders available when it was decided to decentralize teams. Other authorities may have also felt that good management of community-orientated teams required the balance between population size and staff numbers implied but this was not reported as the main influence.

Administrative and political boundaries
In several cases these played an important part in determining the area covered by the team. In Normanton the team's area was that previously covered by the old urban district council. In Docklands the team area was determined by the Docklands Development Board. In Lochend the area was chosen to be conterminous with that of the local community council and the Housing Department sub-area. In Huntly the team area was initially formed on that of the local registration district. In Rye

a major part of the boundaries was determined by proximity to the neighbouring county of Kent.

Referral levels
This was the other main factor in deciding boundaries. High rates of referral from vulnerable client groups were major factors in the initial plans to set up teams in *Honor Oak* and *Whitehawk* and also influenced the decision to establish the *Lochend* team.

TEAM EXPERIENCE

B.1 *Team functioning*

The maximum number of people involved in the main decision-making activities of the teams (i.e. 'key' members) was about twenty (in Normanton) and in most cases was substantially smaller. At this scale the teams seemed to find no significant problems in developing satisfactory relationships between members.

B.2 *Accessibility*

Boundaries created problems of access for the Longbenton team since it had been given responsibility for two separate estates and the team office was located away from them both. There were also some access problems for the Rye team in that it had difficulty serving the more distant villages in its area and insufficient resources to establish any call offices. The other teams had sufficiently compact areas or (Huntly) adequate call office facilities to make access no major problem.

B.3 *Neighbourhoods*

The boundaries of neighbourhoods seem to have been respected in determining the larger areas covered by the teams. Only from the Docklands team was there a complaint of a totally inappropriate boundary in the case of the West Beckton part of the area. Attempts to recognize neighbourhood boundaries were acknowledged in Longbenton, Rye, Whitehawk, and Huntly. Transport links were also regarded as important in Huntly which was the only team to have played a significant part in decisions determining its boundaries.

B.4 *Other agencies' boundaries*

In the experience of the contributing teams two main clusters of other organizations and agencies could be distinguished in terms of the *compatibility* of their boundaries. In the first cluster, where boundaries are generally compatible with those defined by the social services team, are nursery schools, primary and first schools, middle schools, and in some instances secondary schools; primary health care (GPs and community nursing); community police; and a wide range of local voluntary organizations from tenants' associations to churches. In several instances there were also local housing offices. Included in the second cluster of organizations and agencies where those which had much wider catchment areas than the social services team, e.g. the DHSS (social security) office, larger voluntary agencies, and in some instances housing agencies.

Beyond these generalizations, however, it is clear that some teams are much better placed than others. Those with the most compatible boundaries were the two rural teams and three of the suburban estate teams where other agencies as well as social services have acknowledged the importance of establishing a local presence. In Whitehawk, for example, the housing office is next door to the team office, there are several schools on the estate, and an educational welfare officer works to the same catchment area as the team. The DHSS does not have a local office but has assigned a number of staff specifically to deal with the estate. Similarly, in the rural area covered by the Huntly team, school catchment areas and health clinic and housing boundaries all fit well with those of social services. The main problems are with the DHSS whose nearest office is 40 miles to the south-east and the Department of Employment whose office is 18 miles to the north. Both have a call-in office open one day a week in Huntly but on the other four days the social work team find themselves bombarded with their business.

The two teams with the least compatible boundaries, Docklands and Longbenton, are both fringe areas on the edges of the local authorities of which they form part. In the latter, for example, only the first and middle schools and a housing office serve the same areas as the social services team. Particular problems are caused by the location of the secondary school half a mile away in the neighbouring team's patch. Many people consider this too far away and say they 'never go over there';

consequently the team can gain little from the useful facilities of the school. Further difficulties result from health service boundaries. Most GPs have the major part of their practices in Newcastle and the patch is included in the catchment area of Newcastle hospitals.

Building relations with other agencies and networks

Associated with the question of the compatibility of boundaries is the issue of the density of interrelationships which a team will seek and need to operate effectively and the effect of this on the maximum size of the area that it can cope with. In terms of building close relations with the heads of all the schools, the GPs, nursing officers, police, housing sub-office managers, clergy, local councillors, and so on, the leaders of the teams contributing to this book found the size of their team areas manageable. However, when liaison with smaller voluntary bodies and with informal care networks was concerned some of the teams felt the areas were too large and needed some kind of subdivision. (See B.5 below.) The experience of the largest of the teams, Normanton, was that in a town of 19,000, inter-agency contacts could barely be dealt with on an adequate basis.

B.5 Subdivision of team areas into patches

Team response to the issue of subdivision covered a wide range. The smallest, Honor Oak and the most compact, Lochend, felt no need for subdivisions within their areas. The Whitehawk team felt that the advantages of maintaining a single team outweighed those of subdivision. In particular the team manager believed that subdivision would have given less opportunity for specialization, increased levels of stress in workers, made cover for sickness and leave more difficult, and added administrative costs. In Longbenton opinion was divided and a minority felt it would make more sense to divide the team into two sub-units to serve the two quite separate estates covered. Both Normanton and Docklands have subdivided their areas into three patches with separate teams allocated to each. They argue that this is necessary both to facilitiate access by users and to enable the team to build close relations with local voluntary organizations and informal caring networks. By having regular team meetings, joint projects, and in some cases specialization across boundaries, they felt that they could successfully blend the two approaches. The two rural teams both expressed the need for contact points with users in the more remote parts of the areas they served. The Huntly team had achieved this with call office arrangements and the cover offered by the area officers. The Rye team had not yet adequate resources to open the sub-office it wanted in the northern part of its area.

PRACTICE GUIDELINES

The experience of contributing teams points to a number of factors which *ideally* should be taken into account in deciding on the boundaries of community-based teams. Clearly, it will rarely be possible to observe them all but they can be helpful for suggesting directions for new developments and ways in which established teams may modify their existing arrangements.

C.1 *Internal coherence of the team*

■ **Integration within the social services team requires frequent and easy contact between all its key members, or members of the 'core' team.** By the term 'core team' we mean the people directly managed by the team manager or leader. This group has the main responsibility for the leadership of the team and is likely to be the repository of its values. The particular composition of the core team will vary according to the composition and size of the CSW team as a whole. In small teams (e.g. Huntly) the core team may be the same as the whole team. In larger teams (such as those in East Sussex) it may be restricted principally to those managing subsections such as the officers in charge of residential establishments and day centres, the home-help organizers, and the senior clerk. There is insufficient evidence to indicate whether hard and fast rules could ever be devised to establish the maximum number required for cohesion but it would seem that fifteen to twenty team members (the numbers in Normanton) represent an upper limit from this point of view. This in turn suggests different population maxima for teams according to the number of different categories of staff employed within them. It also indicates different approaches in urban and rural areas.

■ **In urban areas, assuming problems of distance are likely to** be minimal, where field and domiciliary staff alone are involved, a core team of fifteen staff would be expected to cover perhaps 20,000–25,000 people.

Where residential and day-care staff are added a core of fifteen staff would be produced by a much smaller area. For example, if the team area included one EPH and one day centre, with between them a management staff of seven, then with a maximum of eight field and domiciliary core members the team could be expected to serve no more than 10,000–12,000 people.

■ **In rural areas** distance is likely to be a major factor restricting the interaction of team members. When lower population densities are also taken into account the preferred population **totals to be covered by rural community-based teams will ideally be much smaller.**

C.2 *Accessibility to users and potential users*

■ **Ideally, teams should be within easy access of those they serve.** The most straightforward way to arrange this, at least in urban areas, is to draw boundaries so that all the people served are within, say, ten minutes walk of the team office. **This would suggest a catchment area bounded by a radius of about half a mile from the office.** In practice this will often not be possible to achieve. Three other guidelines can be used:

● Where larger areas have to be covered, transport patterns – especially bus routes – can be used as an indication of easiest access.

● Alternatively, sub-areas or patches can be established. Local team offices or call offices can then be set up to facilitate access. Alternatively/additionally direct contact can be encouraged with the staff allocated to the sub-team or patch as they go about their daily work in the field.

● Additionally, where the team has no local base, a useful strategy is to seek to make arrangements with other agencies such as health clinics or nurseries for staff to call in routinely to see users on the premises.

C.3 *Respecting locally significant boundaries*

■ **Two kinds of pre-existing boundary are of particular**

importance in determining or modifying team boundaries: neighbourhood boundaries and the boundaries of other agencies with whom the social services team need to liaise.

● *Neighbourhood boundaries*: while social services teams are almost always likely to cover much larger areas than those we have defined as neighbourhoods (Chapter 3, pp. 53-4; Chapter 4, p. 103), it is important that their own boundaries should not dissect neighbourhoods and so create artificial frontiers that make no sense to local people. In drawing up the boundaries of a new team or reviewing those of an existing team it should be a high priority to identify neighbourhoods within and adjoining the proposed or actual team area. Necessary adjustments should be made to the team boundaries accordingly.

● *Agency boundaries*: in initial planning, team boundaries should be drawn with reference to the main collaborating agencies. Where these are incompatible with each other a careful judgement needs to be made as to the priority of different agencies. There can be no automatic assumption that one, e.g. health, is more important than another, e.g. housing. The situation of each team will have to be assessed according to local needs and future plans.

C.4 *Building relations with local agencies*

■ **Team boundaries should take account of the need of team members to establish and maintain close working contact with colleagues in other agencies, local councillors, and others of particular significance**. Again, it is not possible to lay down hard and fast guidelines on how many such contacts an individual team leader or manager might be expected to cope with successfully. Much is likely to depend on the organization of the team as a whole and the possibility of sharing contacts on a systematic basis with other members of staff.

● From available experience it would seem that a ratio of better than one worker responsible for agency contacts and relations to every 4,000 people is desirable if close contacts are to be established and maintained.

C.5 *The subdivision of team areas into patches*

■ **The case for the subdivision of the area covered by a**

community-based team would seem strongest where: the team office is not readily accessible on foot or by a good transport system to a substantial proportion of those it is intended to serve; the area covered is too large or fragmented for the easy development of close relationships with local voluntary organizations and local informal caring networks.

■ **Practitioners have found that in urban areas with reasonably dense settlement, 4,000 to 5,000 is a workable population to aim for in defining sub-areas or patches.**

Locating the office

ISSUES

The local office brings with it clear advantages for both users and other agencies, reduces travelling time for its staff, and can help give them a feeling of belonging to the area they serve. There remain, however, a number of issues (see also Chapter 4, pp. 96, 123):

A.1 the precise siting of the office within the area;
A.2 the type of building preferred;
A.3 the advantages and disadvantages of sharing premises with other agencies;
A.4 the case for having sub-team or patch offices;
A.5 coping strategies for teams which have to operate without a local office.

TEAM EXPERIENCE

B.1 and B.2 *Siting the office and the type of building*

All the teams except for Longbenton have offices within the areas they serve. The Longbenton team shares space with other teams in the area office, some 2 miles from the nearest part of the patch which it covers. Of all the other teams only the Whitehawk team has a purpose-built office. It is centrally placed, close to the bus routes running through the area, next door to the housing sub-office, a library, and a youth club. Two teams on urban housing estates, Honor Oak and Lochend, have offices in converted flats, in both cases sharing buildings with other agencies. The Rye team has a converted shop in a central position near the bus station and post office and the Normanton team is based in the former station master's house, close to the town shopping centre.

The two remaining teams have accommodation on more than one site. The Huntly team has a presence in four separate offices in its thinly populated area. In Huntly and Alford it is represented in the area offices of the local authority where the area officer gives one-third of his time to social work (see Chapter 2, p. 28). In another part of Huntly the two team social workers have an office in a portakabin belonging to the district council and in the town of Insch they have a call office in the local health clinic. The Docklands team aims to have a separate office in each of its three patches. In the North Woolwich patch it has quarters in the old public baths. In the West Beckton patch the team base is a portakabin on the new housing estate.

The seven teams with local bases all feel that they have achieved satisfactory siting for their offices, in central and accessible places. However, the facilities of the buildings used are not uniformly seen as satisfactory. In Docklands the North Woolwich office is cramped and the West Beckton portakabin has the disadvantage of being subdivided into small rooms. In spite of such shortcomings most of the teams argue for the use of buildings which fit into the locality in preference to purpose-built offices which, they think, may seem more alien to local users and less easy to approach.

B.3 *Shared premises*

Shared premises are seen as an advantage by the teams with experience of them, both for the contacts that they bring with the other agency or agencies and for helping to make the approach to the social services less stigmatizing for some users. But they are also experienced as potentially restricting team freedom where reception facilities are shared. In two cases, Honor Oak and Huntly, the more formal arrangements planned by links with other departments threatened to introduce an unwelcome degree of distance between users and staff in the social services team. In Huntly, for instance, a joint initiative between region and district councils plans to incorporate housing and social work in the same building with formal reception facilities serving both offices.

B.4 and B.5 *Sub-offices and strategies for teams without a local base*

The different views of teams on the pros and cons of having sub-team or patch offices have been discussed above (pp. 63–6). The team with no local office, Longbenton, have developed a series of strategies to compensate for this, including building up relationships with local groups and setting up and running their own group and community activities in the area.

PRACTICE GUIDELINES

C.1 *Siting the office*

■ Any long-term development of community social work requires a local base for the team in the area served if they are to achieve their maximum potential.

■ Ideal locations and possible locations may not be the same. Ideal locations will give a high priority to user-access to the team and staff-access to the locality. Depending on circumstances, the most relevant guide to access may be walking distance or public transport routes. In the case of the former, in an urban area, acceptable limits for access are likely to be about ten minutes' walking time or a radius of about half a mile from the office.

■ Possible locations will have to be assessed in the light of not only these factors but also the type of building, the prospect of sharing premises with other agencies, and the establishment of sub-offices (C.2–C.4, below).

■ It is not an essential prerequisite for the initial development of CSW practice to have a community base. Much can be done to overcome the handicap of an off-patch office by the adoption of a high profile in the area served (see C.5, below).

■ Before a team first moves into a local base in an area, a planning period of several months may be advantageous, both to enable the team and the larger organization to work out new policies and strategies and also to make it easier to begin training staff in new methods and procedures before all the pressures which are likely to apply once the team are physically deployed begin to build up.

C.2 *Type of building*

■ **All practitioners of community social work stress the great importance of having adequate local premises** which means not only sufficient space for the ordinary team activities, meetings, writing up, interviewing, filing, and reception, but also room for developmental work. This includes a meeting room suitable for use by local community groups and spare office space for such groups and any additional staff the team may gain, for example for special projects.

■ **Practitioners tend to be divided on the desirability of purpose-built office accommodation as opposed to the conversion of existing premises.** Those favouring **purpose-built accommodation** stress the advantage of having adequate facilities for the whole range of activities undertaken by a community social work team and the contribution of well-planned accommodation to office efficiency.

■ **Those favouring the use of existing buildings** stress the importance of blending into the background. Converted flats or shops are felt to be more acceptable to many users and consequently to make access easier and the team as a whole seem more part of the local scene.

In the final analysis, the choice must depend on the order of priorities of the team and this, in turn, is likely to be influenced by the particular character of the area served and what seems most appropriate to it. It is also important to recognize the constraints which are likely to be associated with securing local premises. CSW teams themselves may have only limited involvement in the selection or design of premises; limited resources may result in premises which are far from ideal; even if resources are available it might not be possible to obtain the ideal premises in the ideal location.

C.3 *Sharing accommodation with other social services agencies*

■ **Proximity will normally help the development of collaborative working relations with other departments such as housing, probation, advice bureaux, and so on, which are a key aspect** of community social work. In particular it is likely to speed cross-referrals, cut out duplication, and encourage joint projects. Further, a common entrance to such a building reduces the likelihood of users feeling stigma as a result of being seen entering a social services office.

C.4 *Establishing sub-offices and call offices*

■ **For rural teams serving a scattered population, with a number of different centres or sub-centres, there is a strong case for establishing a number of contact points.** Other agencies will often be willing to co-operate in this — for example GPs, health clinics, nurseries. The contact points are likely to be just as important for fellow workers in other agencies as for users. By establishing a routine presence the team become available as a part of the problem-solving network of the sub-area.

■ **In urban areas the issue of sub-offices is more controversial.** The case *for* their use is strongest where the area covered by the team contains isolated or fragmented sub-areas which are not readily within reach of a central point and/or which have distinctive problems of their own, calling for special attention. The case is also strong where a team are seeking to work closely with local informal networks in the development of social work from within the community. The case *against* the sub-office approach is that it is likely to lead to the fragmentation of the team. This in turn will weaken the ability of staff to provide support for each other, make cover for sickness and leave more difficult, and restrict the development of special skills.

■ **Consider these arguments in relation to the situation of your own team and weigh up the case for and against.**
A compromise approach practised by some teams is to institute sub-area or patch teams without sub-offices, and deploy them from a central office. Closer contact and support between their members, is thus retained.

C.5 *Community social work without a local team base*

A number of strategies have been developed by teams based outside their area to compensate for difficulties of access, etc.

■ **Establish formal links with other social services agencies which have a local base**, e.g. schools, clinics, churches.

■ **Achieve representation through members of the team on local committees**, e.g. community associations, advice bureaux, *ad hoc* projects.

■ **Set up and run groups for users on the patch**, e.g. mother and toddler club; sufferers' groups; youth clubs.

■ **Participate in local events**, e.g. festivals, fund raising, sports days.

Reception

ISSUES

It is not enough to place an office in a convenient site to make it psychologically accessible as well as physically available to potential users. Much is likely to turn on how the office is advertised outside and what kind of arrangements exist inside to receive callers. These factors give people an immediate impression of how an organization sees its relationships with its users. The following aspects of reception are likely to be especially important (see also Chapter 5, pp. 182, 191):

A.1 how easily identified is the office from outside?
A.2 what hours in the day is it open to help people? When it is closed what alternatives are advertised?
A.3 what is the quality of the reception arrangements?
A.4 how fast is the response to enquiries and referrals?
A.5 how open is the process of handling the enquiry or referral?

TEAM EXPERIENCE

B.1 *Office identification*

All the teams with offices in their areas clearly mark them by signboards on the outside of the building. However, to the outsider the signs do not seem particularly attractive or welcoming. They are generally much smaller than those used outside state schools and less personal in that they do not give the name of the team leader or manager. Nor do they give the uninitiated any idea of what services are offered. The East Sussex teams, though, do have somewhat better advertisements in the form of leaflets which describe the main functions of the services and, with the help of a map, show exactly how to find the office.

B.2 *Duty hours*

The *duty hours* worked vary, mainly, it appears, according to the size of the team. The larger teams such as Normanton and Whitehawk have a duty officer available all day. But the smaller teams such as Rye restrict duty hours to shorter periods. However, in these cases the team receptionist is available to answer calls and can get in touch with a social worker if necessary, in some cases through a paging system.

B.3 *Reception*

While reception facilities in community social worker teams vary between the formal and informal, the logic of reducing barriers between the system and the user points towards informality. There is no evidence that removing physical barriers between the user and social services staff places the latter in any extra jeopardy. Indeed, violence towards staff is extremely rare even in the toughest inner-city area where such informality is the order of the day. In the Lochend team, for example, the only act of violence that is recalled is that of an old age pensioner who, frustrated about some mix-up in shopping done for him by a worker, threw a tube of smarties across the office!

All the teams seek to make the reception facilities comfortable and welcoming but the degree of formality varies. The most formal are in Whitehawk, Rye, and Normanton where a counter or hatch separates the user from the team and the rest of the office is shut off from reception. The least formal are Docklands, Huntly, and Lochend where the caller comes straight into the team area and there is no physical barrier between the user and staff. The Honor Oak team also had a very informal reception area until recently when, as a result of pressure from the Housing Department whose sub-office shares space with social services, a very formal reception area was introduced, with staff and users separated by counter-to-ceiling bullet-proof glass. However, the social services team has fought successfully to return to its former open-door system and will soon be re-introducing informal reception arrangements while the housing office remains behind its protective screen.

B.4 *Speed of response*

All the teams seek to respond quickly to enquiries and referrals. Users calling in duty hours seldom have to wait more than a few minutes before someone is available to see them. Given the high priority in most of the teams to informal helping where no official referral is called for, many callers can be helped straight away and the large majority on the same day.

B.5 *Open and closed methods of working*

The degree of formality/informality in the teams' methods of working broadly corresponds to the degree of formality in reception arrangements. In the more formal setting, for instance in Whitehawk, much of a social worker's dealing on behalf of a client with other agencies is often carried out in his or her own office, away from the reception and waiting area. In contrast, at the most informal end of the continuum, the user coming into the Docklands team is likely to hear negotiations going on in the open office which also serves as a reception area. This arrangement conforms with the team's philosophy which is to try to:

> 'break down as far as possible the physical and emotional separation between the client and the worker; to offer local people the opportunity to observe the set-up and workings of the team and so help to demystify the social work profession; to encourage wherever possible open interviews and through this to help deprivatize personal problems and to build up an awareness of their common causes.'

PRACTICE GUIDELINES

C.1 *Office identification*

■ **Team offices should be clearly advertised with attractive signboards.** The worker in charge of the team should have his or her name displayed on the board. It is also helpful to give some preliminary indication of the nature of the enquiries dealt with on the board or, at the very least, to indicate that enquiries are welcome. Leaflets describing the work of the team, its location, and opening hours can help to familiarize users with their local office.

C.2 *Duty hours*

■ **It is important for teams to find a satisfactory balance between providing duty cover and getting on with other aspects of day-to-day work.** Unless the office is regularly and heavily bombarded with calls requiring a duty officer, it is desirable to reduce the duty hours and thus free time for social work. As long as emergency help can always be found speedily when it is needed (e.g. through a paging system), there is no reason why a social services team should have day-long duty hours, any more than a general practice should.

C.3 *Reception*

■ **Establish a reception area which is consistent with the principles of user-centred CSW;** that is, one which is comfortable (e.g. with easy chairs) and child-friendly (with toys, books), and has access to toilets. The area should also give people a chance to find out about the team and its work (e.g. photos of team members, posters describing team activities) and should display any information material supplied by community groups and other agencies.

C.4 *Speed and character of response*

These are likely to be viewed by users as the most important aspects of their experience of the team.

■ **Where possible the callers should receive attention immediately. Where this is not feasible they should be told how long they are likely to have to wait.**

■ **Whether the enquiry turns out to be relevant or not, callers should feel that the team want to help them.** The attitudes of users in a locality to their team are likely to be shaped by their cumulative experience of the response to requests for advice and help. To acquire the reputation of always being willing to try to help, to accept as an accolade not a badge of shame the role of the last resort: these are keys to acceptance.

■ **Whenever possible users should be given help on the day of their first contact with the team.** To this end it is important that staff dealing with referrals should have the necessary delegated authority to cope with all routine enquiries and referrals.

C.5 *Open or closed methods of working*

■ **Open methods are more consistent with a CSW approach. Unless confidential or sensitive issues need to be discussed, try to see clients in an open, non-stigmatizing environment.**

Referrals

ISSUES

Ease of access, more contact points, more staff in the front line, more delegated authority, and more informal intervention all taken together should mean that the community-based team have the capacity to respond more rapidly to more referrals and to intervene at an earlier stage in the career of a problem.

This approach, however, raises a number of questions about organization and supervision. Some of the most important are:

A.1 which staff should take referrals?

A.2 where should referrals be accepted?

A.3 what authority should be delegated to which staff to take what decisions on referrals? (See also: Chapter 4, p. 116; Chapter 5, p. 182.)

A.4 what degree of informal (unrecorded) action should be encouraged?

A.5 what kinds of records need to be kept?

TEAM EXPERIENCE

B.1 *Who takes referrals*

Most teams encourage all their members to act as a first point of referral. They also encourage workers, at whatever level, to find out as much as they can about the referral at this stage to see whether they can give any immediate help. In all the teams there is evidence that non-social work staff such as clerks and home helps quite frequently respond at this level. However, the most systematic encouragement of such staff to tackle referrals judged to be within their competence is given by the Normanton team. There the unqualified (but very experienced) patch workers filter out most of the problems to do with the elderly and will give advice and help on other problems if they do not seem to require the expertise or authority of a qualified social worker.

B.2 *Where referrals are accepted*

In contrast to most conventionally organized teams, referrals are taken almost anywhere – on the street, at a club, in the shops, in users' homes, on the premises of other agencies, in sum, anywhere the worker happens to be. Research in one of the teams, Normanton, shows that a policy of accepting referrals in this way can make a marked impact: nearly a third of all referrals and nearly a half of the informal referrals were picked up outside the office (Hadley and McGrath 1984: 83). Similarly, staff walking their patches in Whitehawk, Docklands, and Honor Oak frequently pick up referrals on the street and staff in the two rural teams find their cars become known and act as referral points when they are parked in a village or even just seen driving down the street.

B.3 *Delegated authority*

The teams all encourage the individual taking a referral to go as far as possible in dealing with it and, wherever feasible, to respond immediately. This applies whether the worker concerned is the duty officer or the worker on his or her rounds who is approached with an enquiry or request for help. The approach spelled out by the Longbenton team appears to represent the philosophy of all the contributing teams:
Where successful, the team's efforts to achieve a high profile expose it to a bombardment of requests for help made to them personally, face to face, and from which they have no bureaucratic barriers to shelter them. If the high profile is to mean anything these requests have to be met in a constructive way. It is therefore team practice to do as much as possible

immediately, whether giving straightforward advice, making an onward referral to another agency, or embarking straight away on work with a very taxing situation such as a depressed and suicidal mother of three presented by a health visitor when the social worker dropped into the clinic to pick up some bath aides. Where continuing work seems to be needed, this is channelled through the formal allocation procedure, although it is standard for the worker who made the first response to continue.

Such an approach appears to pose few major problems where qualified social workers are involved. However, in those teams placing a major emphasis on the role of ancillaries (Normanton, Docklands) conflict can arise between the capacities of the worker, as indicated by ability and experience, and departmental policies. In Normanton, for instance, patch workers are not allowed to take main responsibility for child care, mental health, or financial cases.

B.4 *Informal referrals and response*

All the teams receive high levels of informal referrals and all try to provide a speedy and, where appropriate, informal response. By their nature, informal interactions are hard to quantify but the research study at Normanton found that over half (55 per cent) of all referrals received in the period examined were dealt with informally (Hadley and McGrath 1984: 74). The precise amount of work which is dealt with informally is likely to depend not only on the policy of the team but also on the style of the individual worker and the shifting pressures on the team to supply the larger organization with 'evidence' of its activities. However, all the teams appear to encourage a first response to referrals at an informal level. In the Rye team, for example, it is accepted that one-off interviews, advice giving, and redirecting people to relevant sources of help do not constitute formal referrals, although they have become an increasingly significant part of the team's work since they moved into their local base.

A number of teams, while encouraging informal work, also try to keep some record of it. This is not the contradiction it may appear to be since such records are kept principally for team purposes and do not involve the completion of a departmental referral form. In Honor Oak, for example, the team write: 'we have our own "unit" form which is used on duty for "one-off" pieces of work or referrals such as welfare rights advice where we feel there is no need for a file — otherwise we might well have a departmental file on most people on the estate!'

B.5 *Formal referrals*

Most of the teams express some scepticism about the value of using a formal referral system as an indicator of the level and quality of work undertaken. As the Whitehawk contributor noted: 'There is continual support outside the referral system. Referrals are a poor indication of work effort. Referrals become formal when client and social worker agree and a discussion then takes place at an allocation meeting.'

However, all the teams had to accept that, given the way in which most bureaucratic systems currently operate, formal referral levels are likely to be regarded as important by their departments and will affect the way the individual teams are assessed and resources allocated. The Longbenton view is reflected in all the contributions: 'It is important for work which is in fact being done to be recorded on the department's normal system — cumbersome though this may be — because it is this system which is referred to by management when considering the deployment of resources, relative workloads, and, indeed, the effectivenes of the community based approach.'

PRACTICE GUIDELINES

C.1 *Who takes referrals*

■ To increase access and speed of response, teams should aim to maximize the number of referral points available to users. Their capacity to do this is likely to depend, in particular, on the range and number of staff directly controlled by the local team, the character of the area served (e.g. urban/rural), and the nature and quality of the team's relationships with other agencies, informal networks, etc.

● Teams are likely to improve their accessibility to users by the integration of all front-line staff – field workers, ancillaries, domiciliary workers, residential, and day-care workers – and their inclusion as channels of referral.
● The effectiveness of these workers as referral points is likely to be enhanced by encouraging their full integration in

the decision-making processes of the team and by maximizing their responsibilities and autonomy.

● All teams, regardless of their composition, can increase referral points by developing close relationships with other relevant agencies and networks, and by encouraging direct contact with them.

C.2 *Accepting referrals wherever they occur*

As a complement to the policy of increasing the number of people who can act as referral points:

■ **CSW teams need to be ready to accept referrals wherever and whenever they occur, rather than confining response to the official referral system.**

■ **Adopting a high profile in the neighbourhood increases the accessibility of staff.** This can be enhanced by:

● establishing daily/weekly visiting routines to particular clients, streets, local organizations, with which people can become familiar;
● wherever possible walking the patch rather than travelling by car; when going by car being ready to stop if flagged down;
● employment as staff of local people (see below, p. 84) who are already well known in the area (some of these workers are prepared to take referrals out of office hours. While obviously this cannot be required, it is a bonus to the team if such support is available).

C.3 *Delegated authority*

The gains from multiple contact points and from a readiness to accept referrals where they occur will be lost if all cases still have to be passed through a formal allocation process before any action is taken.

■ **Community social work teams require a clear system of delegation which gives all staff as much responsibility as they can handle, given their experience and training, and allows them to react directly to problems referred to them.**

■ Experience shows that clerical workers, ancillaries, and domiciliary staff can all successfully give much help and advice when they are the first points of contact with a team.

■ Support for such staff is essential: (i) to clarify which kinds of problems they may tackle in the first instance and which they must in all cases pass on to others in the team; (ii) to enhance their knowledge and skills; (iii) to provide back-up supervision and counselling.

■ The consequent expansion of the roles of these staff has clear implications for improvement in their conditions of service. These are likely to be outside the scope of team management but should be vigorously supported in the wider organization.

C.4 and C.5 *Informal and formal referrals*

Ability to take action informally, that is without entering details into the records of the department by filling in an official referral form, is essential if CSW teams are to respond rapidly and flexibly to request for help and to establish credibility with people in the area served.

■ It should be possible for all referrals to be treated informally unless:

(a) there are departmental requirements to make an official referral, as in mental health and child-care cases, for example;
(b) the case seems likely to require formal procedures to achieve the desired results (e.g. a financial problem or a housing problem require the completion of standard forms and formal contacts with other agencies);
(c) departmental pressures exist to show evidence of formal referrals to justify the work of the team. This last reason, however, unless it is purely temporary, should be resisted wherever possible since it undermines the basis of informal work which is so central to community social work teams. If it is important to senior management to have some kind of detailed feedback on team performance, then the aim should be to negotiate the establishment of methods of evaluation

which positively support the philosophy and mode of operation involved in community social work, not a system which undermines it (see also Chapter 6, p. 209).

■ **Team records of more important informal referrals and contacts with users should be established.** Such records are useful both in a **general** sense, in providing some kind of an overview of the 'unofficial' work of the team for its members, and in a **specific** sense in the case of individual users with whom there is quite frequent informal contact and where cumulatively the contacts may be of more significance than one-off contacts with other users. Such records are also of value when there is staff turnover.

■ **Team records of this kind need to be of the simplest and least time-consuming if they are not to be self-defeating.** A simple card index or ring folder system with a separate card or sheet for each user and a system of brief entries is indicated.

Facilities for community groups and individuals

ISSUES

A.1 *Sharing facilities*

The availability of meeting rooms and various office resources can be crucial in the development of local community groups. Most social services teams have such facilities for their own use and it is logical for community-orientated teams to consider how far they can be shared with the communities they serve. Particular advantages, in terms of the development of a CSW strategy, could include not only the strengthening of local community activities, but also opportunities to work more closely with local groups and the potentially destigmatizing effect of broadening the range of activities based in the team office.

The main problem likely to face teams in seeking to share their facilities are competition with the direct needs of the team; maintenance of confidentiality and security in the office; establishing priorities between different groups applying to use the facilities. (See also Chapter 6, p. 209.)

B.1 *Sharing facilities*

All the teams except Longbenton, which does not have a local office, make some facilities available to local community groups and to individual users. All can offer a meeting room in their own office or make arrangements with a nearby agency for meeting facilities. All teams except Lochend offer copying and/ or secretarial facilities, although the Honor Oak team experience some disapproval for this practice from their colleagues in the housing team who share premises with them. The Lochend team does make its telephone available to users who do not have their own to contact other agencies. Two other teams, Normanton and Docklands, have laundry facilities for washing clothes and bedding too soiled to be accepted by launderettes, and Docklands also make available an iron, vacuum cleaner, and sewing machine. In addition, their offices serve as bases for the team volunteers.

Teams have not as yet experienced serious problems from competing demands of different groups applying to use their facilities. The main problems encountered have been related to the lack of separate equipment and space to be made available to community groups; this gives rise to competition with the teams' work and difficulties over the use of facilities in the teams' own space. Similarly, problems are encountered in sharing team meeting rooms if, as is often the case, community groups meet out of office hours and other parts of the office are not readily shut off from the meeting area.

In spite of these problems, all the teams have noted positive benefits from sharing their facilities and would like to see the process taken further.

PRACTICE GUIDELINES

C.1 *Sharing facilities*

■ Ideally, both building design and resource allocation at team level should take account of the need for opening facilities for community groups.

● Building design should make available a separate room or rooms for local community groups which can, when necessary, be shut off from the team offices.

● Resource allocation should make it possible to equip the community room with furniture and office equipment of the kind needed by the groups likely to use it. Given the variety of different needs in different areas the most effective way of ensuring that relevant resources are made available is to give teams a 'community budget' for this purpose.

● Access to the facilities should be determined on the basis of team policies but these in turn will need to be discussed with whatever constituency currently exists among local community groups.

In practice, however, community social work teams may often have to manage with much less favourable conditions and in these circumstances will have to:

■ **fit community use of facilities into normal office routines.** This process can be helped by:

● agreeing within the team which community groups should have access to what facilities and which members of staff should take responsibility for arranging and monitoring this access, including safeguarding the confidentiality of records, etc., and ensuring that team work is not disrupted.

● allocating a meeting room for use by community groups out of office hours which can be isolated from the rest of the office, if necessary by fitting locks on internal doors.

● seeking to raise funds, if necessary on an *ad hoc* basis, to meet additional costs (phone, stationery, equipment, etc.) used by groups in the initial phase before they can raise their own funds.

The role of local staff

ISSUES

A.1 *Advantages in the use of local staff*

The potential value of integrating and using local people as staff of community social work teams has been touched on in several of the earlier entries in this book. In particular, three main advantages are claimed for this kind of development:

(a) knowledge: local staff are likely to be well-placed to increase team knowledge and understanding of the area and people served through their own daily involvement in and commitment to the locality.

(b) access and referrals: local staff, if successfully integrated into the team, should increase its accessibility to local people, acting as informal referral channels into the organization.

(c) the involvement of local people in the work of the team could help break down the barriers that often exist between a formal agency and its users, and increase the acceptability of the team in the area. (See also Chapter 4, Integration with informal networks, pp. 96–114.)

A.2 *Disadvantages in the use of local staff*

At the same time, a number of potential disadvantages in the integration of local people as team members has been suggested. These include:

(a) fears that such staff might have difficulty in respecting the confidential nature of their work;

(b) anxiety about possible bias in the performance of their duties, related to their position in the local community;

(c) concern that they could come under undue pressure from out-of-hours referrals. (See also Chapter 4, p. 97.)

TEAM EXPERIENCE

B.1 *Using local staff*

All the teams except Longbenton (the only team without a base in the area it serves) have at least some local staff. As *Table 4* shows, the largest categories concerned are domiciliary and ancillary workers. But some teams also have local people amongst their clerical staff and the two rural teams include one or more social workers who live locally.

All the teams with experience of using local staff in integrated roles were positive about their gains from this practice. The most frequently mentioned benefit was the enhanced knowledge in the team of local needs and resources. For example, the Rye team commented:

'This is most important. Local staff have a considerable amount of local information which is often invaluable . . . From them we have learned about the strengths and weaknesses of the extended family networks and other social contacts of many of our elderly clients; we have gained a good knowledge of the ways of the local comprehensive school; we suddenly "find" local clubs and societies in all parts of the patch.'

Table 4   *The employment of local people by the teams*

	Domiciliary/ residential	Clerical	Social workers
Huntly	n/a	n/a	2 area officers* 2 social workers
Longbenton	n/a		
Normanton	home helps street wardens patch workers		
Honor Oak	n/a	clerk receptionist	
Lochend	n/a	2 clerks	
Docklands	home helps family aides		
Rye	home help organizer home helps	3 clerks	1 social worker
Whitehawk	home helps care assistants		

* (For a definition of the role of 'area officers' in Grampian, see Chapter 2, p. 28)

Gains in accessibility and referrals were also experienced in several of the teams. A study of referrals in Normanton showed that both wardens and home helps channelled referrals into the team but that the former, who were much more fully integrated into the day-to-day working of the team, were a far more significant source (Hadley and McGrath 1984: 85). Clerical workers who lived locally were also likely to improve accessibility.

The more general issue of increasing the acceptability of the team in the locality as a whole was mentioned by a number of teams. As the Normanton team put it, 'Localising staff . . .

brings the community into the team, enables local connections to be made naturally, and reduces the significance of the agency as officialdom for clients and their relatives.'

B.2 *Disadvantages in the use of local staff*

The teams have found few disadvantages in the employment of local staff. It was recognized that the issue of confidentiality might need careful handling. Some local workers in Normanton and Huntly had found that they were likely to be approached out of office hours with work problems but had developed coping strategies to keep such demands within bounds. In essence, over a period of time local workers appeared to negotiate informal rules of availability within their networks in out-of-work periods that they felt were acceptable to themselves and others.

PRACTICE GUIDELINES

C.1 *Maximizing the use of local staff*

The potential value of local staff in enhancing the knowledge, accessibility, and acceptability of community social work teams is firmly supported by team experience. However, factors including the degree of integration of such staff, the autonomy of the team, and the strategies adopted appear to affect the actual extent of their practical influence on team practice. Pointers from team experience indicate ways in which effective involvement of local staff can be fostered:

■ **Identify which social services staff live and work locally.** Establish which of these are managed by the CSW team and which are managed from elsewhere in the department.

■ **Where the local staff are already members of the team, seek to relate their work to the specific parts of the area they know best.** The development of sub-areas or patches can be a useful way of organizing this allocation. Encourage them to feed in their knowledge and understanding of the area and its people to the team, e.g. through work on individual cases, through team discussions, and through involvement in local projects.

■ **When new staff are recruited into the team the opportunity to recruit locally should be used.** It is important to look for people whose experience and maturity have won them respect in the local community. Promotion through the posts of home help, warden, and volunteer is one well-proved method of selecting people for the role of patch or neighbourhood worker.

■ **Local staff should be encouraged to develop the role of representative of the team in their neighbourhood and to act as referral points for users, as well as representing neighbourhood points of view with the team.**

■ **The team should seek to ensure that a system of support and supervision is constructed to back up this expansion of staff roles.** Such a system, which might be linked to a related training programme, should seek to deal with the potential problems of bias and confidentiality (see pp. 92–4) which may confront local staff, and also to help staff devise strategies for coping with out-of-hours demands on their time.

■ **Where local people are employed by the social services department and work within the team area but are managed by other sections of the department** (as is frequently the case with domiciliary staff and care staff working in residential homes) **the team should seek to negotiate with higher management for organizational changes leading to their integration in the team.**

■ **Where such integration cannot be achieved, the team should seek to establish close formal and informal links with the staff concerned,** e.g. set up regular meetings with home helps and with care staff in local residential homes, systematically develop informal contacts through work on shared cases.

■ **There could be considerable advantages if at least some of the staff with a local background were professionally qualified. Teams should actively pursue the idea of seconding some of their unqualified local staff on CQSW courses.**

■ **There is a strong case for having a mix of local and outside influences in the team so that both local and professional issues can be considered in a balanced manner.**

The role of local volunteers

ISSUES

A.1 and A.2 *Formal and informal volunteers*

The involvement of volunteers in community social work teams can be at either a formal or informal level. In the former case, volunteers are recruited to work with the team as ancillaries to the paid staff and may take on a variety of tasks across the team area. In the latter case, as informal volunteers, they are likely to be recruited to work in specific tasks concerning relatives or neighbours and to perceive themselves as providing direct help rather than working through the team.

Regular involvement by the team with volunteers of either kind can be seen as having similar advantages to those claimed for the employment of local staff in enhancing the knowledge, accessibility and acceptability of the team, as well as the additional advantage of increasing the practical help available in the area. However, some CSW teams have deliberately refrained from seeking to recruit formal volunteers on the grounds that they emphasize the separateness of the team from the locality and that it is more appropriate to encourage the strengthening of community-based action through informal volunteering and the formation of independent local voluntary organizations.

TEAM EXPERIENCE

B.1 *Formal volunteers*

Docklands was the only team to have a formal volunteer group. This is supported by members of staff who provide supervision as necessary; it has its own base in one of the team offices. Some problems of over-involvement and confidentiality have been encountered but these are felt to be outweighed by the gains in knowledge, acceptability, and resources that the group brings with it.

B.2 *Informal volunteers*

All the teams work in one way or another with informal volunteers in the course of their day-to-day activities, especially through family and neighbourhood networks. For example, neighbours may be asked to keep an eye on a convalescent elderly person recently returned from hospital and living alone or perhaps to undertake shopping for a housebound person living nearby. Sometimes their help is sought also in a wider context. For instance, an Honor Oak team member writes about her own work with volunteers: 'I personally ruthlessly exploit people known to me in many ways, e.g. asking them to work in the toy library, or to help integrate new tenants into existing groups, or to help run play schemes. I have been able to pay some of them for child-care work from Section I money. If volunteers are needed, I invariably know who to go to on the estate.'

Whether any of the contributing teams really 'exploit' their volunteers is another matter. Such evidence as we gathered suggests that they would all share the view of the Normanton team: 'Volunteers in our experience do not, and perhaps should not, become responsible for very difficult clients, such as the chronically sick . . . Ongoing regular work is the responsibility of organized structures rather than individuals.'

Half the teams – Huntly, Whitehawk, Longbenton and Docklands – make use of informal volunteers who work directly with their staff. Huntly usually avoids asking volunteers to work with people they already know. Whitehawk emphasizes the importance of choosing as volunteers people who will be acceptable to local networks. However, this does not preclude encouraging clients to become volunteers: the team find that this can help some individuals to deal with their own problems as, for example, the father who had physically abused his child and later helped to run a disco for local children.

PRACTICE GUIDELINES

C.1 *Formal volunteers*

The advantages of formal volunteers are that they can be deployed more flexibly and widely than informal volunteers and the team can have greater control over their selection, recruitment, and training. Some possible disadvantages have been referred to above (B.2) but the teams deploying the volunteers have not suggested that these are particularly serious in practice.

■ **Probably the most effective way of recruiting new volunteers is through the day-to-day work of the team;** that is, through contacts with families and other community networks, through work with local voluntary organizations, and through clients who want to help others in their turn. Selection will need to take account of acceptability to the local community.

■ **Training, related to the basics of social services provision and to the particular approach of community social work, could enhance the contribution of volunteers.** Some social services agencies have introduced more elaborate training schemes for volunteers (e.g. Probation Associates, Channel, Marriage Guidance). However, it is questionable whether the semi-professional status and practice aimed at by such training is necessary or desirable for volunteers in community social work teams which are seeking to reduce the barriers between themselves and the public.

■ **Where formal volunteers are working directly with users, it may be important to ensure that they are not required to work with people they already know.**

■ **Consideration should be given to making a token payment to team volunteers.** While it could be argued that they then cease to be volunteers, this is something of a quibble since the amounts paid are small and unlikely to be the main motive for involvement. Payment can have the advantage of extending the recruitment pool (see e.g. Hadley and Scott 1980: 79) as some people regard it as evidence that the work involved is taken seriously by the agency. A second advantage is the apparent willingness of paid volunteers to take on more demanding and responsible work. For example, the successful Kent Community Care scheme includes provision for modest payments to neighbours, relatives, and others for the care of the frail elderly living in the community (Challis and Davies 1985).

C.2 *Informal volunteers*

Informal work with individual local people to help provide better services is basic to the approach of community social work. By encouraging mutual aid at this level teams seek to strengthen local networks and their capacity to cope. (See also

Chapter 4, Working with informal networks, pp. 99–101.)

■ **All team members should be alert to the possibility of strengthening their support networks through the recruitment of additional helpers amongst family, friends, and neighbours.**

■ **The negotiation of tasks to be undertaken by informal volunteers needs to be based on a careful and realistic assessment of commitment and capacity.** Further, there may be quite a fine line between the development of collaboration and exploitation. There is evidence that some people are very willing to help if they are only asked but if pressures are exerted on informal volunteers to do particularly demanding tasks which are properly the duty of the statutory service, then the underlying purpose of community social work to enhance the quality of life of people in the community is compromised.

Confidentiality

ISSUES

Critics of CSW have expressed concern that the methods it involves are likely to endanger confidentiality, and so undermine the establishment and maintenance of all-important professional relationships. The grounds for this anxiety usually stem from the small size and local base of the team, and the inference that staff will build up detailed information about a limited number of people which they will share amongst themselves, in particular, the use of local staff may carry the risk of stigmatization by association. (See also Chapter 4, p. 97.)

A.1 The integration of local staff, mainly unqualified workers such as home helps, family aides, and other ancillaries, and of local volunteers, increases the risk that information on users will not remain confidential.

A.2 A local office and the staff working from it soon become well known in a neighbourhood; by consequence clients of the team are more readily identifiable and more at risk of any stigmatization that may be attached to use of the social services.

B.1 *Local staff and confidentiality*

All but one of the teams contributing to this book said that confidentiality was not a significant issue in their area. It is claimed that staff at all levels readily accept the importance of protecting information about users. The Normanton team, for example, report that, 'Staff are fully aware of the sensitivity of much of the information they are given and treat it accordingly.' For them and most of the other teams, employing local people is not experienced as a significant problem.

But one team, Docklands, does regard confidentiality as an issue with this category of worker: 'It is very difficult for local staff to keep everything they might be aware of through their work about their neighbours, friends, and relatives to themselves.' The team had no easy answer to the problem but suggested that it had to keep working at it.

B.2 *Locality and stigmatization*

The loss of confidentiality and subsequent stigmatization through association with a local team familiar to everyone in the neighbourhood are not regarded as problems by the contributing teams. Several of them judged that confidentiality was more likely to be seen as an issue by the professionals than the local people affected. The Honor Oak contributor notes, 'I find confidentiality is an issue for middle-class professionals but local people are well aware how to control it.'

In Longbenton the problem is also seen to be mainly one for the professionals: 'Confidentiality *can* be a problem. But this is not because we work in partnership with local people but in the sense that there seem to be very few secrets from neighbours in any of the parts of our patch. The team have to give up the pretence that the client is an isolated unit.' The same team draw attention to the positive advantages of working locally in negotiating practice round the issue of confidentiality: 'There are opportunities and imperatives in community social work to ask clients expressly for clarification of what they are prepared for the worker to say.'

A difficulty of a different kind is described by the Lochend team which noted the problems that can sometimes arise from not being able to explain the team's action to the local community in order to protect confidentiality in a case. The example quoted by the team is of a family reported for suspected child abuse. The team investigated the case and found it was not substantiated, so the family remained together. Local people were frustrated at the decision but the evidence on which it was based could not be shared with them.

PRACTICE GUIDELINES

C.1 *Local staff and confidentiality*

■ **In both the selection and in-house training of staff the team should give due weight to the issue of confidentiality.** Where local people are recruited into the team without any professional training, particular attention should be paid to their likely ability to respect confidential information acquired through the job. The team's own local knowledge should help them to assess the suitability of a candidate in the light of his or her local reputations.

■ **Workers who know users on a personal basis should be expected to 'declare an interest'.** In all such circumstances users should be given the opportunity to see a different member of staff.

C.2 *Locality and stigmatization*

■ **CSW teams should get to know local attitudes and opinions as part of the process of gaining an understanding of the local culture.** Evidence from the contributing teams suggests that different communities may have different understandings of the nature and importance of confidentiality. The local focus of teams gives them the possibility of initiating a dialogue with groups in the local area on issues of this nature and of talking with users about their views.

■ **Where the team are dealing with particularly sensitive cases, such as alleged child abuse or compulsory admission to a psychiatric hospital, and people in the local area have a lively interest in the matter, the team must seek to explain their position on confidentiality and seek to help people understand why it must be maintained.**

4 Integration

The personal social services represent no more than a single strand in the complex web of relationships and services, formal and informal, statutory and non-statutory, which together provide care and control in the community. The overall effectiveness of provision depends not on one part of this network alone but on how well the whole is woven together.

This perspective is fundamental to the practice of community social work and close collaboration or integration of services and service providers must be a high priority in the strategy of CSW teams. It is helpful to distinguish three main areas for the furthering of integration, although all three are closely inter-related and should be thought of as part of a single overarching structure. These are: integration with informal carers, integration within the social services department, and integration with other agencies.

Integration can be conceptualized in both formal and informal terms. *Formal* integration involves the merging of different services provided by separate sections of a single organization and/or the merging of two or more organizations, or parts of them. In practice, such internal or interorganization integration is not always feasible. Further, where relations between informal networks and statutory networks are involved, it would seldom be desirable even if it were feasible. In such cases, however, *informal* integration can often be achieved. By this we mean the establishment of close working relationships in which decisions are taken jointly and those involved see themselves as part of a common team, even though they do not belong to any one organization or, in the case of informal carers, to any organization at all.

Integration with informal networks

ISSUES

A central feature of CSW is an understanding that informal care is the main source of personal support for the majority of us in the community. Those who seek help from official carers may also continue to receive support from neighbours, friends, and relatives. An awareness of the importance of such informal care is fundamental to the work of a CSW team in a social services department. Important criticisms have been made of this central plank in the CSW platform:

(a) It is suggested that in seeking to rely on informal care CSW teams present a rose-coloured view of modern society. Many areas do not have well-developed systems of informal care. If CSW teams have had successes they have been mainly in the minority of well-integrated communities.

(b) Concentrating on informal care exploits carers who are already hard pressed and confirms women in a subservient, unpaid, and oppressed role.

(c) Social workers deal with the most vulnerable and/or troublesome members of society. By placing faith in care from the community, and investing scarce social services resources in its mobilization, social workers may deprive such people of the professional support they have the right to expect. In any case, meaningful work through informal networks is often not feasible with the most vulnerable users since their own networks are typically very weak.

Advocates of CSW, including the contributing teams, argue that practical experience does not support these criticisms:

(a) Many CSW teams, including some of those represented in this book, operate with considerable success in poorly integrated communities. They appear to have realistic views of the limitations of informal networks as caring entites and to shape their strategies of intervention accordingly.

(b) CSW teams stress the idea of partnership with informal networks and seek to relieve some of the pressures on them through the provision of departmental and other resources, and sometimes through the creation of new resources. Indeed, it is possible to see the introduction of CSW as contributing to the liberation of carers.

(c) There is little to suggest that CSW teams neglect their statutory duties and, where individuals rejected by the local community are concerned, there is evidence to show that the teams work through informal networks on their behalf. Informal networks may not always be caring but they can still be an important vehicle for helping vulnerable people. The strategies which the contributing teams employ in working with informal networks are considered from the following points of view:

A.1 Assumptions and expectations (see also Chapter 3, p. 54);

A.2 Obtaining knowledge about informal networks (see also Chapter 5, p. 165);

A.3 Working with informal networks (see also Chapter 3, p. 92);

A.4 Factors aiding or impeding work with informal networks (see also Chapter 3, pp. 59, 85; Chapter 6, pp. 194, 229).

TEAM EXPERIENCE

B.1 *Assumptions and expectations*

All teams report encountering informal networks, but make it clear that they are not universally caring. The Rye team, for example, described clients whose neighbours wanted them to be taken into care. 'An elderly couple were having considerable problems, and therefore so was everyone else. The wife was in pain, and frequently exasperated with her confused husband. The police were often called to domestic fights and the GP to hear the wife's complaints.' The social services department was lobbied by the neighbours to 'put them in a home'.

Speaking of a parent and toddler group, the Longbenton team discovered that, 'The problematic relationships which exist between members in the real world are reproduced in the group, and can be worked with in a constructive way, diffusing aggression, smoothing out misunderstandings, and engaging in open discussion of conflict.'

The Lochend team have encountered bewilderment and consternation in the neighbourhood surrounding the frustrated expectation that children ought to have been taken into care.

On the brighter side, the Longbenton team discovered a

reclusive and anti-social woman whose next-door neighbours always ordered an extra pint of milk for her to steal from their doorstep. She would from time to time acknowledge her action with an apology. Other recluses were found to have distanced, but still existing, contacts with local networks which could be tapped when necessary for information about their behaviour and whereabouts.

B.2 *Obtaining knowledge about informal networks*

The Rye and Longbenton teams make it their standard practice to find out details about the informal networks of all referrals. Sharing information already acquired by some team members at patch meetings is found to be valuable by the Longbenton and Docklands teams.

Just being around for a while in the neighbourhood flat allows the Honor Oak team to accumulate details of various networks. Through its high profile in the locality, the Huntly team deliberately promotes opportunities for key citizens like publicans, shopkeepers and other gatekeepers' between the informal and formal systems, who tend to be turned to for advice, to pass on referrals to them.

Having local staff within the team is found to be a source of huge amounts of network information by the Rye, Normanton and Huntly teams. Involvement with local groups on the estate has increased the number of informal contacts for the Honor Oak team, and Longbenton give an example of a poorly attended initial meeting of a self-help group including a doctor's wife who then gave the team an entrée into a set of networks which they would have been unlikely to penetrate otherwise. Rye and Normanton also use involvement with community groups as a way of making contact.

Lochend and Longbenton report clients bringing previously unknown friends to groups. They also report obtaining fuller and more accurate knowledge of their clients' circumstances which has in turn enabled more accurate assessments of possible plans of intervention to be made.

A large-scale survey was attempted by the Rye team, but abandoned due to the demanding nature of the task and lack of time to devote to it. As an alternative, they relied on their subjective judgement that there was a need to supplement informal networks for a number of client groups with day care.

The resulting success with a volunteer-run day-care club for the elderly, a large number of small village playgroups, the launching of a Mencap group, summer play schemes, and the beginning of an exciting larger-scale day-care complex to be managed by the local CVS, would indicate that their subjective judgement was sound enough.

It can be inferred from the responses of all contributing teams that their views about collective need and informal caring networks do in fact result from a subjective analysis of the information available, which is for the most part discovered individually, transmitted verbally, and simply remembered rather than written down. The Honor Oak team have found, however, that this system renders fragile information which is liable to be lost on the departure of a team member.

B.3 *Working with informal networks*

All contributing teams acknowledge the need to support informal networks in their caring task. This support may include help provided by negotiating new arrangements with elements of the existing network, help from other informal sources, or help from the statutory services. Whilst teams acknowledge a wish to prevent caring situations from breaking down, they do not perpetuate them at the expense of carers. In all the teams, decision taking about the nature of help to be given is shared with carers and clients wherever possible.

Rye, Docklands, and Longbenton focus, when appropriate, explicitly on the needs of network members, even where these may be seen initially as contrary to those of the person referred. Longbenton describe an elderly woman who became so aggressive towards her neighbours as to be very distressing, but not so as to be sectioned. The worker involved discussed the situation with the neighbours, and although they had attracted attention to their needs by desperate and demanding phone calls and petitions to councillors, one offered to help, and others were receptive to suggestions of how to respond in such a way as to minimize the likelihood of incidents escalating. The worker was, in a sense, regarding the surrounding neighbours as his client, but not at the expense of the woman herself, who received an improved level of help.

The Docklands team have initiated a volunteer scheme which has both assisted their work with informal carers and also created an expanding network of volunteers, as those initially introduced have in their turn introduced others.

The example of the father of a boy on supervision being used as a volunteer driver is quoted by Lochend. Longbenton have utilized clients as helpers at a day centre, indicating that for CSW teams, getting to know 'clients' is a way of discovering local people with strengths.

The Longbenton team have 'allocated' workers to talk to informal 'gatekeepers' such as the sub-postmaster and the owner of the local chippy. They also describe how group work with clients and carers extends the members' networks and sources of help as well as improving relationships among members. Another team initiative has involved the creation of a local day centre for the elderly. This constitutes a place where frail, isolated, elderly people can revive old acquaintances and participate again in the area's ongoing social life. This is an example of community development combining with good day-care practice, within a localized resource, to revitalize decaying informal networks.

The Honor Oak team contributor notes that:

'Because the team is well known and has been in the area a long time, it is rare that we do not know something about someone's support networks. Because of our accessibility and preventive approach, we rarely work in crisis but usually receive referrals early enough for us to test out the strength of supportive networks and the possibility of using informal carers.

When a problem arises or a case comes up for discussion, the decision of how or whether to intervene is influenced by our knowledge of that person's networks and of which block of flats they live in and how supportive the tenants of that block may be.'

An example is given which shows how closely the team is able to integrate its work with informal networks:

Mrs D., a young single mother with two small children, was moved into the area and housed in a very supportive block of flats. Other tenants quickly picked up on her vulnerability and began helping her to settle in. However, they also made us aware of her existence and her aware of ours. For a short period it was necessary to allocate the case on a formal basis but the degree of anxiety generated by the case was greatly reduced by our knowledge that neighbours would be supportive, would keep an eye on the situation, and would make appropriate requests to us for additional help if necessary. When a particular crisis did arise, neighbours accepted that all that could be done formally had been done and that when we went off duty, the support needed to come from them. They were also able to convey to the mother the nature of our preventive approach and so enabled her very quickly to be much more open with us.'

B.4 *Factors aiding or impeding work with informal networks*

Despite the very different situations faced by the contributing teams, they describe a number of common factors which aid or impede the development of their work with informal networks. It is helpful to distinguish between factors which are internal to the team and those which can be located in its external environment.

Internal factors aiding the development of work with informal networks include the level of localization, the use of local staff, team commitment, flexibility, and persistence. The Docklands team summarize the importance of concentrating on a small geographical area by saying 'the localization of the working group enables closer access, understanding, co-operation, and accountability to the local community.' The Longbenton team detail how localization can lead to the accumulation of knowledge about the area served:

'Having fairly compact areas to cover means that the same small number of workers regularly traverses the same ground. This is a major "plus" factor in allowing information to be shared. It is in everyone's interest to listen and remember what a colleague has discovered because the likelihood of being there yourself very shortly is high. It is also very likely that you will be back before long at the block of flats you have just visited, so there is an incentive to find out about very local information. Recently a team member discovered that people in a particular block of flats have developed their own informal alarm system whereby if curtains remain undrawn by 11 a.m., a neighbour will go in to check. This was recorded on the file and included for discussion in the allocation meeting where, again, it will be recorded as part of the minutes.'

The use of local staff as a means of increasing knowledge of local networks has already been mentioned (above B.2). Team commitment to an area, with the trust and confidence that can be achieved over a period of years, is also mentioned by a number of teams. As the Huntly team emphasized, the team should 'be prepared to work on integration over a long period of time'.

External factors which can assist teams in building integrative relations with local informal networks can include the establishment of good inter-agency relationships and interconnections between the informal networks themselves. In Normanton, for example, the team's good contacts with the local clergy bring it into touch with the informal networks associated with several of the town's churches. In Whitehawk 'community cohesion, trust, and family networks' are all seen as factors which can aid (or where they are weak, impede) the development of work with informal systems. Even in the least promising environments some informal structures are likely to exist in the local community for, as the Longbenton team points out, 'Users do not live in isolated boxes. Once some knowledge of informal networks begins to be established, links begin to appear, so that some kind of partial mapping of networks becomes possible.'

Internal factors which are experienced by the teams as inhibiting or impeding their work with informal networks include staff turnover and pressures on time. In the Honor Oak team, for example, it is suggested that there are no 'explicit strategies for integrating with our informal carers — our practice is based on the depth of our local knowledge of networks. This has made it problematic to integrate new staff into the team because we have developed no clear way of sharing this knowledge.' Pressure of time is mentioned by all the teams as a problem in developing work with community networks. In the case of the Lochend team, this is linked with the lack of relevant experience of the social workers concerned. 'The pressure of statutory work . . . coupled with a lack of experience on the part of the social work members of the team has meant that apart from one or two isolated but . . . important initiatives, the 20 per cent weighting (for work with the community) has not really got off the ground.'

External factors impeding development have included professional and trade-union pressures which have made it more difficult to change attitudes amongst staff and create the flexibility in roles that working with informal networks requires.

C.1 *Assumptions and expectations*

■ **Assume that informal networks exist.** Irrespective of subjective evaluations of the extent of overall 'community cohesion', it is certain that informal networks of relationships will exist, and that social services department clients will be part of some kind of network, however attenuated in its extent or caring quality. Whatever the quality of a network, and however isolated from, or in conflict with, other networks it may be, the fact of its existence and its characteristics must be taken into account for effective work to be undertaken.

A helpful model for visualizing networks is given in the work of Terence Lee (1971). He looks at the concept of a neighbourhood from the perspective of the individual, and concludes that people perceive their own neighbourhood as a mixture of a bounded geographical area and the relationships which they have within it. The term he uses to convey this notion is the 'socio-spatial schema'. Neighbourhoods thus defined are of a consistently small size (75 acres), which corresponds to a ten-minute walk from home for an averagely mobile person. The size shrinks with decreasing mobility, but those with greater mobility such as car owners, although enjoying a greater number of relationships at a greater distance, would not include them within their neighbourhood.

Each individual's neighbourhood is unique, though there may be common boundaries – usually obvious ones such as railway lines, fields, and main roads. What planners think of as central, focal points, such as shops, schools, bus stops, and clinics, are often in fact at the limits of individual's neighbourhoods (they go to the shops, but not beyond them). The picture which thus emerges is of a complex overlay of informal networks unique to each individual, a few overlapping at many points, others only marginally, others not at all. (See also Chapter 3, pp. 53–8).

■ **Expect networks to exhibit varying characteristics.** It cannot be assumed that all informal networks are caring networks. Some networks will be more to do with conflict than with care, others most concerned with the passing of information, and still others with influence. Networks which are not primarily caring can, nevertheless, sometimes be involved in the work of the CSW team, though of necessity in an indirect way.

■ **Be aware of costs for network members.** Being a member of a caring or other network will often entail costs for those who are not the primary focus of the department's attention or who are not identified as having or being the problem. CSW teams should not look at networks merely for their caring capacity; as befits their community-orientation they should take into account the needs of others who have not been labelled 'the client', but are involved in problematic situations.

Good traditional practice already acknowledges this issue, for instance by paying attention to the needs of carers of elderly people. CSW teams should consciously develop and extend such practice. Where an explicit authority role is brought into play, perhaps a neighbour complaining of 'nuisance', the conflict between loyalty to the named client and to the rest of the neighbourhood is more stark but it must still be consciously handled without either side being abandoned to the depradations of the other.

■ **Expect to find overlap between networks.** People who are clients in one situation may be carers or helpers in another. Members of a caring network or client group may also be related to networks of influence and information. Teams which are alert to these possibilities will find numerous opportunities to use the various networks to achieve their aims.

C.2 *Obtaining knowledge about informal networks*

CSW teams must move on from a straightforward awareness of the networks of their users which stare them in the face in the course of their everyday work and take positive steps to gather and systematize network knowledge.

■ **Organize user-related knowledge.** Never consider a user in a vacuum, but for every referral map the user's network and consider its contribution to his or her problem or support. Abandoning the term 'client' is a good starting-point. Accumulate your knowledge into a map of networks and identify where overlap occurs. Teams may tend to rely on osmosis, but information thus held is vulnerable to the departure of staff members. An insurance against this is to share all such information verbally at team meetings or through informal interaction. More organized still would be an attempt to diagram networks using techniques such as Network Analysis (Seed 1986).

■ **Encourage an informal open attitude in team members.** People are not always prepared to give information directly about their involvement, and the team members will need to supplement the information they gain from direct questioning by keeping their ears open. A generally helpful stance will also yield more information than an official style.

■ **Keep a log of non-user-related information.** This will apply to networks of information and influence which may, for example, impinge on local political processes. It will also be important as a means of identifying resourceful people on the patch with skills and strengths, as well as informal 'gatekeepers'.

■ **Draw on the knowledge of local staff.** Local staff will already be part of local informal networks, and will often be able to give quick access to community resources, as well as gathering information enabling them to act as an early-warning system.

■ **Encourage team members to become part of informal networks.** This can happen virtually automatically, but in a restricted way, when team members undertake their traditional duties with individual users. To get to know a wider variety of people they will need to supplement such contacts by undertaking community development initiatives and involving themselves as a resource for other agencies in *their* initiatives. Client-orientated group work will also give more ready knowledge of who knows whom and how they affect each other, producing a more accurate and complete picture of users, their strengths and weaknesses.

■ **Subject network information to analysis.** This can be achieved formally and objectively by academic means such as surveys. However, unless academic help can be enlisted, this kind of approach is likely to prove very time-consuming and forbidding owing to the sheer size and complexity of the task.

An alternative approach is to attempt a more subjective analysis of information already available to the team through experience and departmental statistics. Analysis should aim to identify both strengths and common problems within the community networks (e.g. there are a number of single parents in the team's patch who lack family support but young parents in a couple of streets seem to gravitate towards a particular person for help and advice).

C.3 *Working with informal networks*

Teams may work directly with a user's own pre-existing network to enhance its caring capacity.

■ **Work in partnership with networks.** It is important for CSW teams not to colonize or exploit caring networks by placing impossible burdens on them. This will mean making an assessment of the capacity of a network to care, and if necessary, supplementing, or taking over, some of the tasks being undertaken by the network with other, officially or voluntarily provided services. In order to do this it may prove helpful to arrange network or family meetings at which joint decisions are taken as to the distribution of tasks.

Teams should try to work on the basis that they have now become part of the user's network but are available on a different basis – namely as official and paid workers. This status carries some benefits such as reliability and tolerance of difficulties, but also disadvantages such as a certain formality, not being a friend, and limited availability.

■ **Work with network members' needs.** The concept of caring for carers does not need elaboration here, simply the remainder that this is an aspect of good traditional practice which must be an integral part of the CSW approach.

Some carers freely choose to care, but others appear to be trapped by a perceived obligation to continue taking responsibility beyond their resources. Individual counselling often appears ineffective in such situations, and it may be that consciousness-raising group work about expectations of carers will be more helpful in such circumstances.

Caring for non-caring but suffering neighbours is a different but still familiar aspect of the same concept. Such difficulties are sometimes dealt with under a traditional model by invoking 'the interests of the client' as a reason for ignoring the needs of others close to him or her but this is hardly helpful as it tends to increase feelings of frustration, helplessness, and anger towards both client and department. CSW teams should face up to this challenge by seeking opportunities for discussion with network members about their neighbour's situation and any possible legal action, and giving advice to them as to how they might respond in ways which would be helpful to themselves.

Whether confidentiality constitutes a problem is a matter which workers will have to weigh in each case. It is often possible to obtain the client's agreement for such discussions, sometimes with the parameters set by them. On other occasions, for example when someone's mental state is at issue, it may be judged fatuous to invoke confidentiality as the problem and its effects are clear for all in the street to see and endure.

A further problem may be that advice given to network members, although perfectly legal and respectable, would not be in a user's interest. However, the challenge of balancing the interests and needs of different individuals and groups is scarcely new to social workers. They are already in the position of advising parents as to their independent legal rights to challenge decisions that the social services department has taken in what it perceives to be their child's best interests. (See also Chapter 3, pp. 92–4.)

■ **Recognize the potential of local people as a resource.** This is particularly important because lay volunteers can often provide frequent and readily available services with no 'strings' – help is provided simply because the helper wishes to provide it – which an official person cannot match. Unofficial 'gatekeepers', for example, occupy such roles precisely because they are members of the community.

Individuals needing help are devalued if they are regarded in consequence as members of an inferior species, people without strengths or positive qualities. But in reality even the most dependent people usually have something to offer their fellows and CSW should encourage the use of such qualities. This helps both the team and the individual, since being employed in a helpful capacity can foster the notion of self-worth.

As well as working directly with users' networks, CSW teams can undertake effective preventive work by indirectly influencing informal networks not necessarily immediately related to individual users.

■ **Undertake group work with users and carers.** By working with a group composed of users from the same locality, teams will introduce each of them to a more extended network. Group work will also be aimed at improving the quality of interaction among group members, and this will have further positive effects, especially where the participants are already members of each other's networks.

■ **Undertake community development work.** Become involved with non-social services department users in initiating or supporting: mutual-aid groups; resource building; problem analysis; pressure grouping. Teams starting out on the CSW approach will find that a single such effort will quickly introduce them to a number of networks of which they were previously unaware.

Teams will also find that they are then more easily able to assist user-related groups which wish to translate their activities into those listed. Once a number of such initiatives have been taken, the overlapping of networks will become evident, and teams should be alert to the resulting opportunities to link members of different networks as a way of stimulating action.

■ **Be open to input from the community.** Use the team's involvement with informal networks to listen for need, demand, and opinion of your performance so far, and be prepared to make consequent adjustments to team practices. The more the team makes itself available as a resource to the variety of informal networks in the area served, the greater the amount of information which is likely to be forthcoming.

■ **Identify the focus of the team's work in particular situations.** The framework offered by Froland *et al.* (1981) is helpful in encouraging systematic thinking about developing linkages with and between informal carers. They have constructed a useful table (*Table* 5) which is based on the types of linkages observed among thirty agencies, distinguishing different target populations and types of problem addressed.

The kind of helping networks with which agency staff establish links is related both to the nature of the problems concerned and to the objectives of the agency. In other words, the reasons for seeking out informal sources of help are in themselves major influences on the way staff define and identify helping networks. The focus may be on:

(a) a single client or family and the identification of their informal support network;
(b) a particular population group concerned with mutual aid or self-help: this may involve tapping into existing informal networks already providing mutual aid, or attempting to create self-help networks from scratch with existing clients;
(c) geographical contiguity: here agencies locate natural helpers who are key figures in the patch or neighbourhood or promote neighbour exchanges. Some agencies in the study identified existing locality-based networks, others set out to create them. An example of the second approach involved staff in locating 'given' community representatives like clergy, schoolteachers, shopkeepers, and knowledgeable residents, and then organizing them into helping networks.

Linkages are about expanding personal networks, developing mutual aid, and encouraging neighbour ties. Two dimensions to linkages can be identified in the CSW approach to working with networks, horizontal and vertical. The horizontal dimension involves social relationships among people in similar circumstances. Vertical linkage relates individuals to larger social institutions like schools, churches, local government, and personal care organizations. The goals of these approaches are:

(a) to develop connections between formal services and informal systems in order that information about community services and resources should become more accessible;
(b) to make agencies more sensitive to local needs;
(c) To develop the capacity of groups to organize and be advocates on their own behalf.

Table 5 *Opportunities for developing linkages*

| problem focus | elderly | target populations | | | |
		children, youth, and families	developmental and physical disabled	mental health clients	low income and ethnic communities
Individual rights ● access to services ● acceptability and appropriateness of services ● stigmatizing problems	● organize elder forum to identify needs and local resources ● establish linkages between elderly groups in low income housing and local Commissions on Aging	● develop parent advising board to participate in youth and children's services ● establish youth advisory board to provide input to elected officials on youth concerns	● establish Parent Advocates groups to lobby for educational rights for developmentally disabled children ● establish consumer coalition for disabled to advocate for transportation accessibility, curbcuts, barrier free housing	● develop pool of volunteer citizens to help obtain services for returning mental hospital patients ● organize consumer corporation to advocate for mentally ill ● act as advisor to client self-help group	● establish constituency groups among providers, consumers, opinion leaders to identify local resources and organize services ● organize and charter Neighborhood Planning Council to approve or initiate local economic development

Needs					
Needs for material assistance • food, housing • jobs	• recruit local residents to help in home repair for elderly • support neighborhood helpers who provide home aid • contact stores, banks, to improve service to elderly	• foster mutual aid network among abused women to develop co-operative living arrangement • develop network of families in communities to provide temporary shelter care for runaway youth • use lay therapists to act as advocates to ensure that abusive families' basic material needs are met	• establish co-operative living arrangements among severely disabled • develop parents group to assist severely retarded adults to find jobs	• establish citizen/consumer partnership to organize employment and housing opportunities for chronic mental patients	• establish mutual aid groups among unemployed persons to exchange information about job search strategies • develop self-help 'tools and skills bank' to assist in rehabilitating housing • establish neighborhood co-operative to fund local development and provide jobs
Needs for social and emotional support • limitations in social skills	• enlist natural helper in neighborhoods to provide friendly visiting	• recruit and train lay helpers to provide compassionate support to identified child abuse parents	• develop links between parents of disabled children to provide support and advice on raising child	• develop community networks among ex-patients to initiate and plan social and recreational activities	• recruit and train natural helpers to provide informal helping to residents

Table 5 Contd.

problem focus	elderly	children, youth, and families	developmental and physical disabled	mental health clients	low income and ethnic communities
• assistance with activities of daily living	• develop neighbourhood based peer support groups to increase mutual aid	• develop mutual aid groups among single parent families • develop mutual aid group among widow(er)s with dependent children	• consult with and promote self-help groups among retarded, e.g. People First	• develop mutual aid groups for patients • develop mutual aid group and peer telephone network among agoraphobics	• facilitate neighborhood support among residents
Multiple problems • chronic problem • family burden	• develop support groups for adult children of frail elderly	• develop support groups among low income female headed families to exchange day care	• develop exchange networks among citizens, families and relatives of developmentally disabled to provide respite care	• organize volunteers among church groups to provide companionate relationships to chronic patients	• develop resource bank to identify residents who are willing to provide services

target populations

Health related issues • long term care • nutrition • prevention care									
• develop neighborhood networks of mutual aid around meal sites, meals on wheels programs • contact and consult with SRO managers to identify problems • develop patient support groups in nursing homes	• develop mutual aid groups among mothers of infants to exchange information and support • support mutual aid groups among teenage pregnant mothers in schools	• provide support services to family members to sustain the existing help provided • enlist citizen volunteers e.g. youth, neighbors, to develop companionate relationships	• use peer aids to train disabled in skills of independent living	• develop self-help among physically disabled to exchange information on self-care • develop parents groups in conjunction with hospitals, pediatricians to provide support to newly identified parents of developmentally disabled	• develop natural helping teams of neighbors, family and friends and service providers to assist with mentally ill	• consult with board and care operators to improve identification and early intervention • develop patient medication support groups	• identify and consult with group of indigenous leaders to foster community strengths • develop partnership relationships with local businesses, church and neighborhood associations to find local solutions	• establish relationships with local grocery stores to improve availability of nutrition information • identify and enlist lay facilitators to provide first aid and health information

Source: C. Froland, D.L. Pancoast, N.J. Chapman, and P.J. Kimboko, *Helping Networks and Human Services*, pp. 57–9. © 1981 C. Froland *et al.* Reproduced by permission of Sage Publications, Inc.

C.4 *Factors aiding work with networks*

■ **Work for the development of a CSW team philosophy**, including members' ability and willingness to abandon the protective aspects of their professional image and any tendency to react bureaucratically.

■ **Protect staff from the pressures of casework,** which are frequently quoted as a reason for not doing more with informal networks. This is not to say that casework can be made to go away, but that the management of the team can be so handled as to support team members in this method of working despite other pressures. (See Chapter 5, p. 153.) Senior management can also help by publicly supporting this type of preventative work, particularly at times when the team may be experiencing stress or difficulty. (See Chapter 5, p. 182.)

■ **Work to establish the maximum feasible localization of team operation.** Experience shows that, other things being equal, the more local the focus of the CSW team's work, the easier it is for members to build effective links with informal networks in the neighbourhood served.

■ **Encourage team members to share information.** Shared information can help to increase the knowledge of all team members of local networks. This not only improves their day-to-day work and their ability to cover for each other but reduces the loss of knowledge when individual team members leave. Two methods of encouraging the sharing of information are regular discussions of current work at team meetings and the location of teams or sub-teams in common office space.

■ **Maximize the employment and integration of local staff.** Local staff are likely to possess a good knowledge of at least part of the system of local networks and to be acceptable to them. Seek to ensure the most effective use of their knowledge and contacts through their full integration in the work of the team.

Integration within the social services department

ISSUES

There are three different kinds of integration within the social services department:

1 the integration of philosophy and attitude – that is ensuring that everyone approaches their task with a common understanding of aims, objectives, and methods;
2 the integration of roles – the task of seeing that jobs dovetail so that a flexible and responsive service is provided to users;
3 integration of management – the grouping together of a number of different roles under a common management. In the case of CSW the interest is in the managerial integration that takes place on a patch basis – in other words, the different roles which are grouped together on the basis of the area they serve as opposed to being grouped according to differentiation between tasks.

A.1 *Integration of aims and philosophy*

In broad terms all workers within a social services department may share the aim of wishing to promote the welfare of their clients. Nevertheless, where different services are compartmentalized there is a tendency for this broad consensus to fragment as it is translated into detailed action. Different services, with a logic which is irrefutable in terms of their boundaries, invent rules and criteria which serve to exclude certain clients. Staff see their responsibilities as strictly circumscribed by these boundaries and managers see their responsibilities in terms of them, protecting their services and workers from encroachment. At the end of this process, the department's overall aim of providing a service responsive to need can too easily remain unachieved, as users – particularly those with the greatest difficulties – tend to fall between the compartmentalized criteria. (See also: Chapter 5, p. 164; Chapter 6, p. 229.)

A.2 *Integration of roles*

The Barclay Report describes the primary role of the field social worker as 'social care planning'. For this activity to take place, social workers need to assess needs of individuals and families and to assemble a package of services to fit the individual's situation. In order for this to be carried out efficiently, the providers of the different services need to work closely together. It is important, for example, that the role of the home help should dovetail with the way meals on wheels are provided. Similarly it is important that the role of IT units fits with the role of residential units. Compartmentalized services tend to plan in isolation from one another and there is a danger that the roles they design within the compartments will bear little relation to the roles designed for the staff of a separate service. (See also: Chapter 3, p. 76, Chapter 5, pp. 137, 164, 182.)

A.3 *Integration of management*

Under traditional models this will take place at a departmental level some way above fieldwork teams and establishments. This may well leave staff on the ground with insufficient flexibility to link their roles effectively with those of the other departmental workers they encounter in individual situations. Attempts to make these links may meet with opposition from managers and workers who remain loyal above all to the rules of their own sector.

By decentralizing the management of all services to patch level, a common sense of identity with the CSW team and a common sense of purpose (the delivery of services to the patch) are more readily promoted. The single unified management of all services allows for, promotes, and supports adjustments at individual level in pursuance of the aim of a responsive service. (See also Chapter 6, p. 193.)

TEAM EXPERIENCE

B.1 *Integration of aims and philosophy*

The kind of problem which can arise through compartmentalized services is illustrated from the experience of the Longbenton team. A severely disabled man was recently admitted to hospital after a period of two years in which neighbours and the various services had worked very hard, though unwillingly, to keep him at home. When he was due to be discharged, the social worker was confronted by a situation in which the home-care organizer, the domiciliary-care organizer, the district nurses, and the officer in charge of the local residential home, all refused to allow their service to be used. The situation was only resolved when the area manager used his position as line manager to back the decision that the man should be given a place in the residential establishment.

The Normanton team encountered problems with one of the social work assistants who refused to adopt the flexible approach which the team's patch system required. The patch team concerned had to adapt their methods of working accordingly and could make less progress with introducing CSW methods than the other patch teams.

A more serious problem has confronted the Docklands team: the community work posts allocated to it remain unfilled, apparently because community workers have refused to occupy them, feeling that to be identified with a social work team would not allow them to follow their own aims and approach. With other work roles, where staff have fully accepted the restructuring involved in CSW, the Docklands team have achieved much in securing a greater mutual understanding of each other's contributions.

The same phenomenon is noted with the wide range of roles within the Rye team. In Lochend, with community workers based within the team, numerous issues identified by social workers are picked up by the community workers, and vice versa.

In Longbenton, the community development officer serving the area of which the team forms a part shares an office with the team and works so closely with its members that she is treated as one of them. In the same area, the area manager encouraged the three team leaders each to develop a regular liaison with the officer in charge of the elderly persons' home serving their patch. The Longbenton team leader has also taken on some line management functions in respect of the day centre for elderly people set up by the team's efforts. He comments:

'The very striking advantage of this arrangement is that the day centre is providing a service which is highly flexible and takes on all kinds of clients. There is only one effective criterion for admission: the centre must be able to cope with the client. Its scope is considerable, however, and a wide range of problems from physical to mental frailty can be handled. There is an element of ''protection'' for the centre in my dual role. Problems posed by clients of the team who attend the centre are my problems too, to solve within the centre. So there can be no charge against the field team that difficult clients are simply dumped there.'

B.2 *Integration of roles*

None of the contributing teams has abandoned traditional roles entirely, but all seek to 'stretch' them in order to achieve a more flexible and responsive service. This is at some cost to some of the individuals concerned (as in the Normanton experience referred to in B.1); more problems encountered in this area are dealt with in Chapter 5, p. 182.

The Honor Oak and Longbenton teams report the involvement of their administrative staff in community development projects. The Longbenton team obtained agreement for day-centre staff to be paid for sitting with elderly mentally infirm people whilst their carers attended a newly formed carers' group.

The Docklands team have involved all categories of ancillary staff in community development projects and their roles have stretched to include tasks more usually undertaken by social workers, such as giving basic advice, taking referrals, and managing their own workloads. Meanwhile, the staff still retain their former main functions.

Social workers in the Rye team have taken on home-help tasks in order to make relationships, and they also undertake home-help assessments for their own clients. The home-help organizer can apply for short-term or permanent residential care, and the officer in charge of the elderly persons' home can deal directly with a referral for short-term care. The Rye team stress that they do not promote flexibility for the sake of it, but in order to solve problems or cut out unnecessary work or duplication of effort, as when a home-help organizer reassesses a client already assessed by a social worker.

The Lochend team planned to give 20 per cent social work time to community work activities; and community workers would give 20 per cent of their time to selected social work tasks, such as office duty. In this case it was the social workers who found it impossible to break free of their traditional role, citing 'pressure of work' as the reason for not fulfilling the arrangement. Not surprisingly, in the absence of reciprocation, the community workers pulled out of office duty.

All contributing teams are agreed that once staff from all roles have worked within an integrated team for a time, they experience increased job satisfaction due both to a greater appreciation of their colleagues' work and to a reduction in the number of problems encountered in their day-to-day relations with colleagues.

B.3 *Integration of management*

As the Honor Oak and Longbenton teams make clear, problems of lack of integration surface in the very practical form of lack of control over resources. This may be experienced either as a lack of control over the way a role is performed or simply as the failure to secure a place in an establishment.

It is noticeable that the only role adjustments reported by the teams take place where each role falls within the team's responsibility. The Longbenton case is instructive. The team has benefited significantly from having direct control over the day centre, whilst having to go through more laborious processes with other services. The integration of services at area level – still unusually decentralized by normal standards – has clearly allowed some solutions to be achieved once the area manager has become involved.

The widest spread of integration is reported by the Rye and Whitehawk teams, which have the largest number of roles decentralized to the patch level, followed by Docklands and Normanton, again with a large number of different roles within the team, but in their cases without residential or day care staff.

PRACTICE GUIDELINES

From the experience of the contributing teams, it would appear that it is necessary to give managerial control of services to CSW teams in order to ensure that staff will be encouraged or permitted to perform their roles with flexibility. Where CSW teams are not given such control, it is beyond their capacity to achieve role integration. The more services which are decentralized to patch level, therefore, the greater the scope for integration and the greater the potential for more efficient and responsive working.

Ways of overcoming the problems which stem from 'role stretch' are dealt with in Chapter 5, pp. 182–92.

The promotion of shared aims and philosophies within the team is dealt with in Chapter 6, pp. 228–38.

C.1 *Integration of aims and philosophy*

■ **Work to promote a common understanding in the team of the importance of establishing shared aims and philosophy.** The effective development of a decentralized team, sharing responsibility widely amongst its members at all levels, is likely to be substantially affected by the extent to which people are guided by shared goals and values.

■ **Set up a system of participative management in the team** through which common aims can be developed and responsibility for their implementation shared.

■ **Where important differences in perspective exist amongst staff, seek to identify them clearly, work to resolve them where possible, and devise coping strategies where not.**
In new teams it is important not to expect too much too soon. The establishment of common working approaches takes time, even where there is an initial sympathy in outlook. Where such sympathy is lacking it will take longer or may not be possible at all! Genuinely participatory methods of working provide many opportunities for working at differences. Coping strategies for those that can't be resolved can include role modification (for example, not requiring a worker who has difficulty with a particular method or particular client group to cover the same broad spectrum of activities as others but using his/her specialist strengths more intensively).

■ **Where staff prove to be completely unsuited for community social work and their presence in the team seriously impedes its development, take action to find them alternative positions in the organization.**
It is important that seriously disruptive differences in outlook and ability to contribute in the CSW team are squarely faced and not swept under the carpet because no one is prepared to endure the uncomfortable conflicts implicit in them. Few CSW

teams are likely to be large enough or strong enough to function effectively if one or more of their members is actively and persistently hostile to the rationale on which they are based. Where change cannot be achieved, then team leaders or managers should explore with the workers concerned the possibility of moving to another post, outside the team. If this is resisted the matter should be referred for action to more senior management.

■ **In recruiting new staff seek out people already sympathetic to the aims and values of CSW.**

C.2 *Integration of roles*

■ **Aim to establish maximum flexibility in official job descriptions.** Attempts to change job descriptions can be undertaken at any time by the team and its leadership but some occasions are particularly favourable, for example when a new team is set up, when any part of the team or its work is being restructured, and when there is staff turnover.

■ **Support the restructuring of work to create jobs with wider scope and responsibilities.**
As the demands on social services change, the appropriateness of particular jobs may be questioned. Such changes offer the opportunity for creating new posts which are better suited to the challenges of CSW. For example, teams could encourage the merger (which has already taken place in some authorities) of the role of home help and residential care assistant into the new job of care worker. The care worker would be able to function in both domiciliary and residential worlds and to contribute importantly to the integration of services across the boundary between them.

■ **Work actively with trade unions and professional associations for support for more flexible interpretation of roles.**
Opposition from these sources to CSW is linked to understandable concern that workers are being exploited if more is being asked of them with nothing offered in return. The increase in responsibility involved in CSW, which are particularly marked in the grades of the less well-paid workers, should be linked to better pay and conditions, and CSW teams

should be in the forefront of action to secure these. But they should also be ready to use the union and professional association to debate the nature of the changes involved and to underline the advantages which they believe CSW brings to user and worker alike.

■ **Encourage joint working by different categories of staff.** This can be achieved both in traditional casework (the orchestration of social worker, ancillaries, and volunteer, for instance, in working with a particular user), and through project work.

■ **Develop commitment to integrated work through shared decision making.** Encourage the team to develop a problem-centred rather than skill/training-centred approach to the first evaluation of work referred. 'What way should *we* try to tackle this?' needs to be the first response, rather than 'does the matter fall within *my* remit as a such-and-such worker?'

C.3 *Integration of management*

■ **Maximizing the effectiveness of CSW implies that all main services – field, domiciliary, day-care, and residential care – should be decentralized to team level.**

■ **Where such decentralization has not been achieved, teams should press within their organizations for the adoption of policies which move towards it.** Gradualism will do! For example, where only field social work is decentralized to CSW teams, a major step forward would be to incorporate the home-help service.

■ **With the decentralization of services, teams should seek to obtain the maximum feasible control of budgets.**
The team's ability to modify their structures and practices in favour of a CSW approach suited to the locality is crucially affected by the extent to which they can influence their budget and are able to move funds freely between different headings within it. Control of budgets needs to be backed by adequate information systems and administrative support.

Integration with other agencies

A.1 *Team policy*

A large proportion of resources available or potentially available to meet the needs of local communities are neither the property of local residents (informal networks), nor of the social services department, but are controlled by other statutory or voluntary agencies. In order to fulfil the role of 'social care planners', CSW teams will need to use these other agency resources as components of the package of services and resources which they attempt to bring to bear on the problems of individuals and families.

In the same way, few inroads will be made by CSW teams into the broader communal bases of problems unless they are able to co-ordinate their activities with those of other resource controllers. (See also Chapter 6, pp. 193, 209.)

A.2 *Department policy*

Individual problems are the acknowledged *raison d'être* of social work, and CSW teams are likely to find that they are allowed some professional autonomy in implementing integrative strategies in relation to individual users of their services.

But even in relation to users, teams may find that matters of policy concerning relations with other agencies are handled in a different sphere from their own. The stance taken by the department may either impede local efforts to achieve integration, or provide significant support and encouragement. (See also Chapter 6, pp. 209, 228.)

A.3 *Formal integration*

By this term we mean offically sanctioned arrangements by which different organizations combine their activities. As well as, or instead of, combined management, formal integration can also involve other forms of collaboration such as formal joint planning systems and joint decision-making procedures over resources or cases. Such integration can take place at authority, departmental, or team level.

Some local authorities are attempting to promote co-ordination by a comprehensive integration of the management of different departments on a local basis (see e.g. Hambleton and Hoggett 1984). Such radical change holds the potential of major gains in collaboration and responsiveness but is also likely to pose new problems and demands on staff. None of the contributing teams was located in an authority which has adopted integration at this level. However, their experience shows that formal integration can also be applied in more bounded ways which can still enable significant, albeit less comprehensive, gains to be achieved (see also Chapter 6, p. 209).

A.4 *Informal integration*

Many CSW teams are likely to be working in contexts where the level of formal integration is low. They will therefore have to concentrate on achieving integration with other agencies on an informal basis. Such initiatives may often be experimental, although some standard professional practices, such as liaison with GPs, can and should be absorbed into this aspect of CSW strategy. It may well turn out, however, that such informal collaboration has its own advantages and, in particular, that the arrangements made by teams face to face are in fact less rigid and more personalized than those blessed by official agreement. (See also: Chapter 3, p. 63; Chapter 6, p. 209.)

TEAM EXPERIENCE

B.1 *Team policy*

A feature of the teams' approach is the assumption that this form of integration is fundamental to the practice of CSW, and a great deal of energy is expended in attempting to achieve it.

The contributing teams have not, however, gone very far towards refining and developing their policies. Only half the teams make some kind of explicit statement about their policy: Lochend, Docklands, Normanton, and Huntly. The terse statement of the last of these: 'The policy of our team is that we will informally integrate with anybody', would appear to represent fairly the approach of all. Informal integration with other organizations is clearly a mainstream activity of CSW teams, and produces a variety of initiatives. A pattern of similar approaches emerges, but guidelines for effective team policy have to be extracted from the teams' descriptions of what they do.

B.2 *Department policy*

As a rule the local teams are left very much to their own devices in building relations with other agencies. Few of the departments have more than very limited policies for inter-agency collaboration or integration. The Normanton team, for example, says that there is no expectation at senior level about this kind of integration. The same is true in the Rye and Whitehawk teams, although at area level there are several joint initiatives between social services and the district health authorities. Limited plans for collaboration exist in some of the other departments. For instance, in Grampian, the Huntly team report that there are some semi-formal health-social work relationships in a number of health centres. In North Tyneside, the Longbenton team note that formal liaison is confined to departmental level meetings between the SSD and Housing Department, and the SSD and Education Department have both joined a non-school attendance subcommittee. During the 1984–85 miners' strike, North Tyneside set up an interdepartmental officers' meeting to co-ordinate authority-wide support for families thrown into poverty, and the practice of meeting still survives.

The Honor Oak team works closely with a housing sub-team (see B.3). Lewisham, the authority in which it is located, is currently considering proposals for authority-wide decentralization and integration of services. But these are plans for an apparently rather distant future. In the meantime, as elsewhere, the main initiative for local integration is left to the team itself.

B.3 *Formal integration*

Two of the teams have developed elements of formal integration with other agencies. The Honor Oak team shares a joint office with a Housing Department sub-team in a building belonging to the Housing Department. It has also developed close relations with other statutory agencies and is used regularly as a base by both an educational welfare officer and a probation officer who serve the local area. The services collaborate together closely as a team, sharing information, consulting on decisions, and avoiding duplication of work.

The Lochend sub-team also shares premises with other agencies: a sub-office of the Housing Department, the local community council, a food co-operative, and the talking newspaper for the blind. The agencies have separate accommodation within the building but share a common entrance: their proximity means that information flows easily between them and there is a creative atmosphere.

In one other team, Longbenton, a limited form of integration has been sanctioned by the department involving the joint management of a day centre for the frail elderly. The centre is regarded as an independent body managed by a committee of two church representatives and two social services department officers (area manager and patch team leader), with a ward councillor as chairperson. The committee takes all decisions on policy, and is responsible for its own budget, although the staff are employees of the local authority and are managed from the area team.

B.4 *Informal integration*

Most of the teams are working in contexts where formal integration with other agencies plays little or no part in their work, but in compensation they have all made major efforts to achieve greater informal integration. The gains made appear substantial and suggest that this is a field where CSW teams can make considerable progress, even where support from the wider department is not well developed. It may be useful to present these developments in some detail.

In Normanton informal links have been developed with other agencies both at patch team level and by the area team as a whole. The wide range of contacts involved in this work includes churches, Age Concern, tenants' associations, carers' groups, the town council, local political parties, other statutory agencies (housing, probation, education, etc.), various recreational groups such as the amateur operatic society, and the local allotments association, as well as several working men's clubs. The team sees it as a major part of its developmental work to link together many of these different organizations in pursuit of common policies for the local community. For example, the mention of empty premises in the Baptist Chapel by the minister visiting the office on a different errand eventually led to a joint

SSD, probation, and church project to open a drop-in centre for the elderly in the middle of town. The initial thrust for the development came from the SSD team and their knowledge of MSC resources which could be used for the renovation. The Normanton team have also been able to further integration through the access they can give to departmental resources such as transport, staff support, and use of rooms in the team office.

The Honor Oak team, in the much smaller arena of the housing estate which they serve, have been able to develop close working relations with practically all the other agencies located there. In addition to the formal working systems established with housing, probation, and education welfare already described (above B.3), one worker acts as a liaison with the local nursery school to share information, give advice, and pick up early referrals; another member of the team sits on the day-nursery admissions panel. Frequent contact also exists with the community worker for the tenants' association. The team leader attends the monthly meetings of the neighbourhood association with the local GPs and community psychiatric nurses. There is a great deal of informal contact with the housing sub-team which shares office space with the social services team, and there are joint staff meetings every two months.

Both the Normanton and Honor Oak teams have launched attempts to set up community forums to encourage the development of links between organizations and to promote local initiatives. Both have found that the ventures bristle with difficulties but have managed to achieve at least a measure of success. The setting up of the Social Care Assembly of Normanton (SCAN) has been written up fully elsewhere (Butterworth and Cole 1985). Honor Oak has twice established forums for all paid and unpaid workers in the 'people' professions on the estate. Both only survived for a limited period as it proved too difficult to sustain the initial commitment and enthusiasm for joint working which had initiated them.

The Docklands team record informal liaison with nearly all the other agencies operating in their area. In particular, the team have extensive individual contact with other statutory workers and agencies, such as health visitors, schools, and the Housing Department, and with the majority of local voluntary organizations. This liaison is greatly helped by the team's division into small sub-patches, which facilitiates easy informal relationships.

In one instance the team have been able to offer a voluntary organization office space. However, there have been some apparent conflicts of interest with local voluntary bodies, as, for example, when the team used their community care budget to pay volunteers and this initiative was seen as an attempt to entice them away from the voluntary organization they already belonged to.

The Huntly team has used the Gordon Rural Action and Information Network (GRAIN), an organization which it played a major part in establishing, as the principal focus for joint projects with the voluntary sector, including ventures such as luncheon clubs, day centres, single-parent family groups, a volunteer bureau, employment projects, craft co-operatives, conferences, and seminars. GRAIN has a number of standing working parties with whom various members of the team are involved. Apart from GRAIN, the team also have regular contacts with the patch secondary schools, health clinics, community education, and housing.

The Lochend team have very close links with the Lochend Action Centre and the Food Co-operative. A social worker has links involving regular meetings with a primary school. The team as a whole meet with the local DHSS staff periodically, as well as with the health visitors. There is close co-operation, cross-referral, and information sharing with the housing sub-office. Close physical proximity with these organizations, regular meetings, and identified link workers are felt to be important factors.

The Rye team have few regular meetings with local agencies, but close working links have been developed with individuals from other agencies, who are encouraged to visit the office. There is a regular community lunch organized by the team manager, and staff are given specific liaison roles such as supporting a newly formed MENCAP group. The team feel that demonstrating a clear commitment, being open about roles, and feeding back information to other agencies are all important factors for successful informal integration.

Finally, it is worth while quoting more extensively from the Longbenton team's experience, as their examples demonstrate in some detail exactly how informal integration can achieve results. The team aims to achieve such integration with other agencies in two main ways: by formalized liaison and by membership of local committees.

(a) *Liaison*
The team allocate individual workers to meet regularly with other agencies. These include schools, general practices, churches, Age Concern, and sheltered housing complexes. All team members, apart from the clerks, play a part in this strategy. The liaisons have typically started as client-centred ventures where regular meetings have discussed people who are of concern to the different agencies. However, team members have subsequently used the opportunity provided by the meetings to raise more general issues and from time to time this has produced very constructive results, as the following examples indicate.

1. *Liaison with a local church.* The team established liaison with St John's Church in Wideopen and provided useful support for its voluntary visitors and in finding more users for the church's luncheon club. The church volunteers enjoyed working with the team and through their contacts with it gained an enhanced understanding of their value to local people and of the nature of the needs of the elderly in the area. Following these contacts, the church's social responsibility committee invited someone from the department to speak at one of its meetings on what further contribution the church could make. In the discussion which followed, the church offered to consider whether it could help in the provision of services needed by elderly people at risk of entering residential care. Team liaison continued while internal deliberations took place in the church on how it might help. After several months the minister of the church contacted the team leader to offer church premises for a day centre for the elderly. In this way a routine arrangement for liaison eventually led to the exciting venture of a joint managed day centre.

2. *Liaison with a general practice.* A fairly standard fortnightly liaison by a social worker with a GP eventually made it possible for the team to invite a member of the practice to join the steering group of a mental health project initiated by the team. Her close co-operation in an initiative not centred on specific patients is regarded by the team as a particularly important step forward.

3. *Liaison with a sheltered housing project.* The team's link with the project, a social services officer, obtained agreement from the warden for use of the lounge for a regular coffee morning for nearby tenants not resident in the complex and for the meetings

of an EMI carers' group initiated by the team. These arrangements had to be approved by the local housing committee and the good relations built up by the team with the local area housing manager helped smooth the path to their agreement.

4. *Liaison with Age Concern.* Liaison with the local visiting organizer of Age Concern was energetically used to bombard the organization with referrals. These established beyond doubt the need for a more extensive visiting service and for improved day care. As a result there is now an Age Concern day centre on the Longbenton estate and an expanding visiting service.

5. *Unsuccessful liaisons.* Liaisons do not always pay off so handsomely. For example, years of painstaking effort in another general practice have failed to make any impact on one doctor. Again, the very success of the liaison with Age Concern led to its own demise. The expansion of the activities of the organization in Longbenton brought with it more centralized control by the North Tyneside Age Concern. Local Age Concern workers are no longer permitted to make personal contact with staff from other agencies and the close co-operation which the team, visitors, and clients alike found so valuable is no more.

Overall, however, the team's established pattern of liaison has been very productive and even the setbacks and failures have contributed to its learning about the tactics of inter-agency work. Individually, none of the developments achieved is particularly remarkable but taken cumulatively the value of consciously pursuing such liaison is very evident.

(b) *Membership of local committees*
A number of local organizations undertake work which is of particular relevance to the team. The team have accepted invitations from some of these organizations to sit on their committees, with the object of helping them to work more effectively by making their skills and resources available to them. The team hope to have some constructive influence on the organizations' activities in this manner but in no sense seek control. Examples of this kind of involvement include:

1. *Membership of a NACRO committee.* The local NACRO is involved in an employment project on Longbenton. One of its workers came up with a proposal to start a discussion group of an 'intellectual' character for blind people living on the estate.

It became clear to the social services team member that the proposed manner of running the group would make the members feel patronized. The team representative was able to make some more appropriate suggestions for approaching the needs of the group. As a result a working party was set up including a community teacher, the voluntary society for the blind, NACRO, the high school, and the social services team leader. This produced some imaginative suggestions, and possibilities for development were subsequently discussed with local blind people.

2. *The Longbenton Forum.* A loose confederation of local organizations in both the voluntary and statutory sector has attempted to establish a permanent forum for discussion and liaison with Longbenton. The social services team has been able to work constructively with a temporary worker from the North Tyneside CVS in furthering this scheme. An example of its positive results is that the team's EMI carers' group joined forces with the local WRVS in a 'care in the community' initiative.

PRACTICE GUIDELINES

C.1 *Team policy*

■ **Work out a conscious policy of integration with other agencies.**

It is tempting but erroneous to assume that closer physical proximity through being on the patch and more frequent contact with other agencies, will of itself produce integrated working. These are not enough. To make real progress in getting agencies to work together, teams will need to pay close attention to their own thinking and practice, otherwise they will be in danger of finding themselves with an increased number of referrals due to greater accessibility and no strategies to handle them more effectively.

■ **Identify the extent of the team's freedom to integrate work with other agencies.**

Teams may find it useful to distinguish between *operational level integration* – work connected with individuals – and *strategic level integration* – work on planning, intermeshing functions, etc. The latter are normally handled at divisional or central level by social services departments, and are therefore likely to be out of the control of CSW teams, particularly where the other agency in question operates on a wider geographical area. It may nevertheless be possible, with care, for a CSW team to negotiate with a conterminous part of a larger agency, or with a strictly local one, especially if the outcome for them and the social services department can be contained locally. Probably the only way to find out whether your team will be allowed such autonomy for any particular set of negotiations is to try it and see what happens.

Operational-level integration is usually left to individual workers and can be combined into a team effort.

■ **Seek to obtain sufficient autonomy for integrative work.** Through normal departmental channels it may be possible to influence the department to adopt consciously the policy of encouraging local negotiations. Alternatively, sanction for a particular set of negotiations may be obtained. Some already established methods of work may also assist in achieving integrative working (e.g. meetings or case conferences routinely held with other agencies may legitimate integrated working practices at local level). Where it is known that higher-level liaison is taking place, attempt to make a team input into the process by conveying your views to the department's representative or seeking direct representation.

■ **Attempt to develop discussion and co-operation with other agencies over day-to-day casework.** Quite considerable autonomy is likely to be found at operational levels, and negotiations with other agencies can be conducted around individual users with the freedom accorded to the professional to make judgements in such contexts. Arrangements arrived at in one case can, if sufficiently often repeated, become standardized at local level without ever having been negotiated as an issue. Teams may thus be able to achieve a measure of improved integration locally through their day-to-day work on cases.

■ **Identify areas of overlap with other agencies.** This should be a part of the process by which the team shares and discusses information, and can arise out of common casework situations, or from an identification of community needs or resources. A systematic consideration should lead on to the development of team policy.

■ **As a team, legitimize the 'indirect' work of team members.**
Integrative work takes time, and must be given sufficient priority to ensure that it does not always get pushed to the end of the agenda. Team members may be in need of reassurance that this is 'real work' and that it is all right for them to be spending time on it. Recording such work is one way of signalling its responsibility within the team, and a written record of activity can also be used to demonstrate the work of the team to others.

■ **Consciously develop team members' skills.** Skills in integrative activities require the same attention as more traditional skills if they are to improve, and team members may need considerable guidance until they have acquired some experience. Individual supervision and team training should therefore cover integrative working.

■ **Promote a positive attitude towards other agencies.** Areas of overlap are often problematic, particularly with other statutory agencies. It is essential that CSW teams do not fall into the trap of simply blaming the other agency for any difficulties, but look for positive strategies to overcome them. To this end it is necessary to keep on communicating with other agencies despite the conflict which is bound to occur from time to time, and to do so in a non-patronizing way. Work on a long timescale, and continue with strategies even though some reverses may occur. Be prepared for other agencies to use you and your resources constructively, as you are hoping to use theirs.

C(D).2 *Department policy*

Many teams have no choice but to operate in an environment where little account is taken of the need for integrated working. It goes without saying that CSW teams find it enormously helpful when their departments attempt to develop policies which provide a positive framework for co-operative work. Consequently the guidelines in this section are aimed primarily at senior management and carry a 'D' as well as a 'C' prefix.

■ **Legitimize 'indirect work'.** Make sure that teams know that the department approves of such work. Suggestions for action can be made to CSW teams, and they can be asked to record their work and to demonstrate their successes. They will also need the support of senior management when they run into problems which are difficult to solve at local level, or which seem to create difficulties at senior management level.

■ **Involve CSW teams in policy making and negotiations.** Policies with other agencies developed in isolation from the CSW teams may bear little relation to the needs of the workers on the ground, and may in fact hamstring their attempts to create innovative forms of co-operation. It is preferable to take positive steps to discover the views of the team and, particularly where teams are directly affected, to include their personnel in the negotiating team.

■ **Take the initiative to help CSW teams.** If problems are high-lighted by a particular team or anticipated by senior staff, potential minefields can be swept by negotiating at a high level integrative policies which make life easier for CSW teams.

■ **Develop training programmes.**

■ **Allow teams sufficient control over local resources to enable them to negotiate meaningfully at local level.**
It is, for example, useful for a team to know that it can agree to the use of its premises by another agency without having to undertake the time-consuming process of seeking permission.

■ **Encourage teams to experiment.** They can be supported, when difficulties are encountered, by expert advice, and by extra resources for particular projects.

■ **Seek coterminous boundaries with other agencies.** Teams will find that their lives are much easier if they can relate to other agencies on the same geographical basis as themselves. This also helps to iron out problems of liaison at departmental level, as it becomes more feasible to delegate aspects of formal liaison.

C.3 *Formal integration*

■ **Weigh up the advantages and disadvantages of closer integration with other local-authority departments.**
The contributing teams have little direct experience of formal

integration between social services and other local-authority departments. Such contacts as they have, principally with housing, indicate the need to weigh up the advantages of closer collaboration against the problems which can arise over different working methods and philosophies. Teams should aim to resolve any major differences *before* integrating services. Where this is not possible, more limited integration, perhaps involving shared premises but separate working areas and organization, may be preferable.

■ **Weigh up the advantages and disadvantages of closer integration with voluntary agencies.**
The same caveat may well apply to voluntary organizations. Teams can, however, consider sharing premises as a way of promoting physical nearness and as an aid to integrative working. Joint management of specific projects can allow resources to be combined within limited parameters without precipitating wholesale changes in either organization. It may be possible to give formal recognition to locally developed coalitions of agencies and include them in mainstream decision-making and resource-distribution processes.

C.4 *Informal integration*

■ **Involve other agencies with individual users.** This needs to take place at every level within the team in relation to individual users. All team members must be prepared to meet members of other agencies, and discuss problems of job demarcation, plans, and the sharing of tasks.

■ **Create opportunities for face-to-face contact between team members and other agencies.** Informal individual relationships between workers who know each other help to create smooth working relationships. Giving desk space to staff from other agencies and throwing parties seem to have helped.

■ **Formally identify link persons with other agencies.**

■ **Arrange meetings between entire teams.**

■ **Share resources.**

■ **Have the CSW teams represented on management commit-tees of voluntary agencies.**

■ **Work together on projects with other agencies and join in community initiatives.**

■ **Create or support local forums of agencies.**

■ **Remember to oil the wheels of relationships with other agencies** by feeding them back information on their usefulness, trying to resolve conflicts, and keeping in touch.

5 Methods and roles

This chapter looks at the implications for team members of operating within a community social work (CSW) structure. Such a radically different approach, which emphasizes early intervention, localization, and integration of resources, must mean changes in day-to-day working practices from those of traditionally orientated teams.

The changes affect social workers in CSW teams, but also precipitate changes for the other workers within the team. This is most evident where, as part of a departmental CSW initiative, a variety of non-social work roles have been grouped together in the team under CSW line management.

This chapter is divided into three sections. The first explores the skills required of workers in CSW teams and offers a model for their integration into a unified approach to all aspects of a team's work. The second looks at issues surrounding specialization and demands for special expertise within and outside CSW teams, including work with child abuse cases. The third focuses on the role flexibility required by an integrated approach.

The skills of Community Social Work

ISSUES

The CSW approach emphasizes a local basis for social services. It also challenges teams to develop a community orientation, integrate a wide range of services at local level, and broaden their range of methods. Implied in the approach is a critique of traditional methods of organization and intervention (see Chapter 1, p. 4). In the search for new methods, it has to be remembered that the old tasks and functions of social services departments do not disappear. Traditionally understood skills of social workers and other roles are therefore likely to continue to find a place within the operation of CSW teams.

Early in the history of patch team development, it became

clear that established role boundaries began to suffer erosion under the new orientation (e.g. Hadley and McGrath 1980: *passim*), and new combinations of tasks, functions, and ways of carrying them out developed as a consequence. This may amount to little more than a readjustment of existing roles and a redistribution of traditional skills. However, where CSW is adopted as a genuinely radical approach, it necessarily encourages new ways of thinking about tasks and the skills needed to perform them which cease to depend on professional exclusivity.

The unitary approach has played a part in making academically respectable the imperative to go beyond the confines of the individual and his or her family, and understand the work of the team in a wider context. It has proved a workable basis for a patch team's practice (Currie and Parrott 1981) but there is little sign of CSW teams universally embracing the unitary perspective as a means of integrating the various strands of their work.

CSW's drive away from professionalized models of service delivery and traditional ways of conceptualizing skills raises questions about the need to change the self-image of the social worker from that of 'professional therapist' to something resembling the 'social care planner' of the Barclay Report. If ready-made training from traditional sources such as CSW courses does not provide the basis for developing this new emphasis teams must do it themselves.

The skills of CSW will be considered from the following aspects:

A.1 building out from traditional skills (see also: Chapter 4, p. 115; Chapter 6, p. 228);

A.2 an informal style of operation (see also: Chapter 4, p. 115; Chapter 6, pp. 209, 228);

A.3 integrating working methods (see also: Chapter 4, p. 96; Chapter 6, p. 228);

A.4 the unitary approach;

A.5 acquiring skills and staff (see also: Chapter 4, p. 115; Chapter 6, p. 228).

B.1 *Building out from traditional skills*

The contributing teams are clear and unanimous in their recognition that the traditional skills of the social worker – including a focus on individual and family casework – are essential. They are, however, frank enough to admit to some lack of clarity in their own minds about what they mean by 'skills'. When they speak of certain skills being needed, they are often intending to convey that broad bands of activity – such as working with individuals or groups – are needed within the team, rather than that skills as we have traditionally understood them are required unaltered in CSW teams.

The Whitehawk team draw a useful distinction between 'primary skills', such as communicating with people, and the more esoteric 'professional skills', such as casework or counselling. These are often confused, because they can overlap and may lead to false suppositions, such as the suggestion that a home help who is good at communicating with adolescents is performing the same functions as a social worker who is responsible for an adolescent's supervision order.

Staff in the contributing teams have not simply abandoned their old work roles and functions. Where previously a function had to be performed, it will continue to be needed. Thus someone is still required to administer the home-help service, and someone is still needed to investigate allegations of NAI. Nevertheless, community social work is more than an exercise in restructuring or reassembling the pieces of the old jigsaw on a small geographical basis. It implies profound changes in the working lives of the individual workers concerned.

The CSW approach has lead to traditional skills being rethought or extended to meet the demands of the new context. The Longbenton team speaks of a set of 'informal' skills which exist alongside traditional ones. By this they mean that the skills which one would expect to learn on a CQSW course must be applied in such a way that the distance between the professional and the service user is minimized, that access by all on the patch is encouraged, and that flexible switching between different levels of intervention as the circumstances demand is promoted.

By way of illustration, the team cite a worker visiting a teenager recently discharged from care whose neighbours have complained of his disruptive behaviour. A new 'informal' skill in this context might be the ability, on leaving the teenager's flat, to convey for the scrutiny of any watching neighbour, that the worker is not seeking to scuttle away from a difficult situation as quickly as possible but is ready to discuss the matter if anyone wants to approach him. A further aspect of the informal skill is the capacity, in the event of an approach on such an issue, to deal openly with the neighbours or others affected while still protecting confidential aspects of the worker-client relationship.

In a group-work context, an example of relevant 'informal' skills might be the knack of handling an individual user's problems discreetly but effectively during the course of a session. In this way the group can act as a supportive contact point with social workers as well as fulfilling its formal functions.

Informal community skills are seen by the Longbenton team as requiring imagination and creativity. They include the ability to spot connections and opportunities, and to make links between organizations and individuals. A blend of optimism and enthusiasm is needed to encourage things to happen, along with an ability to be sensitive to reluctance and anxiety. The team acknowledge that operating in these ways does make additional demands on staff and requires them to develop new skills. However, they also believe that the development of these new skills pays dividends because their work then becomes less alienating than that of traditionally organized teams which use a more compartmentalized approach.

The Longbenton team also note that placing group work in a CSW context raises questions about the 'psychotherapeutic' basis of group work practice, encourages an outward-looking analysis of the reasons for running a group, and helps to locate a group in the setting of the informal networks of the members and other local resources. The model of self-directed groups put forward by Mullender and Ward (1985) is helpful here. They outline a way of thinking which they have identified in a number of contexts, amalgamating different types of group previously defined in group- and community-work literature. The special character of their approach is that of offering help to social services department clients without restricting the issues to be considered to matters of feeling and relationship. The agenda is handed over to the participants and can be expanded to include whatever items *they* choose to put on it.

The Whitehawk team give an example of a group of mentally ill people who started out by defining their own terms of reference in a rather cautious way but gradually became less and less dependent on external support.

In practising community work skills, the teams have in mind particularly the skill of 'getting to know the area', associated research skills, and knowledge of how to locate and tap resources and funding available to community groups. They also include the skills of setting up groups and helping them to run. They add a special focus (which might not be shared by community workers) to the detail of identifying and working with caring networks and micro-neighbourhoods.

There is a feeling among teams that in some cases they are not doing community work as many community workers might understand it. In taking this view they are acknowledging that their agenda for change is strongly influenced by the major preoccupations of their departments and that they see themselves at the 'community development' rather than 'community action' end of the spectrum of community work.

Group and community work is so central to CSW practice that the associated skills are treated by teams as generalized CSW skills to be expected of all within the team.

The Honor Oak and Longbenton teams, although containing only field social work roles, involve their attached administrative workers in group work and community development work. The Rye team sees it as important for residential staff in their team to understand their role as a community resource and to develop day-to-day involvement outside the walls of the establishment. Within the Docklands team, home helps have taken on a substantial degree of autonomy. This means that they are involved in taking decisions about the organization of their work which would not normally be the prerogative even of their organizer.

B.2 *An informal style of operation*

Linked to the development and extension of traditional skills is the informal style in which the CSW teams deliver the range of services. Teams pay considerable attention to this issue, and it clearly occupies as important a place as group- and community-work skills. To work in such a style is regarded by the teams as a skill in itself, required of all team members. It echoes the concept of 'resourceful friend' described by Bob Holman (1983) but adds the dimension of an acknowledged authority role. It is a testing style for workers, and the ability to adopt it may be less a skill than a matter of personality. There is considerable consistency between the teams in their perception of qualities which constitute the desired informal style. Four elements, in particular, are most frequently identified:

Being flexible: The Honor Oak team exemplifies this quality when it suggests that workers should be 'able to take on a wide range of roles . . . to let whoever is best suited to a task undertake it'.
Working as a team member: The Rye team, for instance, proposes that individuals should be 'responsible for a particular area and be adaptable to the pressures and problems presented'.
Abandoning bureaucratic practices: Examples of this view include the Lochend comment that the 'tell him/her I'm not in' response should not be admissible; the Honor Oak team comment that staff have to learn to cope with being easily available and constantly accessible to the public; and the Longbenton opinion that it is 'necessary to leave behind the role of "expert", make oneself available to people on the pitch, and create less formal ways of relating to clients, colleagues in other agencies, and non-clients alike'.
Being clear and honest: Honor Oak stress the importance of taking on a wide range of roles and being clear in thinking about the scope of each. The public then understands the many hats the worker wears and how to relate to each role. This demands a high level of honesty with the public and a very 'up-front' approach. Similarly, Longbenton argue that it is necessary to be able to explain their own and their client's actions to outsiders while still preserving confidentiality, to engage the co-operation of friends and neighbours, and to offer support.

B.3 *Integrating working methods*

As important as the various individual skills is the ability to combine them into an integrated approach. The capacity to do this is undoubtedly the most important skill for team members and managers to acquire (see Chapter 4 for a detailed account of integration).

The teams differ in the level of detail at which they analyse this issue. The Docklands team try to analyse situations and make decisions in terms of their CSW philosophy. The Normanton team speak rather more specifically of placing people in the context of their network, the community, the social services department, and the wider welfare system. The Whitehawk team describe a system of meetings to define plans of work with families, with the required skills being drawn from a variety of sources such as social workers, family aides, volunteers, neighbours, and statutory agencies. The Longbenton team illustrate the point by describing how they analyse a problem concerning rehousing, common to a number of referrals. In this way they develop strategies aimed at helping the people concerned, for example, setting up a more convenient call point by using their patch contacts. But they also consider a community work response to the underlying problem, for example, bringing together those who request rehousing to form a support group.

B.4 *The unitary approach*

The unitary approach would appear to be the most relevant theoretical model for developing CSW, stressing as it does the need to analyse all the systems which impinge on a problem (e.g. Pincus and Minahan 1973; Goldstein 1973; Specht and Vickery 1977). However, in practice, most of the teams pay the theory little attention, feeling that it does not provide immediate or concrete guidelines to assist with the detail of individual situations. The Rye team do acknowledge that it may be useful for initial assessments of cases, and the Docklands team are unique in claiming to use the approach consciously and constantly. Most of the teams would seem to concur with the view expressed by the Huntly team that all they need to know about the unitary approach is that the majority of problems presented to field social workers are not due to psychological faults in individuals, but can only be understood within the family, community, or societal context in which they live.

B.5 *Acquiring skills and staff*

Contemporary social work training may supply the necessary traditional skills, but by and large it does not, in the teams' experience, equip social workers to operate effectively within a CSW system. There are signs, however, that this may be changing, as some of the teams reported that they have begun to receive students from CQSW courses who have gained an understanding of the CSW approach, have been encouraged to see themselves as community social workers, and have been trained in some of the skills required. Nevertheless, for the present CSW teams must be prepared to undertake much of their own training in CSW methods particularly where their method of working is not officially endorsed by the department. The contributing teams have used a number of methods:

(a) support from fellow team members, either through informal advice and interaction or via structured settings such as team meetings;
(b) individual supervision sessions;
(c) experimentation and invention;
(d) team training events.

The Docklands team feel that training should be locally based, interdisciplinary, and a regular part of the working routine. Broader-based national or regional sessions should be seen as a necessary and useful occasional supplement, with a regional forum as an opportunity for teams operating on a similar basis to come together every three months or so. The services of an external consultant would assist teams to identify issues for training and discussion and could also help them to discover sources of local expertise.

The Longbenton team have had fruitful experience from training outside social work, in management studies, which has provided valuable input on techniques of problem solving, creative thinking, and team work.

As for recruitment, the Normanton and Longbenton team advise a policy of selecting staff who appear to be predisposed towards the required way of working. The Huntly team suggest that this process can be aided by choosing candidates who have had previous experience of CSW as workers or students, and getting them to talk through a project. Involvement of the whole team in selection is an important way of helping to ensure that the new worker can readily fit in as a team member.

PRACTICE GUIDELINES

C.1 *Move on from traditional skills*

Workers bring with them the skills which they have developed in their former roles. These should not be thrown away as strengths must be sensibly utilized. Opportunities for extending traditional roles should be sought, and preciousness about role boundaries should be avoided.

■ **Use traditional skills.** The functions which needed to be performed in traditionally organized teams do not appear under a CSW organization. Team members will have developed a range of skills clustering around their previous functions, and the division of labour in a new CSW team should be determined accordingly. Legal and departmental requirements also have to be taken into account in deciding which team members can undertake certain functions.

■ **Include a broad range of traditional roles within a CSW team.** This has the effect of bringing together a number of different skills and styles and increases the opportunity for sharing and learning.

■ **Distinguish between task and skill.** It is important to recognize the difference between carrying out a function (such as working with an individual) and the skills required to perform the function successfully (such as counselling skills). There is no need to assume that social workers are the only team members who have the skills to help individuals simply because they have traditionally carried out this task. Social workers will possess skills in that area, but there will be occasions when these skills do not have much impact, or when social workers cannot gain an individual's trust because of their authority role or the kind of person a particular social worker happens to be.

The same applies to community workers and home-help organizers. They have had certain tasks to carry out, but this does not mean that other team members cannot learn or share their skills, or that they cannot learn new skills which will better enable them to carry out the CSW team's task of delivering a range of services to a small geographical area.

■ **Distinguish between professional and non-professional approaches.** A helpful way of achieving this is put forward by Professor Jerôme Guay (Guay 1984: Chapter 2; Guay and Lapointe 1985: 73–5), who suggests that professionals are differentiated by their ability to observe themselves rather than simply to react, and by their emphasis on strategy and deliberate planning. The proper role of the professional, he argues, is to plan the strategy of intervention. Within that plan, particular tasks can be shared with any non-professional who is known to have the necessary capacities and acceptability to users. He also emphasizes that in many circumstances professionals are ill-suited by their status as officials and outsiders to provide direct help themselves and in such cases non-professional help is better.

A social worker responsible for exercising a supervision order, for example, should therefore consider his/her primary responsibility to be planning the strategy of intervention with the family, defining the specific tasks to be undertaken in pursuit of the strategy, identifying the people who will undertake the tasks, and ensuring that the activity of all the individuals involved is properly co-ordinated. The receptionist may perhaps take on an advice- and information-giving role, whilst a home help, a volunteer, and another social worker might include the young person in the youth group they are running. The supervising social worker would take on the role of counselling the parents about strategies for control of the young person.

■ **Look for new combinations of task and skill.** It follows from the preceding guideline that although traditional roles may provide a basis for dividing up work within a CSW team, the boundaries of these roles should always be questioned. For example, consider what happens at reception. Should callers be received by 'a receptionist' or could this be a task for social workers? Could it continue to be carried out by a receptionist, but can his or her function be expanded to include active help at the point of reception? What should be the limits of this help? What are the new skills that receptionists will need to learn to enable them to undertake this new task effectively and with confidence?

Again, it can be asked whether home helps *need* to be programmed by the hour. If not, how will their work be organized? Will they do it themselves, and if so what additional skills will they need? Do they possess them already, but just not use them? What is an appropriate set of tasks for a home-help manager?

■ **Use an analytical approach to find new combinations of task and skill.** A helpful way of visualizing this approach is to consider it in the form of a figure developed by Seyd *et al.* (1984: 92–3) from the work of Whittaker (1983), and presented here with some further adaptation. *Figure 9* is in the form of a matrix constructed upon the level of intervention and the kind of task being undertaken.

The vertical axis indicates the level at which the worker is intervening. The first three levels 'person', 'family', and 'group', are self-explanatory. They are the levels of intervention with which traditional social work is familiar. The remaining levels may be less familiar and call for some explanation. 'Network' is used in the sense defined by Warren (see Chapter 3, p. 53). It is a level of intervention which is essential to the practice of CSW. 'Agency' can mean the social services department itself or another statutory or voluntary agency. CSW implies that the attention of the team should be focused on the analysis of common elements of individual problems. This should lead them to consider actively ways in which they can work more effectively with and through other agencies. 'Patch' indicates the area covered by the team, viewed as a collection of people living within a geographical entity.

The horizontal axis indicates the type of task being undertaken: *Agent of authority* indicates an aspect of social services department work which it is important to acknowledge explicitly – investigating, monitoring, supervising, checking. *Agent of change* indicates an attempt to alter behaviour. Techniques used could range from family therapy, counselling, and task-centred casework, to persuasion, report writing, and political lobbying. The others are *information giver*, giver of information to users and others; *broker*, mobilizer of resources; *advocate*, one who acts on behalf of users; *network system consultant*, assisting through pre-existing support systems; *entrepreneur*, creator of resources.

Each box represents a role which the matrix defines as a given task undertaken at a particular level of intervention. For example, the top left-hand box represents the role of the agent of authority in respect to a person (for instance, a worker who checks on an at-risk child). The figure serves two purposes:

Figure 9 *Role matrix in client centred and community social work*

level of intervention \ task	agent of authority	agent of change	information giver	broker	advocate	network system consultant	entrepreneur
person	X		X	X		X	
family		?					
group		?					?
network							
agency		?					?
patch							?

Adapted from: Seyd *et al.* (1984: 93) (See discussion on pp. 147–50.)

(a) It illustrates how CSW builds on to the traditional roles of social work, including familiar functions rather than replacing them. The traditional roles appear as unshaded boxes at the top left of the matrix, and roles which are new or receive special emphasis in CSW are shaded.

(b) It assists in reconceptualizing roles and leaving behind traditional preconceptions about how tasks cluster into occupational roles.

● **Use the diagram to define the work to be done and the roles of the team.**

The first step in using the figure is to define the work to be done in terms of the matrix roles. This should quickly lead CSW teams away from the concept of 'the case' because work connected with any single 'case' will appear in many of the boxes, indicating a number of roles that need to be undertaken. Looking along the axes may also suggest either ways of achieving aims in 'the case' based on the community-orientated tasks and levels of intervention, or ways of considering common problems illustrated by 'the case' which would need community-orientated intervention. The second step is to decide which team member can best fulfil the identified roles.

An example from Honor Oak may help to show how the diagram can be used.

Elsie is an 83-year-old living alone who normally keeps herself looking very smart. The CSW team first got to know her when they helped in rehousing her on the estate, following eviction from her previous home. One day a social worker noticed her walking aimlessly about the estate, looking very grubby and thin in contrast to her normal appearance. The social worker contacted Charlie, the local volunteer who runs the lunch club, to share her concern about Elsie and found that he too was worried about her. The social worker agreed that she should visit, but before she did so, Elsie wandered into the lunch club and asked if she could eat there. Charlie immediately booked her in. The next day Elsie failed to turn up at the lunch club. The social worker called at the flats where she lived but could get no reply from her over the intercom controlling entry to the block. A neighbour let her in and they found Elsie in her flat. It transpired that Elsie did not understand how the new intercom entry system worked so this had to be explained to her. It was clear that she had forgotten about the lunch club and seemed to be suffering from some short-term memory loss. The social worker negotiated a system for the neighbour and others to bring Elsie to the lunch club every day. Charlie agreed to keep an eye on Elsie's attendance and report back to the social worker if necessary. A home help was assigned to assist with washing and shopping.

In this situation, the social worker has played the roles of 'agent of authority', by intervening where risk was perceived, and of 'broker', by organizing the lunch club resource. She has also been an 'information giver' over the new entry phone, and a 'network system consultant' by organizing the support of neighbour and friends and the monitoring by the lunch club (all marked by × on *Figure 9*).

The team can use the figure to extend the limits within which the situation is being considered by looking at each level of intervention in turn and thinking about the tasks along the horizontal axis. For instance, should Elsie be advised to visit her doctor concerning her short-term memory loss? And what of Elsie's family? Could they take a more active part in her support? Who would act as the 'agent of change' with them? Are there any groups in existence or which could be brought into being which would assist Elsie or others in similar circumstances? Is there a team member or a local resident who is interested, for example, in starting a coffee morning in the neighbourhood flat? Looking at the patch as a whole, is the one existing lunch club adequate, or does it only effectively reach one small micro-neighbourhood? Who will begin to persuade the social services department to make available resources for more? (All marked with ? in *Figure 9*.)

In theory, each box should be considered in every situation. Readers may like to try expanding this initial scenario until they have filled all the boxes in the matrix and assigned the roles to various personnel. Be imaginative. See how much work you can think up for a team leader, and have fun creating outrageous tasks for a home-help organizer. Having done that, try it with a real situation confronting your team now.

■ **Recognize the value of non-social work skills.** Bearing in mind the need to distinguish between roles and skills, and acknowledging the possibility of overlap between different roles implied in *Figure 9*, it is essential to consider the potential contribution of non-social work skills to the various tasks traditionally undertaken by social workers.

It may, for instance, be possible for home helps, without needing to behave like social workers, to intervene as change agents with individual clients. They may well have developed a good rapport with the people concerned through their practical work as home helps and be able to use social skills developed in their own life experience to provide advice and support.

■ **Encourage group and community work skills.** The more team members who can take a part in promoting community work or can participate in groups, the wider these tasks will be shared. This is particularly vital in the case of social workers, since they handle the department's major responsibilities *vis-à-vis* individuals. An alteration in the methods which they use is likely to have a large impact on stressful areas of work.

■ **Encourage all team members to see their own work in context.** All team members need to see their role in relation to the overall task of providing a set of services to the patch. A consequence of this should be that role boundaries begin to be constructively questioned and team members look for different ways of carrying out their tasks which allow their better integration with those of other team members.

C.2 *Develop an informal style*

To enable a CSW team to be genuinely accessible to the public, all team members must divest themselves of those elements of a 'professional' or 'bureaucratic' style which tend to distance local-authority officials from the people they serve. Teams speak of the desired informal style from a number of different angles, but all regard it as a general skill required of all team members.

The ability to develop certain aspects of informal practice appears to be especially important:

■ **Be flexible.** Team members should be able to operate confidently in a variety of settings and be capable of a variety of responses. Thus social workers should not refuse to cook a meal if they are available when such help is needed. They should happily stop to receive referrals in the street but they should be able to defer confidential matters to a confidential setting, without alienating the referrer. Social workers with large numbers of similar cases should be capable of undertaking group work, without having to rely on a groupwork specialist.

Team members should not feel threatened when another team member takes on an aspect of their role or when they themselves have the opportunity to extend their new role boundaries.

■ **Be capable of responding in more than one way at the same time.** In the parent and toddler group, for example, switch as required between groupworker and caseworker roles when a parent approaches you about an individual problem. Is the problem a group one? Be prepared to tolerate talking about your casework in the group if a parent raises the issue.

■ **Don't be bureaucratic.** Don't insist on roles. Don't retreat behind barriers (reception window, slow procedures, 'tell them I'm not in'). Don't stand on your dignity. Do attempt to find solutions and then find ways in which the solutions can be accommodated by the rules later. (But be aware of situations where strict observation of rules must take precedence.)

■ **Be clear and honest.** With team members visible on the patch in a variety of roles and settings, it is vital to be clear about the role a team member is playing at a given moment, particularly where this is an authority role. The abandonment of bureaucratic defences will increase the number of occasions when such issues have to be confronted face to face, and will broaden the range of settings in which they occur.

■ **Work as a member of a team.** This is aimed particularly at social workers who may have been encouraged by their training to view their mode of operation as that of the independent professional. The CSW approach needs workers who can see their responsibilities as extending beyond the confines of their personal caseload – who can in fact abandon the caseload altogether as a means of defining activity. Anne Vickery (1983) lists some attributes required of willing members of a co-operative team: enjoyment in working with others; ability to tolerate and work with conflict; willingness to share; valuing joint decision making above autonomy; willingness to be accountable to peers as well as manager; ability to value and be explicit about other people's skills; ability to consider your own role flexibly in given situations.

C.3 *Combining methods in an integrated approach: a model for action*

A full implementation of the CSW approach cannot be achieved simply by 'adding on' group work and community work as optional extras to casework. These must be seen as alternatives to the traditional ways of tackling the major responsibilities of social services departments. They should not be compartment- alized as methods but should interact with one another, each set of activities drawing on and contributing to the others.

A model is presented here (*Figure 10a*), together with a case study from the Longbenton team to illustrate it, which attempts to suggest how a creative relationship can be established between casework responsibilities and alternative methods. The model is complex and consequently it is presented in three stages, each summarized in a figure, beginning with work with individuals and families which is likely to be the starting-point for all social work teams.

The boxes in *Figure 10a* represent the various kinds of activity in which the CSW team should engage. The lines between the boxes represent the processes linking the activities. The direc- tion of flow is indicated by an arrowhead. A two-way flow is shown by a diamond shape. The arrowheads and diamonds are labelled with a letter which refers to the commentary on each figure.

Figure 10a *Developing alternative methods, stage 1: starting with families and individuals*

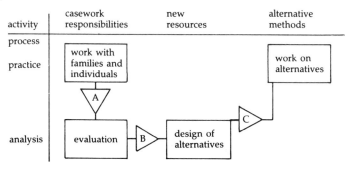

The boxes are arranged in horizontal rows according to whether the activities are to do with practice, analysis or the community. They are also arranged in vertical columns according to whether the activity relates mainly to casework responsibilities, new resources, or alternative methods.

Commentary

We start in the top left-hand corner with *work with individuals and families*. All teams are likely to undertake this work but CSW teams must move from simply doing it to analysing systematically what it is that they are doing.

Example
Fiona Cameron is 27 years old and the mother of four children. Her marriage broke up and she went with the children to live with her parents. In the space of a couple of months, she discovered that she had a severe blood disorder, her mother died, and support from the rest of her family evaporated. She neglected her condition and was admitted to hospital for emergency treatment. The children were received into care and placed with foster parents. Fiona recovered, her children were discharged from care, but then the pattern repeated itself. Fiona became depressed and her children were received into care again.

Evaluation (A). This process needs to be carried out in a way which goes beyond a case-by-case review to embrace an analysis of the team's caseload as a whole, looking for common patterns in the problems concerned, noting links in relationships and evidence of resources.

Example
(a) On an individual basis, the social worker seeks to relate Fiona's circumstances to *Social Origins of Depression* (Brown and Harris 1978). This study identified four underlying factors, at least one of which must be present for depression to occur (lack of intimate relationships, no employment outside the home, three children under 14 at home, loss of mother before the age of 11). These are termed vulnerability factors (VFs). In addition, there must be present a precipitating factor, which, when added to the underlying VFs, causes depression to occur (severe life events, such as death or a loss,

or severe difficulties such as housing or financial problems).
These are called provoking agents (PAs). Fiona has recently
undergone a series of severe life events which are believed to
be acting as PAs. In addition, she possesses three out of the
four VFs. The children had to be received into care and placed
in a distant part of the borough for lack of a local alternative.
(b) On a caseload basis, the social worker considers whether
other depressed women's situations are illuminated by the
model and whether other receptions into care have been of a
similar nature.
(c) On a team basis (through team meetings and informal
interaction), knowledge about individuals and families is
shared and knowledge of the area is integrated into the
decision (impressionistic knowledge, a student's project on
psychiatric hospital admissions from the patch, discussions
with GPs at liaison meetings). The team also looks at the
number of receptions into care which have been needed to
cope with sudden crises. There are *no* local foster parents.

The team concludes that work with the family is ineffective in
dealing with the most common underlying VFs (lack of intimate
relationships and lack of employment outside the home). The
team is not at present aware of any relevant existing community
groups but there would appear to be a considerable number of
women suffering from some degree of depression. The team
does not undertake many compulsory admissions to care and is
proud of the way it uses alternative supportive resources to
prevent them. Nevertheless, a significant proportion of admissions are unconnected with the neglect or abuse of the child
concerned and a local resource would reduce the disturbance
and disruption for the family and possibly allow more flexible
arrangements to be achieved.

Design of alternatives (B). Evaluation is likely to reveal common
needs and problems and the team should search for ways of
tackling them collectively. To do this it will need to engage in
the design of alternatives through group, network, or neighbourhood levels of intervention (see *Figure 9*). The term 'alternative' is used in this sense in *Figures 10 a–d* to represent the
whole range of possible CSW strategies.

Example.
The team reviews two strategies for dealing with the VFs identified:
(a) building up knowledge of and close links with a variety of community groups so that women could have a choice of possible activities, and offering a personal introduction from the team to help overcome initial nervousness. The team feels that this will be a very long-term strategy because it has not previously assembled systematic knowledge of different groups and does not have contacts with them.
(b) starting a women's group, initially with team members taking a lead but hoping to establish it on a self-run basis. This strategy is preferred because it can be adopted immediately.

Work on alternatives (C). The team will then need to determine what resources will be required if the alternatives chosen are to succeed. It may be wise at first to choose alternatives which are not too greedy of resources, or which use resources which are readily available. Having determined on an alternative which looks viable the team should then proceed to put it into effect.

Example
Fiona's social worker and another social worker involved with several similar situations are chosen to work with the group. They negotiate with the occupational therapist and community development officer from outside the team to join the project. The community development officer obtains a room free of charge in the local high school with access to a number of leisure and craft facilities, thanks to her previous involvement with a number of other projects there. All four work on the overall plan for the group and the programme for the first few sessions. Another member of the team offers to do some duty in order to allow Fiona's social worker to attend a crucial final planning meeting. The team leader negotiates for the two social workers not to be rotated for duty on the day of the week when the group meets.
 The team leader and Fiona's social worker engage the family placement team worker for their area in designing a local fostering campaign, based on the distribution of leaflets and posters at identified key locations.

Figure 10b *Developing alternative methods, stage 2: integration of casework and alternatives*

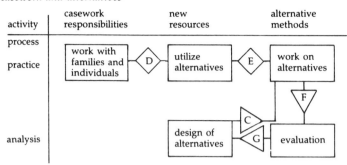

Utilization of alternatives (D). The focus now returns to work with individuals and families. All team members will need to make sure that they refer users to the alternatives wherever relevant, and that they make use of the new resources as a part of their case plans. There will inevitably be a time-lag between the evaluation which identified the need and the provision of an alternative as a resource for the team. As a result, the original individuals or families may no longer be in a position to take advantage of the resource but other individuals and families will be. CSW teams need to be able to plan ahead in this way and think in time-scales which are much longer than those usually required in casework if such resources are to be available when they are needed.

Once an alternative has been established as a resource, it should both become a more effective means of achieving goals and release the time and energy of team members for the development of further alternatives.

Example
The team had been trawled for referrals when the group was first mooted but by the time it actually starts, the number of women referred is disappointingly small. The team has to be reminded about the group and subsequently numbers begin to pick up. Fiona herself does not attend the group after the first session, which she found very demanding, but later her depression lifts, mainly because her new boyfriend moves in with her.

Flexibility of roles in work on alternatives (E). By making sure that the alternatives are used in work with individuals and families on caseloads, the same social worker can be both case-worker and alternative worker. This is time saving and helps to broaden the perspective of the workers by giving them direct experience of new methods of working. Further, other team members, who are not qualified social workers but who may be involved in the alternative methods employed, may often under-take what amounts to casework with the users concerned and in this way save the time of the social worker. Social workers in CSW teams have to learn not to be precious about such sharing of roles and to communicate knowledge and perspectives freely within the team so that this kind of work is appropriately done.

Example
Fiona's social worker is working with the mother of another family who attends the group. This woman establishes a rapport with the occupational therapist, who takes on the role of counselling and supporting her. This saves the social worker a considerable amount of time, as she does not now need to make so many home visits and can concentrate on strategies concerning the children. The occupational therapist also feeds in advice on this subject, reinforcing the social worker's efforts and making them more successful. After some weeks, the social worker feels that the occupational therapist's work is so effective that she can withdraw from active involvement while continuing to monitor the family's situation through the group and the children's school.

Analysis and evaluation (F). Teams should analyse the results of their alternative methods with the same rigour as they use in the initial analysis of their work with individuals and families.

Example
In the early life of the group, few people attend, and most newcomers do not stay. The group workers have to look again at the programmes for the sessions, and the conditions governing membership of the group. Initially the meetings were based on a problem-solving approach, and access to the group was restricted to those who had been referred by other professionals and were felt by the group leaders to be suitable. A number of requests to bring friends had been turned down.

The campaign to attract local interest in fostering through

leaflets and posters has failed to elicit a single response. It is felt that the approach has been too impersonal, and that the team would need to find ways of getting closer to possible sources of recruits.

Feedback to design of alternatives (G). The product of the evaluation should be fed back into the design of new alternatives.

Example
In consultation with the group the workers decide to arrange programmes on health issues which have been requested by the members and to accept informal access to the group through the members' own networks.

The team opt for an intensive attempt to develop contacts with local neighbourhood networks through involvement with the working men's club, but the project is placed on ice as the team has to carry a social worker vacancy for a few months until a trainee returns qualified.

Increasing knowledge of the community (H). Work with individuals and families and with alternatives will increase team members' knowledge of informal networks, and of needs and resources in the areas served.

Example
During Fiona's initial crisis, her social worker had called round to her flat one day to find that she was out but a neighbouring family, supposedly looking after the place for her, was busily engaged in stealing everything movable. The social worker persuaded them to put back the stolen goods and through subsequent contacts with the family and from other enquiries established that it formed the node of a network of people living in the neighbourhood who were engaged in petty thieving, drug dealing, and other nefarious activities. Discreet contacts with the police revealed that they already knew something of the network's activities but had not felt it their business to inform the team. Nevertheless, knowledge of such 'negative' networks is as important to CSW teams as information about positive resources if they are to build up an accurate view of the environment in which they are operating and provide relevant help and advice to users who may be part of such networks or come into contact with them.

The team hope, but have not yet demonstrated, that if they can establish good contacts with the working men's club, they will get access to new networks which may help to strengthen their resources.

Figure 10c *Developing alternative methods, stage 3: integration of local knowledge*

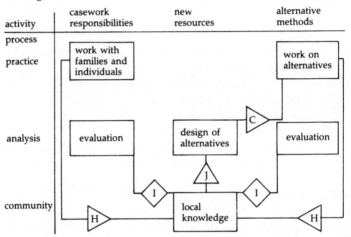

Knowledge and evaluation (I). Knowledge of the community can be used to inform the evaluation of work with individuals and families and of work on alternatives. This evaluation in turn can increase the general knowledge of the team about the community.

Example
The knowledge gained by the social worker about Fiona's neighbours begins to explain a number of events among young people known to the team, and to indicate that an initiative on drug abuse is required. From the team's contacts with other voluntary agencies and with informal networks, the group workers have observed that the women's group members have developed some close and supportive relationships among themselves and are appearing less depressed. However, there is still a measure of dissatisfaction among other agencies with what they consider to be the inadequate record of the team in helping harassed neighbours of mentally ill people. The team attempt to analyse the criticisms.

Knowledge and alternative design (J). Knowledge of the community is also fed into the design of alternatives.

Example
The team integrated their knowledge from a variety of sources about depressed women to determine that the women's group should be a priority (see p. 156). Their lack of knowledge about the networks in which they were trying to find foster parents contributed to the initial failure of the recruitment campaign. On the other hand, the practical knowledge gained by the community development officer about facilities at the local high school enabled the women's group to be established in a suitable venue with a number of resources available free on site.

A view of the complete model (*Figure 10d*) shows the many interactions between the different activities, and the process links between practice, analysis, and community orientation, as well as the way in which alternative methods and new resources feed back into work with individuals and families.

Figure 10d *Developing alternative methods, stage 4: the integrated model*

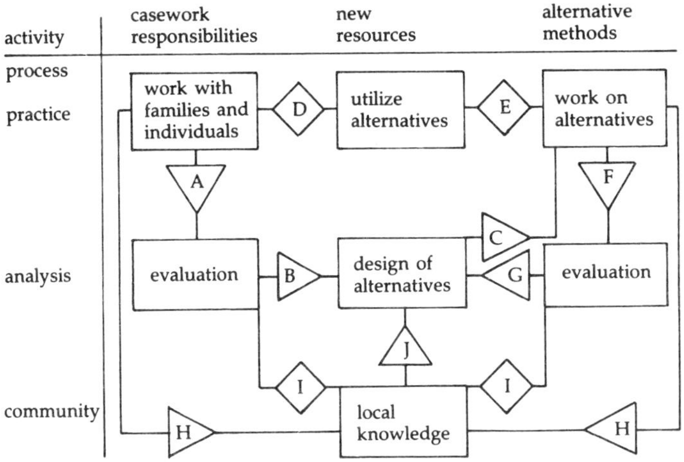

C.4 *Consider using the unitary approach*

Teams who find themselves having difficulty in making headway with the CSW approach may find it helpful to consider the various systems in a more rigorous way, using the unitary approach as described in the literature (see p. 143 above).

C.5 *Acquiring skills and staff*

A plea emerges from the teams described here for CQSW courses not only to train students thoroughly in group and community work, but also to provide them with a conceptual framework and self-image conducive to working in a CSW system. In the absence of suitable official training, CSW teams have no option but to organize their own.

■ **Adapt training to specific local conditions.** Nearly all teams are made up of different sets of roles, have available different departmental resources, face different departmental constraints, and work in widely different areas. Training will need to reflect these different contexts and should be used to analyse and try to solve problems which face a team.

■ **Engage in team building.** One of the major problems facing CSW teams is the need to mould a number of different sorts of worker, often with different experience and expectations, into an integrated unit. This problem can only be dealt with effectively by the team as a whole.

■ **Use consultants.** Consultants have proved invaluable as objective observers of progress or lack of it, and as advisers on team development. They can be used for special team-building efforts or on a regular basis in the process of ongoing evaluation. Suitable consultancy may take some finding, but it may be possible to locate someone with relevant knowledge and skills from other CSW teams, from sympathetic social work or community work courses, or from community-based projects.

■ **Use material from management studies.** There are some useful ideas on creative thinking – a must for those alternative design feedback loops – problem solving, and team building. (See suggestions for introductory reading, p. 204.)

■ **Organize regional training.** This helps teams to feel that they are not alone, encourages them to see problems in perspective, and allows some cross-fertilization of ideas and approaches.

An example of a regional scheme established to encourage the development of CSW is the NISW's Practice and Development Exchange (PADE). Regional networks have been set up through PADE in London, the Midlands, Yorkshire, North-east England, and Scotland. (Contact through NISW, Tavistock Place, London.)

■ **Develop training on the job** through informal interaction between team members and by means of team meetings and group supervision.

■ **Encourage those supervising other staff to articulate the model in individual supervision sessions and also when discussing day-to-day decisions.**

■ **Involve the team in selecting new staff.** Discuss vacancies as they arise with team members and review job specifications with them. Those who will be most directly concerned in working with the new member should take part in short-listing applicants and, where possible, in the interview process.

■ **Wherever possible choose new staff predisposed to a CSW approach and with some practical experience of its development.** In interviewing applicants with experience of CSW get them to talk through a project with which they have been involved.

Specialization

ISSUES

The CSW approach envisages local teams equipped to provide a wide range of services to a small geographical area. The team members are required to possess a matching range of knowledge and skills.

Nevertheless, it is hardly feasible for community social workers to carry in their heads *all* the detailed knowledge they might need in the different fields of activity covered by the personal social services, or to be effective in working in depth with every sort of problem that might be encountered. The case for retaining an element of specialization in departments which have adopted CSW in all their front-line teams is a strong one.

The most appropriate way of integrating specialization with CSW, the experience of the contributing teams would suggest, is to develop a system analogous to the medical model where primary care is provided by general practitioners and community nurses, and the role of specialists is to take referrals from these workers when required.

Specialist back-up to a generalist primary contact may be achieved by the inclusion of specialist workers in CSW teams, or by the formation of separate teams of specialist workers. In a situation of scarce resources it is not uncommon for departments to choose to organize generically at the expense of much specialist support; CSW teams are then left with the task of organizing their own expert support.

A.1 *Specialization within the team*

Specialization is most often considered in terms of client groups. Within field social work teams, this is normally bound up with the concept of organizing work according to cases and caseloads. In this approach team members often operate in isolation from one another. Specialization thus conceived would seem to cut across the CSW approach with its emphasis on teamwork and on viewing the services provided by the team as an integrated whole. The question which is therefore posed is whether a CSW team should tolerate specialism within its ranks at all. The answer from the contributing teams would appear to be 'yes' as long as methods can be found to share specialization knowledge and skills, and integrate them effectively within a CSW perspective. (See also: Chapter 4, p. 115; Chapter 6, p. 209.)

A.2 *Relating to external specialists*

Specialist teams exist even in many decentralized departments to serve groupings of users who are thinly scattered. Others are created because it is easier to obtain resources for a special, clearly identified focus (such as the discharge to the community of long-stay hospital patients, foster-parent recruitment, guardian *ad litem* work) than merely for strengthening existing fieldwork teams.

For whatever reason, specialist teams seem likely to continue to exist alongside CSW teams, and it is therefore necessary to consider the factors which influence the relationships between the two, and the steps which CSW teams and their departments can take to ensure efficient joint working. (See also: Chapter 4, p. 115; Chapter 6, p. 209.)

A.3 *The impact of new legislation*

The recent legislation requiring experienced and specialist workers to perform certain functions in the fields of child care and mental health reflects both a dissatisfaction with some social work practice and an attempt to ensure high standards of practice within the caseload model. This may well presage similar demands for other, as yet unfavoured client groups. On the face of it, this would seem to reinforce the caseload-orientated approach, to challenge the generic approach of CSW, and to exert pressure on departments to organize their teams along specialist lines. For these reasons, it is important to examine what effects such demands are having on CSW teams.

A.4 *Working with child abuse*

The previous section of this chapter has argued that CSW is not simply an optional addition to a team's responsibilities, but makes a directly related contribution to work with families and individuals in need or at risk. By this token, CSW must be as relevant to NAI as to any other area of work, yet it often seems difficult for people to make such a connection. Part of the reason for this may be that CSW is regarded mainly as a preventive philosophy, whereas NAI work is seen as reactive.

In BASW's recent publication *The Management of Child Abuse*, the Project Group acknowledges the influence of social, structural, and political factors but clearly states that the reality for social workers is that for individual cases there is no alternative but to react to the immediate implications of risk (BASW 1985: 4–5). Moreover, the caseload model of the individual worker personally responsible for the child and family is nowhere more heavily emphasized by departments, public opinion, and the media. Each successive public inquiry into child abuse tragedies has called for greater expertise, experience, and training for social workers handling such cases. Thus pressure is great for NAI to be another area of specialization.

The impact of CSW on working with NAI will depend partly

on whether the root causal factors suggested by BASW are at all accessible to its preventive strategies, and partly on whether its techniques offer more effective ways of intervening reactively after abuse has been identified or alleged (see also Chapter 4, p. 97).

TEAM EXPERIENCE

B.1 *Specialization within the team*

The teams speak of specialism in three senses: client-group specialism; work-role specialism; and community-orientated specialism.

Client-group specialism
None of the teams has members who are formally identified as client-group specialists. However, only the Normanton team stated categorically that *no* specialism occurs, and this can perhaps be accounted for by the use of small patch teams each possessing only one qualified social worker.

All the other teams have members taking a noticeable preponderance of certain types of cases. This is accounted for in Huntly, Docklands, and Longbenton in terms of allowing members' personal preferences some rein. The process would seem to be the almost accidental outcome of case allocation in Huntly and Lochend, whilst in Docklands, Rye, and Longbenton it is more deliberately planned. The Longbenton team feel that this reduces stress by allowing members to work in those fields in which they feel most at home, and the Docklands team believe that it is essential to take into account individual's different skills and experience.

The Longbenton team distinguish between specializing in cases and developing special interests. The latter is viewed as assembling expertise and detailed knowledge in a given field which is then expected to be applied in an integrated way in casework, group work and community work.

Work-role specialism
Teams combining different categories of staff roles acknowledge that their members continue to specialize in terms of their role. Some problems in this area are dealt with in the third section of this chapter on Role flexibility. Huntly views community social

work itself as a possible specialism. Honor Oak, Docklands and Longbenton stress the need for all team members to practise all three traditional methods: case/family work, group work, and community work.

'It is not desirable to have people specializing in community work and casework, because the very essence of the CSW system is to get all those engaged in actually providing the department's services to be involved in relating to the community. It is this community focus which helps break down professional and bureaucratic barriers and allows a creative variety of links to develop.'

Community-orientated specialism
The Honor Oak team are unique in reporting specialisms arising according to the networks with which a given team member happens to be familiar. However, Longbenton, Docklands, and Honor Oak all acknowledge that the specialisms which their members do develop must reflect demand for such expertise from the patch. Another kind of community specialism is represented in the Lochend team, one member of which specializes in a particular school, and undertakes all work connected with it (casework, liaison, and community development).

B.2 *Relating to external specialists*

Their location
With no internal specialists, all terms are put in the position of having to relate to specialist workers managed outside their own team. The organizational distance varies from team to team. The Lochend team, being a sub-team, have access to several specialist colleagues in the main team, to whom they feel quite close.

At the other end of the spectrum, the Docklands team inhabit a wider organizational world in which centralized specialist teams cover the whole borough. This is also the case with Normanton. The Huntly and Longbenton teams are in authorities where specialist staff of any kind are few and far between.

Relationships
A number of teams stress the need for identifying useful specialists and forging good working relationships. The

Lochend team, despite enjoying good relationships with many specialist colleagues in the wider team, notice that the use made of them varies with their responsibility and informal familiarity. The Rye team work with some specialists who have a brief to cover the patch and are often in the office. These relationships are not problematic. Where specialists do not keep in frequent touch with the office, however, the team feel the specialists' clients become alienated from the CSW process. At Honor Oak no problem has been found in using specialists as advisers and co-workers.

The Docklands team find relationships easiest where specialists see themselves as advisers to the patch workers, but conflict has occurred where specialist teams control resources needed by community social workers for local people. Here, the CSW team give primacy to the flexible use of resources to meet identified local need and come up against the wish of the centralized specialists to apply standardized central policies. The Docklands team feel that their mode of operation is alien to the specialists, and because of communication problems created by the different management structures involved it is difficult for the specialist to come to understand what the CSW team is trying to achieve.

The Normanton team are concerned to retain responsibility for all service provision, in the sense of being answerable for its quality, including that of the specialist workers, and therefore see themselves rather as agents for the community, engaging the services of specialists on its behalf.

The Longbenton team have worked closely with the IT unit in its patch (but managed by, and serving the area as a whole). The unit owes its existence in part to the resource-building efforts of the team in identifying and helping to negotiate a suitable location, and two workers from the team were seconded to work part time in the unit for its first year of operation. The close link has continued, with team members running evening groups and the unit responding to demand from the area by making alterations to its programme to meet the needs of young people actually being referred.

Their value

All of the teams affirm the value of specialist workers. Honor Oak, Rye, Docklands, and Normanton express the view that the existence of, and co-operation with the CSW team is necessary for specialist workers to function to their highest potential. The Rye team note that some clients of specialists become labelled by their problem, rather than being seen as whole people who have a particular problem. In this way an individual may be seen as 'blind' but other difficulties – or strengths and potentials – he or she may have may be overlooked. The Docklands team propose that specialists should all be decentralized into CSW teams, being line managed by the CSW team leader whilst having access to a centrally based adviser for reference and co-ordination. The Longbenton team are most explicit in their view of the positive value of specialist expertise:

> 'Departments are often so short of resources or imagination that they feel they have to choose between CSW and specialism as if they were exclusive alternatives. Specialist knowledge, expertise, and ideas are vital, and it is important that these should be available to CSW teams. When team members have been on training courses in specialist subjects, the beneficial effects on the team's work have always been noticeable. The strength of the CSW system is its ability to exploit this knowledge and expertise in combination with knowledge of the community.'

B.3 *New legislation*

Particularly in the larger teams, mental health legislation has not caused too many problems. Demand for compulsory admissions is fairly low and, in any case, response to it is seen as part of the range of duties to be carried out within the patch and therefore something that the teams are willing to take on. It fits with the models for specializing within CSW teams outlined above.

The need to handle the extra work created by the guardian *ad litem* legislation is mentioned only by the Rye team for whom it has been a major problem, slowing development as a CSW team.

The Longbenton team have managed until recently, along with the rest of the area, to avoid having any social workers nominated to the guardian *ad litem* panel, but this fortunate state of affairs is about to cease. The Docklands team are not troubled about new legislation for which there is a low demand from the patch. One team member is an approved social worker (ASW).

The Huntly team have to call in an ASW from Inverurie. In the

Honor Oak and Longbenton teams most workers are ASWs. The Honor Oak team stress that it is preferable for statutory mental health duties to be undertaken by a patch worker familiar with local conditions and personalities, but they are not so happy to be called off the patch to perform statutory functions.

The Normanton team take pains to enable non-qualified workers familiar with the clients concerned to participate and play a leading role in compulsory admissions, but fulfil the law's requirements by having appropriate qualified workers oversee the admission and sign the forms.

B.4 *Working with child abuse*

From the information provided in Chapter 2, it can be seen that the patches covered by the majority of the contributing teams are areas of significant deprivation, of the kind likely, according to BASW, to produce a high incidence of child abuse. All the teams report that they feel pressurized by the demands of 'statutory work', among which child abuse plays a large part. It is clear from the team's responses that they do respond within the traditional casework model so far as investigation, immediate action, and subsequent monitoring and intervention are concerned. The need for a qualified worker to take case responsibility is found by some teams to be at odds with their policy of encouraging non-qualified staff to maintain a high level of involvement and responsibility, but the majority of teams see little difficulty in arranging for the case to be co-worked in such situations. The problem identified by nearly all teams is that the unavoidable demands of child abuse casework tend to block, or significantly circumscribe, the ability of the teams to step away conceptually or practically from casework. As a result the teams can offer relatively few examples which show the CSW approach directly affecting child abuse work.

At the preventive level, the Honor Oak and Lochend teams give examples of supporting parent and toddler groups, and it would be possible to list a large number of child- and family-orientated initiatives mentioned elsewhere in this book. All would qualify as 'preventive', given the broad nature of the definition of child abuse adopted by BASW: 'when the basic needs of the child are not being met through avoidable acts of either omission or commission' (BASW 1985: 4).

The Whitehawk team describe a process of meetings to discuss referrals of children and families involving other agencies and community members. The fact that this takes place at an early stage helps to accustom the participants to working together. This, it is hoped, makes NAI case conferences more effective and encourages more co-operative decision making in child abuse cases.

A parent and toddler group was set up by the Longbenton team specifically to work with families on caseloads where there was felt or known to be a risk of abuse. The group helped to establish close and informal relationships between social workers and parents, which both assisted and survived the exercise of the department's authority role. The group members have acted as a resource for each other, and the information gained at the group has enabled a number of allegations to be investigated both quickly and relatively painlessly.

The teams from Lochend, Honor Oak, Normanton, and Longbenton all state that their interaction with informal networks has opened up to them sources of information about particular cases where abuse has been alleged or has occurred. This has enabled them to respond more quickly and appropriately.

PRACTICE GUIDELINES

C.1 *Specialization within the team*

Although the CSW approach is avowedly generic, specialized skill and knowledge are still essential for high standards of work. The experience of the teams suggests a number of ways in which this expertise can be encouraged within the team, without compromising a generic and flexible approach.

■ **In teams new to CSW consider the use of weighted caseloads.** This approach means starting out from a traditional view of the work of a team as client-orientated and caseload-organized. Team members can be encouraged to build up a caseload including a large proportion of a given client group, or of cases requiring a particular method (such as behaviour theory techniques).

This is a good method for the early stages of development, since it allows team members a measure of choice and personal preference, and does not of itself create particular threats or fears, being close to the way in which non-CSW generic workers and members of client-group teams will have worked previously. It is necessary, however, not to drift into compartmentalization of the different client groups or work methods, and this way of working must be used in conjunction with the integrated approach outlined earlier (see p. 153).

The weighted caseloads must, of course, not only be developed on the basis of worker preference or experience, but also relate to an analysis of need and demand. Weighted caseloads can be moved gradually towards the more community-orientated model of special skills and knowledge described below (p. 173) by encouraging team members to consider alternative methods in relation to their client-group weighting.

■ **Encourage the development of core specialisms.** This method of constructing specialisms within CSW teams begins with a client-group or work-method orientation. It may start from a development of a weighted caseload or work-role specialism, but does not necessarily need to do so.

Team members identify an interest in a client group or work method and take particular responsibility within the team for assembling information on developments, legislation, resources, and methods, and for developing skills in the area. They are then encouraged to share this knowledge and skill with the rest of the team (by informal discussion, team meetings, co-working). They also take responsibility for initiating developments in the area of their core specialism. Examples of such developments would be: a group needed for depressed women (stemming from mental health core specialism); a requirement for a local family centre (stemming from under-5s core specialism); the opportunity to utilize unused space in a moribund community centre (stemming from community work core specialism); the need for more intensive relations with the local high school (stemming from court work core specialism). The probability of overlap between developments and client groups should be consciously explored by the team as a whole, so that maximum use is made of new resources, and people needing them are viewed holistically and not as labelled categories such as 'depressed women', 'young mother', or 'potential user of community social facility'.

Core specialists must actively seek out other team members' knowledge and skill, and tie them into their analysis and approach to specialism. They must, conversely, actively sell their own core specialism to other team members and be prepared to put their skills and knowledge to the service of other client or community groups.

■ **Work towards the adoption of network specialisms.** This is an out-and-out community-orientated way of constructing specialism within a CSW team. The professional construction of reality is abandoned and teams look outward to the patch to identify specialisms based on the networks of relationships which they can observe in their area. At the simplest level, this could include regular liaison by identified team members with other voluntary or statutory agencies (GPs, first school, or tenants' association) for example, or with local establishments (such as a sheltered housing complex or day nursery).

At a higher level of complexity, such liaison can be extended to include all (or most) casework generated from the liaison, plus group work and developmental work. Thus the network specialist becomes an expert in, for instance, a particular school's facilities, staff, extra-curricular activities, pupils requiring court reports or family work, etc.

The above examples are 'official-site-orientated'. Certainly such sites do provide a focus for informal networks, and this will be a productive way of identifying many of them. Not all networks are official-site-orientated, however, and teams should consider identifying specialisms in networks focused on unofficial sites, such as: the adolescents who congregate in Joe's Café, those who share a stairway in a block of flats, the people who are known to the woman at No. 53 on the corner.

There are other categories which may provide a focus for networks, for example: young black women; solvent abusers; widows. Team members can consider specializing in such networks as long as they are aware that their existence must be thought of as provisional. It is rather like thinking in terms of client groups (except that these are not professionally recognized as such), or communities of interest, and there may not be any real interaction between the people labelled by a selection of characteristics. Nevertheless, team experience would indicate that thoughtfully chosen labels of this nature may reveal a network of real relationships within a patch.

Although it is convenient to distinguish between these three ways of specializing within a CSW team, it is not necessary to stick rigidly or exclusively to them. A weighted caseload can ease almost imperceptibly into a core specialism. Specializing in a network may well relate closely to a client group or to a core specialism, and it may be sensible to cluster network specialisms with a particular core specialist.

Specialisms do not need to be the exclusive property of a single individual. It will often follow naturally from the sharing ethos of a CSW team that a specialism will be co-worked. In the same way, a given team member will probably undertake more than one specialism, so that the possibility exists, and should be exploited, of an overlapping network of special interests which will serve to further promote the sharing of knowledge and skills, and cross-fertilization between ideas, initiatives, and use of resources.

■ Seek to break down barriers between roles.

This will apply to those teams which include non-social work roles, sometimes because of historical accident (you just happen to have a community worker or a worker for the blind within the team), or because the department has deliberately included a large number of roles within a team as part of a decentralization programme. A CSW team will be seeking to break down the traditional barriers between roles and allow all team members to contribute their skills to work with individuals, families, groups, and the community. It is a helpful way of 'unfreezing' role boundaries to envisage the different roles as core specialisms. Thus, just as a social worker might specialize in work with adolescents, undertaking case work, group work, and development initiatives, and may also use his or her group work skills with mentally ill people, a receptionist will specialize in receiving callers to the office, and may also undertake work in that context with an individual adolescent or group, may take those particular relationships and skills into a non-reception group setting, and may undertake a development initiative with the adolescent core specialist.

This way of viewing roles should accord equal respect and status to each role, while recognizing the need to differentiate functions and accommodate different skills, styles, and experience, and also allowing the role holders to develop their work flexibly, in a satisfying and integrated way.

C.2 *Relating to external specialists*

As well as striving to build up knowledge and expertise within the team, all the CSW teams studied here are in the position of having to relate to non-member specialist workers. It is essential that CSW teams find efficient ways of gaining access to the resources controlled by specialists (e.g. residential places, day care, funding), or possessed by the specialist workers themselves (e.g. skills, knowledge, person hours).

Especially in departments which are not working as a whole towards a decentralized CSW approach, it will be necessary for CSW teams to take some initiative in promoting productive working relationships. Some of the guidelines suggested here and in C.3 below apply equally or primarily to departmental management. These are marked with a 'D' prefix.

■ **Participate in allocation processes.**

The fact that a resource is managed by specialists does not have to mean that decisions on its use are left entirely with them. For example, CSW teams may be able to influence allocation processes by attending appropriate meetings. It may be possible to get the department to open out allocation processes officially by raising the issue in appropriate forums. Informal arrangements may be achieved through negotiations and discussion, or a consistent display of commitment and interest. Good relationships with establishments located on the patch may enable those particular establishments to pioneer flexible admission arrangements tailored to local needs, or encourage experimentation in using the facilities for a variety of neighbourhood-related purposes.

It is important to have team members participate on departmental working parties examining services to client groups.

■ **Work for sympathetic allocation criteria.**

If criteria for allocation of resources are sympathetic and responsive to need as demonstrated by CSW teams, then control over the actual allocation itself is not required. This can be accomplished as explained above, either by informal negotiation or by influencing formal departmental processes.

■ **Manage resources at patch level.**

On those occasions when new resources are created, there

will be opportunities to assume responsibility for managing them within the CSW team. This is most likely to occur if the new resource has been obtained as a result of a patch initiative (when it may well be possible to build local management into the initial design). Complacency is to be avoided, because just as you are interested in attracting management to the patch, so others may be interested in creating another specialist team, or centralizing management.

Conversely, there are times when no one seems to want the extra work entailed in managing a new resource. If it is on your patch, seize the opportunity. You will be able to use your control to manage the service in an integrated way, and may set a precedent.

■ **Create informal lines of communication.** Whatever the formal structure and however remote specialists may seem, it is always possible to improve working relationships by informal methods. It is well established that informal relationships are what make organizations tick and these are always open to influence by the CSW team.

A CSW team member can be identified as liaison person with a specialist team. This can sensibly be part of a core specialist or caseload-weighted role. The liaison person then takes responsibility for managing the team's relations with the specialist team, handling referrals, carrying messages, clarifying difficulties, discussing issues. Alternatively, or additionally, a specialist can be invited to perform the liaison function on behalf of the specialist team.

Specialists can be invited to team meetings either as a special effort or as a regular arrangement. Invitations to attend specialist team meetings should be accepted, and can be actively sought (e.g. to discuss a contentious issue or a CSW initiative).

Peripatetic specialists far from their home base can be offered desk space, use of the telephone, toilet facilities, etc., in the team office in a warmly welcoming manner. CSW teams should try to find out the routines of the specialist workers so that they can have a reasonable chance of contacting them when necessary. If no routine is apparent, try to establish one, e.g. suggest that they work in the local area on set days or always drop by on Wednesdays on the way home. Request specialist workers to co-work cases with CSW team members or offer to co-work on their cases. Put forward suggestions for initiatives on the patch in the appropriate area of specialism to be worked jointly between CSW and specialist teams. Where departmental management is consciously promoting a CSW-based system, organizational structures and lines of communication can be formally set up to influence good CSW team-specialist relations.

■ (D) **Promote geographical proximity.**

The simple fact of geographical distance between specialist and CSW teams will tend to increase the psychological distance. Whilst some separation may appear inevitable, it can be minimized. Each CSW team could be given its own specialist, if a sufficient number exist. The specialist could relate laterally, possibly with the help of an adviser to draw together departmental issues. Alternatively, a system could be constructed by which specialists spend part of their working week actually present in CSW team offices. Or a specialist team might be located permanently in a single CSW team office.

■ (D) **Monitor specialists' allocation processes.**

By ensuring that resources respond sensitively to need identified by CSW teams, the 'ivory tower' syndrome can be avoided.

■ (D) **Set up systems which ensure that CSW and specialist teams have to communicate.**

CSW and specialist workers ought to have to meet to discuss referrals, allocations, and planning. By establishing that all referrals must initially be received by a CSW team, the CSW and specialist teams can be forced to confer with each other. Setting up cross-groupings of workers to allocate resources will also encourage a meeting of perspectives.

Both CSW and specialist teams will have contributions to make to service planning and new initiatives, and these can be brought together by establishing representative planning groups.

■ (D) **Organize specialist teams internally to relate to CSW teams.**

One specialist team member can be assigned to relate to one or a grouping of CSW teams in terms of case work, group work and developmental work. The specialist teams' information systems can be organized on geographical lines. Specialist resources can be organized in catchment areas which relate to CSW team boundaries.

■ (D) **Frame the specialist role in relation to CSW teams.**

The polarization between CSW and specialist teams can be minimized if the relationship to CSW work is borne in mind in the formulation of specialist job descriptions. Specialist workers should be expected to relate to CSW teams as part of their duties and should seek to act as advisers and co-workers with CSW teams. They should also be asked to view their clients as whole people, and to see them in the context of the wider networks to which they belong.

C.3 *New specialist legislation*

The Mental Health Act (1983) affects people living in the patch and its enforcement is an integral part of social work activities and duties. CSW workers are in no way exempted from applying its provisions simply because of their local involvement and they are well placed to act effectively as approved social workers (ASWs). The guardian *ad litem* panels, on the other hand, specifically exclude workers with a previous connection.

■ (D) **Encourage CSW involvement in statutory mental health work.**

In larger CSW teams, one or more team members could become ASWs. They should co-work statutory mental health cases with their non-approved colleagues to ensure that detailed previous knowledge is brought to light. Where specialist approved workers have to be brought in to support a CSW team, the situation should be co-worked with a community social worker for the same reason.

There seems little advantage in making locally based workers leave their patch to undertake these duties for other teams. This should only happen in order to cover for absence and such substitution should be to a standard pattern to enable a neighbouring worker to become familiar with his next-door team.

■ (D) **Discourage the use of CSW resources for guardian *ad litem*.**

This work is by definition irrelevant to the CSW team and

would therefore only be a distraction to the members. It would be preferable for a specialist team to be created. It might be possible to enable interested community social workers to undertake this work if their missing hours could be substituted.

C.4 *Working with child abuse*

■ **Subject work with child abuse to the same community-orientated scrutiny that is applied to any other type of case work.**

The responsibilities of working with child abuse are perhaps more onerous, and the risk of public exposure is certainly greater, than in other areas of social work activity. Nevertheless, it is not fundamentally different in other respects, and should be subjected to the same sort of evaluative processes as those advocated in the first section of this chapter (pp. 153–61). The benefits which flow from integration with informal networks and other agencies, from integration of services at patch level, from the localization of services, and from the creation of alternative methods and resources are all applicable to child abuse.

■ **Develop 'preventive' strategies aimed at children and families.**

It must be remembered that although some child abuse cases are starkly horrifying, much of the work undertaken in this area concerns situations which are far less clear cut. There are allegations without apparent substance, differences of opinion about the significance of particular events, different views as to parents' capacity to change. In such contexts it may be debatable whether abuse is taking place at all, and all the more important for the team to behave towards the 'suspect' families in the same way as they would approach other problematic situations.

BASW draws attention to stress experienced by parents (BASW 1985: 5) and to the needs of children for physical care and protection, for bodily growth and the exercise of physical and mental functions, for love and security and the opportunity to relate to others, for new experiences, and for intellectual development (BASW 1985: 4).

It is not necessarily beyond the scope of a CSW team to undertake developmental community work which makes some small inroads into the causes of stress. At a limited local level, practical help with welfare rights or housing can be delivered by the team or by other agencies such as advice centres which the team attract to, and support on, the patch. Similarly, action groups can directly address these problems as well as being a means by which local people can seek to claw back to themselves a little power and influence.

Children whose basic needs are not being met are more difficult to look after. If CSW teams can help to create resources such as parent and toddler groups and youth groups, they may both help parents in their struggle to meet their children's needs in the face of severe practical difficulties and deprivation, and contribute to the reduction of stress on the parents themselves.

■ Develop 'reactive' strategies according to the principles of CSW.

At the hard end, when abuse is evident or strongly suspected, CSW's major strategies of integration, localization and alternative approaches should pay dividends.

Integration with informal networks. By being in touch with informal networks, and building up an overall picture of relationships within them, the team can gain information on which to make more accurate and realistic assessments (see for example, Blom-Cooper, 1986: 133). Such contacts may also make it easier to provide support to a family by working with its network, perhaps to build it up, perhaps to help change the way it operates, or perhaps to feed in information. A non-official person may well be more acceptable than a social worker to a family suspected of child abuse.

Leissner (1986) develops a similar approach, arguing strongly that the social context of the family in child abuse cases has been ignored, perhaps because of an over-prioritized respect for the principle of confidentiality in situations where neighbours in fact already know more than the professionals. He suggests that social workers should, as a conscious strategy, seek good working relationships with neighbours of actual or potential abusers, listen to what they have to say, spend a considerable proportion of the working week in the neighbourhood, and demonstrate that social workers are concerned with helping people with the practical difficulties of their lives. At the organizational level, Leissner argues that a substantial proportion of social workers' time should be set aside from case work to allow: (a) new workers to get familiar with their neighbourhood; (b) established workers to participate in neighbourhood work; (c) the initiation and support of children's safety committees to encourage neighbourhood involvement and representation. Qualifying training courses should provide an obligatory community fieldwork placement, and in-service training programmes should seek to second social workers for six-week community projects.

Integration with other agencies – the improved working relationships which result from CSW teams' efforts to liaise closely with other organizations – can also produce better information, and can reduce tension and increase understanding and co-operation in the stressful circumstances of a child abuse investigation.

Integration within the social services department. When a wide range of service is available under a common local management the speed of access to them is improved and the flexibility of their application increased.

Localization. When services are local, they are more readily available to clients both in a practical and a psychological sense, and the involvement of parents is made much easier.

Alternative methods and resources. Group work and co-working help to share the load and reduce the anxiety which child abuse situations arouse. The other benefits of saved time and more effective work continue to apply in child abuse cases. Directly useful resources such as family centres can sometimes be successfully argued for through the department or in conjunction with voluntary agencies.

■ **Follow the department's child abuse procedures at all times.**
At the risk of stating the obvious, it must be emphasized that nothing that has been said here is intended to imply that child abuse procedures can be set aside at any point. Rigorous investigation and handling of proven cases is fully compatible with a search for alternative approaches which emphasize community orientation. Social workers have to learn to accept their ambivalent professional status as simultaneously agent of control and source of help.

Role flexibility

ISSUES

Departmental policy is likely to be the main factor affecting what CSW teams can achieve in the development of role flexibility. It will influence the number of different roles combined within a team, the level of support or difficulty which teams encounter when role boundaries are blurred, the number of rules which teams feel they are expected to observe in allocating tasks between personnel, how staff perceive any changes, and the reaction of the unions.

It has been suggested (Pinker 1982: 248) that broadening out the task of social workers will serve only to divert a scarce resource from its proper purpose of delivering statutorily required help to individuals and families. Departments which hold this view may force adherence to traditional expectations of social workers and discourage the flexible deployment of staff.

On the other hand, if some tasks traditionally undertaken by social workers are shared with non-social work staff, space may be made for social workers to broaden the range of their activities. Teams may be able to use the previously untapped skills and aptitudes of non-social work staff and so extend the resources of the team, whilst ensuring a proper level of support for non-qualified team members.

However, irrespective of arguments about the quality of service which may result from flexibility, individuals and unions may well object to such profound changes in working practices because they perceive them as potentially exploitative, or because they believe other structures are preferable, or because the challenge to the status quo is threatening.

The issues to be considered are:

A.1 authority policy; (see also: Chapter 4, p. 155)
A.2 the social work role; (see also: Chapter 5, p. 164)
A.3 non-social work roles; (see also: Chapter 3, p. 76; Chapter 4, p. 115)
A.4 staff feeling; (see also: Chapter 4, p. 115)
A.5 union reactions. (see also: Chapter 4, p. 115)

B.1 *Authority policy*

The authorities governing the teams vary in their attitude from *laissez-faire* to rigid adherence to job descriptions. All teams have nevertheless managed to achieve a degree of flexibility, though teams such as Longbenton with few roles are relatively restricted in their scope.

Honor Oak do not know what their authority's policy is in this respect. However, social work job descriptions are very wide, appear to cover all desired activities, and the District Officer has rarely interfered.

Job descriptions are strictly adhered to by Wakefield and North Tyneside. The latter has, however, recognized that rigid job descriptions can inhibit delivery of the best possible service and intends to unify the home-care (home helps) and domiciliary care (intensive personal-care tasks) services. In the Normanton team, departmental policy does not, in practice, prevent a flexible approach to most tasks. Flexibility is the official order of the day for the authorities of the Rye, Huntly, and Docklands teams — though in differing contexts. The Huntly team feel that this is a long-standing tradition in a rural authority, where staff have been thinly spread and are expected to turn their hand to anything, including rounding up sheep!

Newham's official policy as seen from the Docklands perspective is to provide broad guidelines rather than detailed job descriptions, and to clarify particular practice issues as they arise. This has assisted the innovatory efforts of the Docklands team, allowing freedom for local negotiation, for example in expanding the role of family aides to encompass different client groups.

Where the Docklands team have identified departmental policy as the source of restrictions to the flexibility they consider essential, they have openly challenged practice on specific issues through official channels and have gained positive changes, for instance in the scope of the home-help role. Many issues identified in this way have yet to be tackled, however, since the process is proving lengthy.

The policy of East Sussex is tailored to their patch system and aims to establish generalized job descriptions which give a clear outline of responsibility levels so that grades can be set, but which allow maximum freedom in tackling tasks.

Overall, the teams give the impression of having sufficient autonomy within their varied functions to make significant attempts to broaden staff roles, whether or not their departments have consciously adopted this policy.

B.2 *The social work role*

All teams would appear to subscribe to the philosophy of broadening the social work role, as outlined by the Longbenton team: 'team members have to have broken out of the individual caseworker mould, and to have the capacity to see themselves as group workers, community workers, and servants of the community.' Some extra supervisory and representative functions are also added to the social work role. In the Docklands team, social workers take on management roles such as representing the team leader at departmental or community meetings and supervising the family aides. In Normanton, too, supervision of patch workers and of the caring aspects of the domiciliary staff roles is undertaken by patch leaders who are social workers. They are also to be found programming home helps and representing the team at community meetings.

In the opposite direction, the Huntly team believes that it is important that social workers should be prepared to undertake practical tasks. Normanton patch leaders scrub floors alongside home helps, Docklands social workers put people on to commodes and undertake home-help and meals-on-wheels assessments, and Longbenton social workers undertake manual tasks with home helps and volunteers in situations where support seems needed. A social worker in Rye initially undertook to work as a home help for a particular client in order to build a relationship in a problematic situation.

All the teams are very aware of departmental requirements that social workers should shoulder the responsibility for particularly risk-laden work. Huntly, Rye, Normanton, Lochend, and Longbenton acknowledge that they take into account their departments' expectation that certain 'statutory' cases will be handled by qualified social workers. The Huntly team would take into consideration all available options in allocating a case involving NAI, depending upon its seriousness and the feelings of any unqualified worker involved.

The Longbenton and Normanton teams conform to departmental policy in 'statutory' cases where an unqualified worker is involved by ensuring that in all instances a qualified worker co-works the case, and takes overall responsibility for it.

The Lochend team have encountered problems in bringing this flexible approach to reality. It was originally intended that social workers would undertake community work tasks, and that community workers would share in duty, but pressure of case work has prevented the social workers from making this move, and the community workers, who have a strong sense of identity as a separate group, have not begun to do duty.

B.3 *Non-social work roles*

It is clear that all non-social work roles within a CSW team are broadening out to include some functions which have traditionally belonged to social workers: being allocated a case, attempting to achieve change with an individual or family, providing information when on duty or in reception.

In the Docklands team, administrative staff are expected to do telephone and reception duties, take referrals and present them at patch meetings, open and close premises and organize repairs, and manage the loan of equipment to clients.

Honor Oak administrative staff are active in running or assisting local groups. Although such tasks are included in their job descriptions, this aspect of their work is not adequately understood by district administrative staff. In consequence, the local staff often feel under pressure when undertaking group work as no extra help is provided to cover their 'normal' duties.

The Longbenton team clerks were given permission by their (administrative) line manager to participate with the social work team in a community social work project. As a result, one has become company secretary of the Longbenton Mental Health Resource Group.

The Longbenton team have frequently arranged for their Day Care Centre organizer to assess potential users for her resource. The Rye team similarly allow the officer in charge to deal directly with a referral for short-stay care at her establishment when no other service is required. The home-help organizer may also undertake this function. The Normanton patch workers share in office duty, although a qualified worker is always available. Patch workers also undertake community work.

The Docklands team have extended the family aide role to

take in all client groups, to allow them to be allocated cases, to negotiate financial matters, to complete referrals, to help out by taking telephone calls and at reception, to present cases at patch meetings, to run and manage groups, and to represent the team on local groups. The home-care organizer also helps with reception and telephone calls, runs projects, and represents the team at local meetings and senior management meetings. The home help integration scheme has had particularly far-reaching effects, in so far as home helps have been given their own sub-patches within which they themselves decide with whom they should work, and how.

B.4 *Staff feelings*

Staff appear from the teams' accounts to experience a greater degree of job satisfaction – at least once initial changes are established.

Responses from the teams indicate that although non-social work staff may not have a social worker's skills, they have other skills acquired through means such as their former occupation or general life experience. In many instances, these skills may be as appropriate or more appropriate, than social work skills. Non-social workers have shown that they can handle responsibility and welcome the opportunities it brings. Furthermore, in teams where sharing, teamwork, and mutual accessibility prevail, the level of support for such workers is higher and more immediate than in traditional set-ups.

Normanton, Docklands, and Longbenton all report job satisfaction among their workers, though in the Longbenton team it took about eighteen months to materialize. In Normanton, work satisfaction has been shown to be particularly high amongst the patch workers, unqualified ancillaries who undertake much of the front-line work of the team (Hadley and McGrath 1984: 203–9).

In the Docklands team, the non-social workers expressed satisfaction at what they saw as progress in their jobs, when they found that at last they were being trusted to do what they knew they were capable of, and that their worth was being recognized by the professionals. The social workers have experienced the more practical tasks as a breath of fresh air, and all staff have welcomed the greatly improved mutual understanding born of sharing and overlapping tasks.

The Rye team feel that staff are reassured by clearly under-standing their principal responsibilities and feeling they are being sufficiently supported when they step outside these.

However, a number of teams expressed dissatisfaction with elements of the situation existing when information was contributed to this book. The Docklands team were particularly concerned: (a) that a particular post with which an individual identified would disappear as a result of the broadening of others; (b) that staff might end up having to cope with tasks for which they had not been prepared by experience or training; (c) about the *extra* work which CSW demands and generates; (d) about the unfair pay structure which remained linked to the former circumscribed duties.

The Normanton team were also concerned at the injustices of the current grading system. The Longbenton team suffered from the department's Level 3 quota system which means that social workers could be arbitrarily barred from receiving the financial reward owed to their range of work and independent mode of operation. Senior management had recently suggested that non-qualified workers (SSOs) should abandon the work they were doing which overlapped with that of social workers. The SSOs were very angry and felt demeaned by the suggestion that they were not capable of such work.

B.5 *Union reactions*

The unions could be expected to take a keen interest in these developments, but have not figured prominently in the experi-ence of most of the contributing teams. Union policy does not appear to play any part in the lives of the Huntly, Lochend, or Honor Oak teams.

The Rye team are aware of the directive from NALGO warn-ing against role flexibility being used to provide cover for unfilled and redundant posts. The manual union is watching the situa-tion carefully, in particular the issue of combining care attendant and home-help roles into care worker posts. In Normanton, the unions have raised the issue of the flexibility of ancillary workers' roles with the management of the department.

In Longbenton the unions have created no problems for the team. During protracted discussions about proposals to restruc-ture the department, NALGO has taken pains to assist in the process of professional debate by focusing attention first on the issues of improving service, and by making it clear that it would exert all efforts to safeguard staff interests once the questions involved had been settled.

The Docklands team feel that the unions have tried to encourage workers to stick to their job descriptions in pursuance of the principle that you don't take on extra responsibilities without securing a regrading. Fortunately for the development of CSW, because of the authority's policy of broad guidelines, there are no detailed job descriptions for people to stick to, and union attempts to curtail these developments have come to nothing. More recently, however, the union offered to help the team if they should wish to get management to review the remuneration of its ancillary staff.

PRACTICE GUIDELINES

Role flexibility is clearly crucial if CSW teams are to achieve a broader, more imaginative, and better integrated method of work, allowing the strengths and styles of non-professional workers to be utilized to their full potential. Breaking down traditional role boundaries, nevertheless, creates problems for both workers and management. These must be addressed if CSW is to be firmly established and teams are to operate at maximum efficiency.

C.1 *Authority policy*

Departmental attitudes will necessarily influence the tactics used by teams in their search for flexibility. Where policy is at odds with practice, conscious strategies need to be developed to deal with the resulting tensions.

■ **Identify the policy of the department with regard to adherence to job descriptions.**

It is essential to be aware of the environment within which a team operates, as it will help to determine the appropriate level of flexibility. This is not always obvious, and may only become apparent through experimentation. It is important to be clear about the source of any difficulty in developing flexible roles. Team members' difficulties will need to be approached through techniques of team management, whereas departmental problems can be faced by measures suggested in the following guidelines.

■ **Reduce conflicts with the department by observing departmental requirements.**

This is particularly important where teams are going it alone: it will reduce anxiety among senior management and induce confidence that the new approach is not unduly risky and the staff not irresponsible. An imaginative way in which this can be achieved, whilst continung to allow flexibility, is co-working, which permits non-social work staff to undertake work with, for example, at-risk clients alongside a qualified social worker. The non-social worker may in this way take on a major part of the work, while overall responsibility remains with the co-working social worker. It may also be advantageous in some cases to allocate a social worker to a case where the service being offered is in fact group work.

■ **Do not use the practice of CSW as an excuse for avoiding traditional tasks.**

Management may well object to an alternative task being carried out if it is used as an excuse for not doing something else. Departmental requirements must therefore be seen to be met by social workers in CSW teams in order to obtain the freedom to broaden the role.

■ **Work to change departmental policies through the official departmental forums.**

If a team policy is adopted by the department, it becomes much easier to work with problems experienced by individuals who have previously been reluctant to concede the need for such a policy. It also removes any problems caused by having to work to a formal structure that did not accord with CSW practice.

■ **(D) Senior management should seek to create broad job descriptions.**

Job descriptions should take account of the drive towards flexible methods of working inherent in CSW systems. It is therefore necessary to describe roles in a way which allows as much freedom as possible with respect to the detailed tasks to be undertaken, and which will allow for roles to overlap.

C.2 *The social work role*

■ **Exploit the broad and ill-defined nature of the social work role.**

The definition has always been wide (you never know when some new piece of legislation is going to come along) and invariably contains some catch-all clause such as 'any other duties required by the area manager'. Moreover, there is some uncertainty as to how to describe the social work task. Group and community work skills have been included on CQSW courses for some time, and it is widely accepted that the practice of group or community work is part of the social work role, 'if only there is time'.

Similarly, more practical tasks seem on the whole to be undertaken without difficulty by community social workers to help them build relationships with a particularly vulnerable person. Such acts, if ever noticed, can be justified in casework terms, and provide an important means for social workers to become more involved with non-social work staff. This can improve relations within the team and allow more opportunities for non-social work staff to begin to participate in what social workers are doing. It also allows support to be given to non-social work staff in difficult situations.

■ **Develop strategies to help social workers not to remain bogged down with 'statutory work'.**

Articulate very clearly that the alternative methods involved in CSW are legitimate and should be scheduled into diaries in the same way as visits to clients. If necessary, allocate some fixed time each week for team members to be freed of case work (e.g. one day per week), but recognize that if the arrangement is too rigid it is more likely to crumble at the first inconveniently timed emergency.

Imagine that the team have no alternative but to manage without one worker who is on long-term sick leave. Then use the strategies devised to cope with the situation, but with the worker present and with their time freed.

Establish that each team member has a legitimate right to be involved in one alternative project. Initially, at least, choose projects which are likely to reduce social workers' caseloads. This should free more time for further alternative approaches.

Begin with projects which look as if they will be relatively easy to establish and will allow early pay-off. There is nothing more draining of morale than a high-priority project which is time-consuming and difficult to set up and which, even if successful, will tie up team resources for a long period before any headway becomes apparent. Do not be reluctant to start with only the knowledge about clients and the community which the team already holds. Ambitious surveys will absorb resources for some time without actually making any inroads into casework tasks.

C.3 *Non-social work roles*

The shift in non-social work roles is more visible than that of social work roles and more obviously conflicts with existing job descriptions. It implies a greater level of responsibility and autonomy which is not reflected in pay scales.

■ (D) **Staff should be properly remunerated for the work they undertake.**
The broadening of non-social work roles to include elements of social work activity necessarily raises the question of whether it is possible to continue to pay staff at a rate designed for closely circumscribed roles. This issue has been highlighted by the operation of CSW systems because changes in role have been made explicit, but improvements in service under any system generally require staff to work to higher standards of individual responsibility.

■ (D) **Management must make clear where responsibility rests.**
Where roles overlap it is particularly important that responsibilities for decisions and their consequences should be clearly defined. Low-paid staff should not be left with levels of accountability which their pay does not match. Further, support systems must be provided for such staff when they are expected to operate in complex situations whether through line management or by setting up systems of co-working as outlined above.

C.4 *Staff feelings*

■ (D) **Management seeking flexible working must demonstrate the positive value they attach to high-quality work at all levels.**

This will create a climate which encourages staff to attempt to improve their practice. It is particularly damaging to the morale of non-social work staff if management imply in response to union pressure that they are only capable of working in a closely supervised, constrained way.

C.5 *Union reactions*

■ **(D) Management must take care to consult with unions prior to embarking on any restructuring.**

It will be inevitable that restructuring on a CSW basis will demand considerable changes in job descriptions and working practices, and these must therefore be negotiated with unions beforehand.

This may well be a source of conflict, as it has been in Hackney, and, initially, Islington. However, unions will not necessarily behave in stereotypical, dyed-in-the-wool ways, but may well see that the proposed changes represent opportunities for their members to achieve greater job satisfaction and broader experience leading to enhanced opportunities. The changes in East Sussex and Humberside were not blocked, and the unions in Islington were won over to the decentralization proposed there.

■ **Teams should seek to involve unions as partners.**

For a start, this is better than having them block efforts to secure change. Further, it may help to secure fairer remuneration. Many branches are interested in the professional implications of proposed changes and wish to forward the interests of their members by participating and representing their members in the professional debate.

6 *Management and development*

Introduction

The development of community-orientated methods of working and the structures which they require brings the effective management of people and resources into the front line of service delivery. Traditionally in social services there has tended to be a wide gap between operational practice and management. The distinction between *managers*, responsible for administration and policy, and *professionals*, responsible for the delivery of services to individuals and families, leads to organizational tension and often mirrors the 'them' and 'us' conflict between management and workforce common to many parts of commerce and industry.

In structures which give responsibility for a particular geographical area (patch or neighbourhood) to a group of practitioners, this tension cannot go unresolved. No longer at this level is it simply a question of 'managing', for example, a collection of cases through the process of professional supervision. The responsibility for a whole community implies the need for decisions concerning resources, priorities, planning and development, and the need for management of such processes. The leader of the community social work (CSW) team is responsible for an organizational unit in a way that an intake or long-term team leader is not. Issues of management and hence the management style and capabilities of those who carry responsibility in the front line take on a new and larger significance.

This chapter focuses on the main challenges likely to be facing the managers of CSW teams. While it is aimed primarily at team managers and team leaders, given the strong case for a team approach made throughout this book, its target is also the membership of teams as a whole. In addition, because of the importance of integrating the CSW team into the larger organization of the department, senior management is likely to have a particular interest in this part of the book. We have therefore included, in addition to the Practice guidelines (C), a section headed Organizational guidelines (D).

The chapter, of course, cannot attempt to serve as a general manual on management. Readers interested in wider aspects of the art will need to refer to the extensive literature on the subject. We have recommended below some of the texts which we ourselves have found most useful (p. 204). The four main themes which we address here are: management within the team; team management, the wider organization, and the community; evaluation; change and development.

Management within the team

ISSUES

Three main issues emerge from the experience of the contributing teams in this area: the scope of team management, the appropriate style of management in CSW teams, and leadership skills.

A.1 *The scope of team management*

The opportunities open to any particular team to develop a CSW approach will be in part determined by the overall structure of the organization of which it is a part and the style and approach favoured by those directing the organization. The dynamics of relationships between the individual CSW team and the wider organization are considered more fully in the next section but the nature of internal management of CSW teams cannot be properly examined unless the scope for local decision making is first established. In particular it is important to distinguish between situations where CSW methods have been adopted at team level within an organization which is still structured and managed on conventional client-centred lines, and those which form part of a departmental scheme of decentralization. What are the constraints and opportunities of these contrasting situations, in terms of the differences in the tasks delegated to teams, in systems of monitoring and control, and the impetus represented by the general style of management of the organization as a whole? Does CSW need a particular organizational climate in order to survive? (See also: Chapter 4, p. 96; Chapter 5, p. 116.)

A.2 *Management style*

Most exponents of CSW have insisted, both on the grounds of the values which it embodies and the practical demands it makes for collaboration, that its successful practice requires a participative style of management. If CSW is premised on the need to support the enabling or empowering of service users, then staff in CSW teams can reasonably expect a similar measure of respect for *their* needs for development and self-determination as employees. Pragmatic factors advanced to support a participative approach relate to the devolution of responsibilities and decision making in CSW teams. This cannot function unless there is a high measure of trust and willingness to pool information and work freely in the give-and-take of a team. Such involvement can only be expected, it is argued, where participative management is the norm.

On the other hand, the setting in statutory social services remains hierarchical and bureaucratic. CSW teams, like any other kind of team in a statutory department, are ultimately responsible to the chief officer of the organization, and through him or her to its political controllers. Even in the most devolved system, authority has been delegated, not given away and those responsible for directing the wider organization have a duty to determine its policies, manage its resources, and maintain its standards of practice. Can a balance be struck between those two sets of demands? Is participative management possible in state bureaucracies? (See also Chapter 4, p. 115.)

A.3 *Leadership attributes and skills*

Some critics of CSW have argued that it makes excessive demands on its front-line managers (e.g. Pinker 1982: 247) and have implied that it is unlikely that sufficient people of the calibre required could be found to staff social services departments run on these lines. What qualities and skills are needed in practice to provide effective leadership of the CSW team? To what extent might they be cultivated and developed where they do not already exist? (See also Chapter 5, pp. 137, 182.)

TEAM EXPERIENCE

B.1 *The scope of team management*

The experience of the contributing teams illustrates a variety of structures and forms, and reveals significant differences in outlook and approach within the wider organizations in which they are located. As well as political and organizational differences the teams' experience indicates that there is no one particular management style which underpins all the initiatives described.

The teams fall into two main categories according to the structures of the departments of which they are part and the styles of management followed in the wider organization. The two East Sussex teams both define a system of delegation and decentralization which spells out clearly the responsibilities of local teams and which embodies a number of devices to ensure that central management is informed in some detail about important aspects of their work. Yet it is also clear that within this system teams have been left a considerable measure of autonomy, and can and do develop local initiatives reflecting their assessment of local conditions and needs.

In the other six departments organizational systems seem to be less clear-cut and a variety of departmental structures and differences in styles of management is in evidence at middle and higher levels. Nevertheless, whether by chance or design, all appear to leave some room for the development of a considerable measure of local decision making, if there is sufficient commitment at team level to use the opportunities presented.

The Longbenton team offer an example of this situation. Teams in North Tyneside are required to follow departmental policies and procedures wherever these have been defined. However, when policies which affect team members are under discussion in the department, they are encouraged to contribute their views. In all other aspects of their work they are allowed to develop their own approach so long as it fits within the general policy framework of the authority. The team manager comments: 'This is a clear model with the major advantage for the subordinate of being able to predict the limits of one's discretion, as well as knowing in advance the areas in which the team can proceed without interference.'

B.2 *Management style*

The management style of the wider organization within which the contributing teams are lodged is generally experienced as authoritative rather than participative. One manager comments, for example, that in his department 'although not formally enunciated' the most favoured style appears to be an authoritative one. 'There is not enormous sympathy with participative or democratic management models, as the conventional wisdom is that managers are there to manage.' Yet in spite of this there is 'recognition that allowing staff to contribute to management tends to get the best out of people'.

Another contributor points to a style of management which is defined from the top of the organization as participative but which 'viewed from the base of the pyramid looks authoritative'. Nevertheless, this system, like that of the other teams, leaves considerable scope for individual teams to adopt different styles of management. The Rye team manager describes a situation in which there is a place for both styles within the same organization:

> 'There appear to be two main styles of management endorsed by the department. On the one hand is a fairly authoritative style practised by senior management, with expectations that first-line and middle managers will adopt a similar stand. In contrast has been the push for team-building programmes, with training officer support, and consequent encouragement for a participative style of management at fieldwork team and establishment level.'

Experience within the contributing teams themselves for the most part indicates a firmly held view that a participative style of management is required in the implementation of CSW. Participation in decision making is clearly of particular importance for CSW teams where collective responsibility and flexibility of working are distinguishing features, compared with the individual responsibility and demarcations of more traditional ways of working. Throughout the teams a participative approach is characterized by the holding of team meetings where decisions concerning referrals, cases, work allocation, needs, priorities, objectives, and community issues are shared. There is a clear commitment to the involvement of team members and to team discussion of issues, accompanied by a recognition that there will always be some situations where there can be little discretion in the decision made.

The view from Docklands exemplifies the nature and value of participation.

'A participative approach to management is one which enables staff to mature and develop as a team. Through shared ownership of decisions staff are more likely to be motivated and committed to task goals. All decisions are discussed, even if at the end of the day it is clear that the leader will make the final decision. From the leader's point of view a participative approach is one where the difficulties of the management role can be shared with team members and understood by them.'

A number of standard mechanisms appear to be used in all the teams to ensure that there are regular and significant opportunities for discussion of team policies and shared decision making. These include a weekly meeting of the main staff group where current developments in both the department as a whole and different sections of the team can be shared, and new initiatives can be proposed and considered. Some teams, as for example the Normanton team, also have additional meetings for sub-groups within the larger team, including the separate patch teams, the ancillary staff, and the social workers. All the teams engage in project work in which, typically, several workers, often from different occupational categories, combine to tackle particular tasks such as establishing a youth club, starting group work, or co-operating with a local voluntary agency to set up an advice bureau. A further means, described by several teams, of developing and maintaining all members' participation is the day or weekend away when the whole team takes time out together to review aims, practice, and achievements, and make plans for the future in the light of their evaluation.

In at least one team participation has been used in the key area of staff recruitment. The importance to a team approach of ensuring that there is maximum cohesion among individual members is self-evident. The Huntly team have, however, taken participation in this area one step further: 'our senior has just been promoted . . . As a team we have been involved in compiling a job description for the post and again as a team are involved in the interview procedure. Hopefully, we will therefore obtain a senior that we want. It is obviously very important that the team end up with someone with whom they can work.'

Limits to participation

It would be misleading to assume that participation is always appropriate or to confuse a participative approach with a democratic or *laissez-faire* approach. Participation does not mean fudging issues through an insistence on consensus nor does it necessarily exclude the exercise of authority through imposed decisions in areas outside the scope of the participative process.

In the experience of the contributing teams two main factors appear particularly likely to limit participation: the special problems faced in the period of transition from traditional methods to CSW, and the no-go areas defined by expectations and practice in the wider organization.

Several of the teams described the need for strong leadership in the early phases of the change to new methods of working. In Normanton the area officer said, 'Certainly, in the early days of the team a more direct approach was needed to take people through changes.' The Longbenton team leader echoed this view in commenting that 'the management style of the team must in its early stages have appeared more controlling because the CSW philosophy was not common property'. The manager of another team (Rye), the most recently established of those contributing to this handbook, gave an example of a change in practice marking the end of a period of transition: 'Until now I have undertaken to lead all the discussion sessions but now I feel this can be appropriately shared with team members.'

Team leaders and managers define two types of decision making which are from their point of view 'no-go areas', this is where they are not prepared to share their authority with their teams. The first of these concerns the defence of the structures and methods required to develop CSW. So, for instance, in one team the manager vetoed a proposal to establish a permanent duty officer since he judged the change would undermine the sharing of responsibilities and knowledge that he was seeking to establish in the team. Others have resisted suggestions to re-establish formal specialization at team level.

The second and more commonly encountered no-go area is marked by boundaries defined by the wider organization.

Examples of the issues and procedures set off-limits in this way include practice for handling statutory cases such as child care referrals where non-accidental injury is suspected, compulsory admission to care, and the management of financial matters. In such areas, it is the responsibility of the team leader or manager to ensure, whether reluctantly or otherwise, that practice is in line with departmental rules.

B.3 *Leadership attributes and skills*

While much emphasis has been placed on participative management in CSW teams, it is clear that CSW team managers are key figures in the successful development of a decentralized approach. They have either been instrumental in implementing a bottom-up development or have been placed in the front line of wider organizational change. In both cases they are responsible for developing and implementing new concepts. There are few precedents on which managers in this situation can draw and little training to which they can turn. The teams all acknowledge the significance of the leadership role and emphasize the importance of personal commitment to the ideals of CSW in general and to the team in particular.

The contributing teams refer most frequently to two aspects of leadership in CSW: personality characteristics and leadership skills.

Personality characteristics
Personality characteristics needed included 'charisma' (Whitehawk and Normanton), ability to give 'guidance and direction' (Rye), 'determination' (Longbenton), and 'vision' (Docklands). However, a note of caution about accepting a view of leadership based centrally on personal attributes was sounded by one contributor. Any notion of CSW which depends on the 'cult of the personality' of the team manager or leader would give an inadequate picture of both current practice and future potential. While special demands may be made on leadership qualities in a period of transition to a new method of working, in the end CSW teams must eventually acquire the capacity to 'survive through the inherent qualities of CSW as a better way of doing things' and not depend for all time 'on the personal qualities of a particular leader to prop them up' (Longbenton).

Leadership skills
The experiences of the contributing teams indicate something of the particular challenges that are involved in managing a CSW team. The increased level of autonomy of the teams, the freedom to determine priorities locally, the assumption of responsibility for finance and resources, the need to develop new methods of working and new relationships, and the presence of external constraints, all pose their demands. Three types of skill are identified as being of special importance: interpersonal, entrepreneurial, and political.

Interpersonal skills. Team leaders and managers have the responsibility for building their teams into cohesive units and maintaining their effectiveness, once established. Both in transition to CSW and afterwards, contributors stress the importance of giving people time to develop and build on their strengths. They also emphasize the key role played by groups in CSW, both in the management of the team and in its work with other agencies and users. The development of groupwork skills by all members of the team is considered a high priority.

Entrepreneurial skills. A CSW approach with its emphasis on prevention and care in the community challenges established structures and the appropriateness and level of existing service provision. In developing resources at the local level the CSW team manager, therefore, is unlikely to be successful unless he or she finds new and different ways of meeting the needs identified in the community: 'A preventive or proactive organization needs to use its ingenuity in discovering different responses to situations if it is to be successful. *Entrepreneurial* skills when dealing with the variety of human and social situations thrown up by a social services department must be a necessary concomitant of flexible practice' (Normanton).
  The entrepreneurial skills of teams are often demonstrated through project work. One of the contributing teams makes the distinction between *'safe' and 'unsafe' social work projects.* The former are characterized as acceptable projects for which financial resources can be sought through established budgetary channels, e.g. luncheon clubs, playgroups, IT groups. The latter are 'projects that, it could be argued, are peripheral to social work practice or are high risk politically, e.g. tenants' groups, welfare rights projects, unemployed groups, and other employ-

ment initiatives'. It is in the approach to 'unsafe' projects that the team may need to engage in entrepreneurial activity such as using another agency or organization to front the development of initiatives for which resources would not be directly available via the team.

It is evident from the teams' descriptions of their work that they see an entrepreneurial approach as meaning being pro-active rather than reactive, being ready to break with existing practice, knowing one's way around organizations and systems, being opportunistic and enthusiastic. In this sense it is important for *all* members of CSW teams to be *entrepreneurs* since they will all be involved in developing ways of working which are not necessarily facilitated by existing organizational structures and systems.

What particular bundle of personal characteristics and experiences may predispose one person to be more entrepreneurial than another is not evident from the material contributed. However, it seems highly significant that most teams could call on the experience of members who had previously operated in community work settings and that some had the direct help of community workers.

Political skills. The general consensus of the contributing teams is that negotiation and maintenance of 'diplomatic relations' with such outside bodies as voluntary organizations and other statutory agencies and with councillors are key features of the CSW team manager's role. 'Dealing with community associations and voluntary organizations requires an understanding of how they function. . . . Dealing with key people in the community requires yet another set of skills since quite often individuals can be very powerful, e.g. MPs, local councillors' (Whitehawk).

To a large extent the need for political skills is generated by the teams' involvement in entrepreneurial activity where such endeavours as the establishment of alliances, the negotiation of resources, and the discreet lobbying of those with influence form a growing part of their activities:

'It is important to know when developing a project who are your potential allies and who are possible enemies, who would support a project and who would be against it. To obtain this type of information it is obviously necessary to meet either formally or informally individuals involved in various organizations and thereby sound out feelings. It is therefore extremely important to develop an acute political awareness of the area in which one works as knowing the right person at the right time can often ensure the success of a new project.'

Through formal and informal contacts with a variety of people able to influence policy and by the development of a set of alternative, more politically acceptable proposals, one of the contributing teams is engaged in acquiring a key resource, a conventional bid for which had been rejected by the wider organization.

PRACTICE GUIDELINES

C.1 *The scope of team management*

■ **Establish as clearly as possible the scope and limits of team decision making.** Find out which policies and procedures of the organization apply to teams, the circumstances where teams are encouraged to develop their own approaches, and the nature and extent of the no man's land where neither applies but the ingenious team may find space to develop their work.

■ **Seek to gain recognition for the limitations and possibilities of team management so established, at all levels within the team.** It is an essential prerequisite of successful CSW that a realistic appreciation of the degree of team autonomy in the wider organization should be shared by all team members.

■ **Where appropriate, undertake negotiations with the wider organization to extend the scope of team management.** Departmental policies and practice should not be regarded as immutable. Where the team's experience shows there is a good case for increasing team autonomy, this should be presented to the appropriate level of departmental management, backed by relevant evidence and in a manner that reflects an understanding of the constraints faced in the wider organization. Don't just moan about other parts of the organization which appear to work against you – try to do something about them!

C.2 *Management style*

■ **Work to build acceptance of the need for effective management of people and resources in the CSW team.** Management is still a dirty word to many social workers who too readily see it as nothing more than a device to curb their professional independence. Whether or not such a view could ever be seen as relevant within a statutory service, it is clearly counter-productive in a CSW setting where coherent team policy and practice are prerequisites of effective working.

■ **Establish an understanding of the main components of the management task.** It cannot be assumed that staff, whether professionally qualified or not, will have any systematic understanding of the main functions of management. The main processes can be shown to be common to all formal organizations: defining goals, planning their achievements, setting up structures and procedures, and evaluating the outcomes in terms of the original goals. An appreciation of how these activities are undertaken in the department as a whole as well as within the CSW team can form the basis for intelligent debate on the role and influence of the team in the wider organization, and of the desirable and possible decision-making structures.

It is not possible in this handbook to examine in detail how teams might explore the nature of the management function but as a starting-point there is a substantial literature on which they can draw. Some books which we have found particularly useful in this field are those by Mintzberg (1973), Handy (1981), Kast and Rosenzweig (1981), Kotter (1982), and Peters and Waterman (1982) full details of which are given in the References (pp. 248–51).

■ **Evolve a participative style of management related to the stage in team development.** In the areas which are open to team-level decision making, the values inherent in CSW and the type of interpersonal relations it requires predicate the development of participative methods of management. The principles underlying this approach to management have been identified by Likert in his book *The Human Organization* (1967) as including supportive relationships and group decision making in semi-autonomous work groups, linked together in overlapping structures, with high performance aspirations.

These principles appear to be well recognized in established CSW teams. However, the transition to them where a team has previously been operating on more hierarchical, one-to-one systems of management is likely to have to be gradual (see below: Limits to participation, p. 206).

■ **Build supportive relationships.** Participative management is founded on the principle of supporting individual staff and helping them to gain significant satisfaction through their work. Stated at its most ideal, Likert suggests a principle of supportive relationships:

'The leadership and other processes of the organisation must be such as to ensure a maximum probability that in all inter-actions and in all relationships within the organisation, each member, in the light of his background, values, desires, and expectations, will view the experience as supportive and one which builds and maintains his sense of personal worth and importance.'

(Likert 1967: 47).

● In applying this approach, seek to build on the existing strengths of team members. Do not devalue or undervalue skills which may be more characteristic of other ways of working. Seek to find ways in which they can be used in the team, and opportunities for the development of a broader skill base can be created.

■ **Group decision making in semi-autonomous groups:** involvement in group decision making means that everyone can share in shaping the goals of the team and forge the basis for collective responsibility. Each group is linked to the rest of the organization by people who are members of more than one group. Group decision making, however, should not be confused with those 'systems' in which committees meet endlessly and never seem to come to any definite conclusions. To quote Likert again:

The group method of supervision holds the superior fully responsible for the quality of all decisions and for their implementation. He is responsible for building his subordinates into a group which makes the best decisions and carries them out well. *The superior is accountable for all decisions, for their execution, and for the results.*

(Likert 1967: 51)

● Developing this approach means that the team should set aside time for regular meetings, that the responsibilities of the group should be clear, and that the decisions of the group are binding on its members. Team leaders and managers should seek to ensure that all team members feel comfortable about participating in the meetings and that risks of domination by the more articulate are avoided. The relationships of sub-groups, such as project teams, to the main group need to be clearly defined and tied into its meetings.

■ **High performance goals.** The success of participative management turns on the identification and acceptance of high performance goals by all, or at least most, of the members of the team. Such commitment may result as part of the natural evaluation of a team towards CSW, where the decision to work in this way is taken by the members themselves. Where CSW teams have been created through political or managerial decisions, the achievement of consensus may present problems. In these circumstances the team manager should:

● seek to establish the extent and nature of such common ground as does exist by methods such as group discussion, training exercises, and days out;
● attempt to tackle the problems so identified (e.g. lack of knowledge and understanding can be tackled through discussion, training programmes, visits to experienced CSW teams, or visits from their staff; personal anxieties about the new demands of CSW, can be approached through similar methods and also supportive supervision);
● be patient. Don't force people into rapid change. Adaptation to new methods of work may be demanding and should be expected to take time.

■ **Limits to participation:** there are two major limiting factors to the development of participation in the CSW team, both of which need to be clearly understood by its members:

● limits set by the wider organization over the extent and nature of decisions delegated to teams; for example, central controls maintained over expenditure, over procedures for handling certain types of referral such as NAI cases;
● limits set by the stage of development of the team: extensive sharing in decision making requires a high degree of

consensus on values and methods of working and may involve the acquisition of new skills in a team. A team making the transition to CSW may take time to develop in these ways and participation in such teams needs to be introduced gradually, keeping pace with change, not racing ahead of it.

C.3 *Leadership attributes and skills*

■ **It is the overriding responsibility of the team manager or leader to ensure that the team operates in a manner which ensures the achievement of its goals.** To this end, he or she requires the skills and understanding of the general manager, to see that all the essential ingredients of the managerial process are established and maintained, from goal setting and planning to evaluation.

■ **However, in an effective CSW team, leadership cannot be the monopoly of its official head alone. Other members must be ready and able to take initiatives in different aspects of its work.** This calls, in particular, for the development of competence in interpersonal relationships, and entrepreneurial and political skills.

■ **Interpersonal skills must include those required to maintain the effective functioning of the team.** Team managers and members alike need to understand the importance of team cohesion for goal achievement. Awareness of group processes and improved team functioning can be helped by:

- setting aside time for the team to review its functioning;
- using an outsider with group skills to act as a consultant on the functioning of the team;
- giving the members of the team a significant say in decisions affecting its composition and management.
- involving the team as a whole in the recruitment and selection of staff.

■ **Entrepreneurial skills need to be widely developed in the CSW team.** Team members can be helped to acquire more innovative styles of working by such means as:

- making time for projects and other entrepreneurial activities in work programmes and for their review in team meetings;

● wherever possible ensuring that at least some of those recruited into the team have had experience of community-orientated work;

● providing for mutual support in new activities by arranging for two or more staff to share responsibility for each undertaking.

■ **CSW teams must seek to develop a good understanding of the political context in which they operate.** CSW teams are inevitably drawn into both organization and party political worlds. They have to learn to operate politically and understand the ways in which these worlds work. In particular, they will have to learn how to balance the accountability they are likely to feel towards their particular neighbourhood or community with the accountability they have as part of a local government organization to the hierarchy and to the elected representatives.

ORGANIZATIONAL GUIDELINES

D.1 *The scope of team management*

■ **The effective operation of CSW teams require the establishment of clear guidelines on the nature of the authority delegated to them.** This in turn has implication for the publication of a framework of departmental policies and practices. These issues are related to the degree of autonomy vested in the teams and are examined together in the next section of the chapter.

D.2 *Management style*

■ **A policy aimed at developing CSW requires a participative style of management in front-line teams.** Senior management should aid the emergence and growth of such a style by:

● actively supporting team managers in the introduction of participative methods;

● backing the introduction of relevant training programmes for management and team development. (See also: Change and development, p. 228.)

D.3 *Leadership attributes and skills*

■ **Leadership qualities of those managing CSW teams are crucial.** Senior management should seek to select managers able to meet the needs of the organization in terms of both tasks and people. In doing this it should be prepared to break established patterns of simply promoting or selecting the best social work professional. Home-help organizers and heads of residential homes, for example, may be as well or better equipped to meet the demands of the job. Important qualities include the ability to:

- motivate staff;
- innovate and use resources creatively;
- establish credibility and respect with other agencies.

■ **Make adequate provision for management succession.** One cost of a successful programme of management development is staff movement through internal and external promotion. Strategies for preserving continuity of leadership might include:

- arrangements for staff to take on acting responsibility for more senior positions in the team;
- secondments within the organization;
- the cultivation of collective responsibility within the team (see p. 197).

Team management, the wider organization, and the community

ISSUES

In organizational terms the CSW team manager has a pivotal role; he or she is responsible for balancing the needs of the local community and the team against the needs and demands of the wider organization.

A.1 *Autonomy and accountability*

One of the major issues to emerge as a consequence of decentralization is the achievement of a balance between local autonomy of CSW teams and the need for consistent standards and overall control within the wider organization. While local needs and priorities do vary from one community to another, requiring different emphases from neighbourhood teams, there are common organizational requirements which have to be recognized. Such requirements relate to the political context in which organizations operate and the policies to which they consequently commit themselves, the budgetary situation which prevails, and other external factors such as public expectations following child abuse tragedies. (See also: Chapter 4, p. 123; Chapter 5, p. 165.)

A.2 Isolation

High levels of autonomy for local teams risk entailing isolation from the organization as a whole and in particular from relevant developments in practice in other sections and groups. Are there ways in which such isolation can be reduced or overcome without abandoning the measure of self-determination gained?

A.3 Links with the community: political dimensions

CSW teams serving clearly defined areas would seem to be more likely to become involved in political issues than traditionally organized teams. Councillors may well find it easier to make direct contact over individual cases and may come to develop a particular interest in the team serving 'their' constituency. The team, on their side, may want to gain the support and protection of their local representatives for their work. But such relationships may turn out to be full of pitfalls for the unwary. In particular, how far can contacts of this kind be developed before they are perceived as subverting the accountability of the social services department to the social services committee and the council?

A.4 Links with the community: the involvement of users

Perhaps the most important of the new relationships and links which CSW teams must aim to forge with the community is that with the users or consumers of service. Either directly or indirectly, the aims of a decentralized approach can only be served if there is greater involvement of users in the determination of needs and services. This is explicit in models of decentralization which originate from a political commitment to local democracy and implicit in an approach which is preventive and which seeks to support informal caring systems. But in either model how far can this relationship be one of account-ability to users, given the continuing hierarchical structure of the social services department?

Secondly, how does the CSW team cope with the potential tension that can be created by the client-participator dichotomy? The CSW team seeks to establish partnerships with members of the local community, to look at the resources which exist in it and to engage in the helping process people who may in differ-ent contexts be known as clients. However, the team will still be expected to fulfil statutory duties, including such potentially contentious matters as child care and mental health work and in this role will continue to be perceived as an agent of social control. (See also: Chapter 3, pp. 59, 60; Chapter 4, p. 97; Chapter 5, p. 137.)

TEAM EXPERIENCE

B.1 *Autonomy and accountability*

The experience of the contributing teams indicate the different expectations and behaviour of the partially and fully decen-tralized organizations. In those departments where only part of the organization is decentralized or where teams themselves are only partly decentralized the prevailing culture appears to be that CSW teams can go their own way so long as the *important* aspects of their work, individual cases, do not fall below minimum standards. For example, the Huntly team notes: 'Minimal levels expected are that all statutory work is carried out, i.e. reviews, court reports, etc. Most important is that child care practice is professionally competent.'

In some organizations minimum levels of performance are viewed in very broad terms. In Normanton, for example, these are defined as 'not to embarrass senior management or the committee' and accepting that 'statutory cases must match up to basic legal requirements'. The Longbenton team perceive the requirements of their wider organization in similar vein:

'Minimal satisfactory standards of team performance are expressed in terms of work on individual cases. . . . A team also has to fulfil its commitments to the area team by way of the duty rota and liaisons on behalf of the area as a whole. . . . Apart from these areas, and assuming they are being satisfactorily handled, the team has no demands made of it in terms of its work being monitored, and can therefore develop other ways of working so long as the minimum criteria are met.'

The comprehensively decentralized East Sussex social services department sets more explicit performance standards and detailed financial controls. Teams are expected to keep within agreed budgets; targets are set for residential care budgets, home-help hours, Section 1 payments and travelling expenses, and for all budgets which are within the managerial control of the CSW team manager. A management information control bulletin containing a wide range of detailed information about financial performance and services is published monthly and discussed at area, divisional, and departmental management team meetings. The Whitehawk team manager describes how this system impinges on him:

'Minimum levels of team performance that must be ensured to keep senior management satisfied are related to a whole series of client, staff, and financial issues. Reviews need to be completed on time, and are subject to disciplinary procedure. Complaints procedures, professional standards, staying within budgets, allocation of hours within residential establishments, no overtime working, no car travel excess, no subsistence claims above normal, health and safety checks, fire drills, home-help hours, staff development reviews, and many other standards need to be achieved. . . . It is in these areas in particular that the (patch) team manager role quite clearly is very different from that of the team leader.'

It is clear from all the teams, however, that so long as they operate within the standards set by the wider organization there is considerable scope for innovation both in terms of developing more appropriate responses to the needs of the community and in securing and creating resources within the CSW team. Given the resource constraints exercised in the public sector the CSW team is likely to be working within rigorously defined service limitations. Its assets, staff, home-help hours, cash, buildings, etc., are likely to be fixed. One way of securing additional resources is to look outside the organization: 'Entrepreneurial thinking about MSC projects, Pathway schemes, Community Programmes, and other projects in the field of employment all help to bring new resources to the patch team' (Whitehawk).

B.2 *Isolation*

The contributing teams do appear to be somewhat isolated in their day-to-day work from other teams and sections in their departments. In Normanton this is explained in terms of the fact that CSW was a bottom-up development in an authority still organized on more conventional lines: 'In our situation we had no alliances with other teams since we were pioneers.' But isolation also seems to be experienced in East Sussex where *all* the teams are decentralized. As the Rye contributor put it: 'The team is largely self-sufficient.' However, action can be taken to reduce isolation. All the teams emphasize the importance of regular feedback to members by management and anyone else possessing information, about developments in the wider organization. Membership of common-interest groups considering, for instance, new methods of intervention or a crisis such as the miners' strike which affects several areas covered by the local authority can also help reduce isolation. In Lochend another strategy used is for members of the sub-team to travel to the office of the area team two or three times a week to share lunch with workers there.

Further, while CSW teams may experience a sense of isolation from their own organizations they may well be developing stronger relationships elsewhere. In particular, close contacts are likely to develop with other agencies and organizations serving the local area and these may come to constitute new reference groups for the team. In Whitehawk, for instance, the team manager notes: 'The team manager peer group is no longer necessarily based in social services. It could, in fact, be with headmaster, housing manager, and others rather than team colleagues.' The same can also be said of other team members as well.

B.3 *Links with the community: political dimensions*

Contact with elected representatives is reported by all the contributing teams. Such relationships are not formalized at the local level: there are no official forums of either a consultative or executive nature. However, on an informal basis the CSW teams find that local politicians figure much more prominently in their work. In Normanton, for instance,

'local district councillors and parish councillors have been very involved with the team at the local level. The nature of the relationship is curious. On the one hand councillors come with referrals and an expectation that they will be speedily dealt with to enhance their credibility with constituents. On the other, they are often aware of their lack of knowledge of professional and organizational issues and thus shy away from becoming too embroiled in issues.'

Longbenton also describe contact over cases and other work with representatives: 'At the local level there is contact over individual clients. . . . There is also contact with councillors through involvement with local groups. This will often lead to discussions with them over policy issues.' The Rye team manager has a regular arrangement for meetings with the councillor representing the town: 'The local county councillor on the social services committee calls to see me every six to eight weeks to share perceptions of the patch and its problems.' These informal relationships with councillors are viewed positively by the teams but may have to be handled cautiously for, as the Lochend contributor put it, 'using politicians to redress departmental grievances is regarded as a cardinal sin and is not contemplated lightly although it does happen.'

B.4 *Links with the community: the involvement of users*

The team all appear to be developing closer links with users or consumers of services. Although there is at present no formal or official user representation or involvement in the team's activities, it is possible to see in the areas served by some of the CSW teams signs of the development of quasi-institutional forms of involvement. In some cases, independent voluntary organizations supported by the teams are beginning to provide a forum for users. In Normanton the Social Care Assembly of Normanton was established jointly by the team and local organizations (see Chapter 4, p. 127). The Huntly team is closely involved with a voluntary agency, the Gordon Rural Action and

Information Network (GRAIN), which acts as a forum for team members and users of service to work together: 'GRAIN is very much part of our team network and users are represented through this organization which is directly accountable to the general public at its annual general meeting.' As well as these formal links with local interests which exist in only a minority of the team areas, all the teams point out that they are frequently and regularly exposed to user views of their services through the groups they run for particular clients and through collaboration with a large number of self-help groups and other voluntary agencies.

PRACTICE GUIDELINES

C.1 *Maintaining effective relations with the wider organization*

■ **The team need to recognize the importance of the wider organization of which they are a part and the ways in which developments in the wider organization can affect them.**

● The team manager has the prime responsibility for developing this understanding: as an effective general manager it is a key part of his/her role to process information about the wider organization on behalf of the team.

● In addition, all other team members who acquire information about developments in the organization outside the team in the course of their work should be encouraged to feed it back to the team through the regular team meetings or other suitable mechanisms.

■ **The team should ensure that it is effectively represented in the wider organization.** Team managers should give management meetings a high priority in terms of preparation and engagement and seek to influence the organization through them.

■ **Teams can also have influence within the wider organization through demonstrating a willingness to be a 'test bed' for new ideas and developments.**

■ **Teams should seek to identify the basic performance**

standards required of them by the organization. Ensure that they are understood within the team. Where systems or processes are not already prescribed, establish ways of monitoring the team's performance against these standards.

■ **Maximize the flexibility of the team's operation.** The CSW team should seek to use their resources creatively in order to respond to the needs of the community they serve. They will have to find ways of operating flexibly and adaptively, ways which do not depend upon formal and official organizational processes and structures. Freed of many of the constraints of the larger, more bureaucratic organization, the local manager is in a position to use existing resources in new ways and to seek additional resources and support in ways which may be opportunistic rather than planned.

● To achieve this flexibility it is important for the team to *know their way around* the wider organization. It is important to know about budgetary systems and resource allocation processes.

● Teams should seek to identify sources of funds, e.g. grants to voluntary organizations, urban aid, special development funds, research money, trusts, etc. The use of certain traditional budget heads, e.g. home-help hours or Section 1 payments, may need to be challenged.

C.2 *Isolation*

■ **Teams should devise strategies appropriate to their own context to deal with the threat of isolation.** Some means of tackling isolation adopted by practitioners in decentralized departments are:

● building close contacts with teams serving adjacent areas, for example, based on sharing staff or resources for particular activities, and by developing joint project work;

● promoting joint training programmes within the wider organization which bring members of different teams together;

● establishing common-interest groups across the authority, relating for instance to special areas of knowledge, new methods of integration.

In pilot and priority area teams where the department otherwise remains centralized:

- seeking to establish a forum for meetings with other pioneer teams inside and outside the authority.

In both contexts:

- through regular liaison with other agencies serving the local area, building up peer support groups;
- tapping into regional and national networks exchanging information on CSW, for example, the National Institute for Social Work's Practice and Development Exchange.

C.3 *Links with the community: the political dimension*

■ **Establish the nature of team accountability to the elected representatives of the authority.** What kinds of formal contact are permitted? Can team managers and leaders, for example, communicate directly with councillors over individual cases or wider issues? Whatever the *formal* guidelines on these contacts, what discretion is allowed in *practice* in making informal contacts?

■ **Within the scope allowed by the guidelines established, seek to build close relationships with local representatives and help keep them informed of the work of the team and about local issues.**

C.4 *Links with the community: the involvement of users*

Formal representation of users or the wider community at the level served by CSW teams is not yet provided for in the British political system. Nevertheless, local teams can do much to promote relationships with both.

■ **Teams should seek to use all means at their disposal to develop contact and dialogue with the communities they serve in general and their users in particular.** Some steps that can be taken include:

- Publicize the team's work either through a team newsletter or through negotiating space in, for example, the local free paper. Ask for views.

● Hold team open days; open up the office. Attend public meetings relating to community issues; be seen to be involved.

● Work with voluntary organizations; get to know their views. Get to know the views of other professionals and the agencies which they represent.

● Use groups to get feedback; encourage them to think about the services they are receiving and what might be more appropriate ways of helping them.

● Encourage the establishment of self-help groups. Carers' groups, for example, can be very effective forums for finding out what the issues are relating to the care of a range of dependent people.

● Work with such groups to influence policy locally.

● Within existing service provision ensure that users' views are taken into account. Do residents of old people's homes, for example, have access to an official forum such as a residents' committee in which they can express their views and contribute to the running of *their* home?

ORGANIZATIONAL GUIDELINES

D.1 *Autonomy and accountability*

■ **Give front line teams the maximum feasible autonomy to apply departmental policy.** If CSW teams are to be effective they must be given the widest scope to develop their resources and respond flexibly to local needs. It may be possible to increase the degree of authority delegated as the teams develop and mature.

■ **Establish a clear system of delegation.** Greater team autonomy must not be confused with a *laissez faire* attitude on the part of senior management. The nature and limits of the responsibilities delegated to teams needs to be spelled out clearly.

■ **Set up a comprehensive two-way information system.** CSW teams are responsible and accountable to the wider organization. Information systems should be established which give them the data they need on matters such as practice guidelines, budgets, and other resources. They in turn will be expected to supply information to enable the wider organization to manage its resources, balance the needs of different localities, and plan and develop services.

■ **Organizations should ensure that there is a management structure which facilitates communication up and down the management line.** Hierarchies should be as flat as possible in order to encourage the maximum interchange and understanding between local team and central management. Local managers should be as involved as possible in the *collective management* of the organization through regular formal management meetings, specific project groups, policy planning, and service development forums.

■ **Organizations need to establish clear frameworks for CSW teams to operate in.** Such frameworks will relate primarily to policies, performance standards, and budgetary targets. The publication of comprehensive operational instructions can help this process where they are based on the realities facing front-line workers and embody sufficient flexibility to respond to changing conditions.

It is important that the local team is aware of what is expected of it and of what direction it should be taking in its overall development; the tendency not to be able to 'see the wood for the trees' at the local level is difficult to avoid. Given a clear view of the overall strategy of the organization, the values on which it is based, and explicit performance standards, teams will be able to determine their priorities locally and to establish practical objectives.

■ **Teams should be given the maximum feasible level of control over resources.** Local budgets should be established. Successful organizations tend to delegate responsibility in order to achieve flexibility in response to local conditions. Innovation and experimentation will not flourish where there is tight central control and no local access to resources.

D.2 *Isolation*

■ **Take action to minimize the isolation of front-line teams.**

Organizations seeking to decentralize on a wide scale, establishing neighbourhood offices, will need to be aware of the potential for isolation of CSW teams. For some organizations this could become a serious problem with implications for staffing and recruitment. Some consideration will need to be given to how both social and professional isolation might be minimized.

● Encourage inter-team contact to share ideas and experiences.
● Develop good communications within the organization through departmental meetings, management papers, policy documents, bulletins, newsletters or in-house magazines.
● Bring people together through training and specific task or project groups.

■ **Take action to minimize the isolation of specialists.** The number of specialist staff in decentralized organizations is likely to be reduced and they are likely to be spread more thinly over the areas served. CSW should enable their work to be more effectively integrated with that of generic front-line staff but they may become more isolated from professional colleagues sharing their own specialism. To counter the negative consequences of such isolation, encourage the development of specialist interest groups within the authority, support contacts with specialists in other agencies, and facilitate attendance at training and refresher courses.

D.3 *Links with the community: the political dimension*

■ **Establish guidelines on contact between local teams and elected representatives.**

● Formal processes should be developed on as local as possible a basis.
● Teams should be in no doubt concerning their scope and freedom in official dealings with politicians.

D.4 *Links with the community: the involvement of users*

■ **Encourage teams to develop a dialogue with their users and the wider local community.** Ultimately, if the values of a decentralized approach are to be carried through to a logical conclusion, it will be necessary to create structures which enable the people in the areas served to participate fully in the management of their affairs, including the personal social services. The political and constitutional issues involved in bringing about such changes mean that they are hardly likely to be achieved in the near future. But there is no reason, in the interim, why management should not stimulate the development of as much contact and discussion as possible, and so help prepare the way for more radical change in the future.

Evaluation

ISSUES

Evaluation in organizations is concerned with establishing the extent to which organizational objectives are achieved. In almost all organizations it is possible to make a useful distinction between the basic objective of survival, what Miller and Rice (1967) have called the *primary task* which must be given first priority, and other objectives which can be pursued once survival is assured – the *mission* task. However, in a non-profit organization, such as a statutory social services department, where the ultimate test of profit and loss cannot meaningfully be applied, it is often difficult to identify relevant measures of performance which can form the basis of evaluation and to agree appropriate priorities between different objectives. Not only may views on the *purposes* of a service differ – for instance, should it seek to be primarily preventive or should it concentrate on dealing with those already in crisis? – but it may be difficult to define precisely the nature of the outcome desired – for example, what would constitute effective preventive or reactive work in a particular field?

Given such difficulties, and an increasingly constrained political and economic climate, it is perhaps understandable that the managers of such non-profit organizations have tended to concentrate on evaluation which is mainly limited to *input* measures, focusing in particular on areas of practice which are felt to be most likely to have an impact on their public credibility and ultimately their survival. In the personal social services this has meant the use of input data on referrals, home-help hours, bed occupancy, and comparisons of the costs of different types of intervention. It has led to a particular emphasis on inputs in the most politically sensitive areas, notably child care, but again with a concentration on input data such as the numbers in residential and foster care, the proportion of reviews carried out on time, and so on, rather than on the much more difficult questions of the quality and effectiveness of the interventions made. This approach tends to have been reinforced, particularly in its 'value for money' aspects, by the work of the government's Audit Commission (Audit Commission 1985; 1986).

In this section we consider how these issues have affected the contributing teams' development and practice of CSW. We then suggest guidelines, based in part on their experience and in part on expected future trends, on how CSW teams and the organizations managing them might develop evaluation of their work. It seems clear to us that the development of CSW teams represents an opportunity for organizations to establish systems of evaluation which go beyond measures of input without becoming too embroiled in detailed evaluative studies of broad service areas. First, the evaluation of the team as a unit means that it is possible to examine the relationship between the agency and a particular community. This would seem to have rather more potential for success than attempting to evaluate the effectiveness of an organization through an examination of the impact of individual workers on individual clients. Secondly, CSW teams are much closer to the consumer and it is through the greater involvement of users of service that evaluation will attract the most significance.

These themes are reflected in the two main issues which emerge from the experience of the contributing teams (see also Chapter 4, pp. 96–114):

A.1 the nature of the objectives and related methods of evaluation prescribed by the wider organization, and the manner in which these impinge on the operation of the CSW team;

A.2 the evaluative criteria and processes used within the teams to assess their work in areas not assessed through the evaluation required by the wider organization.

TEAM EXPERIENCE

B.1 *Evaluation of team performance by the department*

In all departments this appears to be limited principally to input measures. However, it was evident that these measures were considerably more complex and wide-ranging in East Sussex, the one department to have comprehensively decentralized its services. This department, also, is the only one to have begun to move into closer scrutiny of more qualitative aspects of performance through the institution of departmental inspections.

Teams were asked about the *minimal* standards of performance which they had to meet to satisfy their departments – in other words, their primary tasks. In Normanton 'minimum levels of team performance are of two kinds. Firstly, the requirement not to embarrass senior management or the committee. Secondly, statutory cases must match up to basic legal requirements.' Similar criteria appeared to operate in most of the other teams. For instance, the Longbenton team leader commented: 'Minimal satisfactory standards of team performance are expressed in terms of work on individual cases. This work is quite closely monitored in some contexts (NAI, statutory child care, admissions of elderly to residential care) by means of procedures and reviews.'

In East Sussex, as we have noted, a longer list of performance criteria is mentioned by teams. The Rye team, for example, listed: 'Child in care reviews, general response to referrals within a few days, regular case reviews and clear case planning; management of budgets within targets including all aspects of residential care (staffing, food, capitation, etc.), home-help hours, stationery, travelling expenses, etc.'

These and other data about areas, teams, and individual establishments are published in a monthly management control information package. This, where relevant, compares targets and performance as, for instance, in actual and allowed expenditure under the Children and Young Persons Act (1969), bed occupancy levels, children in care reviews completed and uncompleted.

However, beyond such *input* measures none of the teams believed their work was being systematically reviewed by senior managers. While some regretted this, all acknowledged that the present system left them considerable freedom: 'Beyond this area teams may develop according to local needs and tastes. Thus the team manager has considerable scope for innovation' (Normanton). 'Apart from these areas, and assuming they are being satisfactorily handled, the team has no demands made of it in terms of its work being monitored, and can therefore develop other ways of working so long as the minimum criteria are met' (Longbenton).

B.2 *Team evaluation*

All the teams use team meetings to evaluate their work on a regular basis. The teams regard internal evaluation as a particularly important precondition of their development: 'Internal methods of evaluation take the form of regular team workshops and navel-contemplating sessions to see if the thing is working. As a matter of team practice, all areas of work must be subjected to constant review. Weekly team meetings in Lochend are unsparingly self-critical of the way the structure is functioning or otherwise' (Lochend).

Most of them also set aside whole days when they can meet away from the office for a major review of their work. The Rye team, for example, 'take a day out once per year to review objectives, team systems, etc., and set new objectives. We can review performance against minimum standards, objectives achieved or not, mitigating or other factors within our control or not.'

The importance of preventive work is widely acknowledged but difficulties were found in producing convincing ways of measuring it. The Normanton contributor notes:

'One major problem with using objective criteria for evaluation is the fact that as the department is largely geared to caseload and reactive measuring techniques, indirect team work is not considered relevant for measuring purposes. Thus prevention techniques lack effective evaluation tools. The tendency is to work more impressionistically than is desirable.'

However, another team uses information on type of referral as an indicator of progress in this area: 'As a team I think we measure our value by non-crisis referrals which show the value of the preventive work that we do' (Huntly).

The teams do not claim that the methods they use are always very systematic or that record keeping is always adequate. The Longbenton team leader notes:

'Informal evaluation is a continuous process and takes place internally. We have used a day-out technique plus regular team and section head meetings. Casework, issues, and projects are discussed at team meetings and in individual supervision sessions. Minutes are taken at team meetings and so they provide a record of developments. We are not systematic in this, and there is no pattern in our reviewing, which is undertaken rather subjectively and without our having formally defined our criteria. Implicitly, our criteria are based on an improved standard and range of services to enable people to remain in their own homes for as long as they wish.'

PRACTICE GUIDELINES

C.1 *Evaluation and the wider organization*

■ **Establish procedures or methods for responding to the evaluation demands of the wider organization.** Meeting these demands is likely to be a precondition for freedom of action in other areas and should be given a high priority by the team. When the particular criteria used by the wider organization are experienced as counter-productive in terms of the effective practice of CSW, seek to have them modified or changed and promote evaluation which is *relevant* to community social work.

C.2 *Team evaluation*

■ **Identify appropriate objectives as part of the overall team plan.** These objectives should be clear and as measurable as possible so that it can be established whether or not they have been achieved. More detailed guidelines on objective setting are included in the section of this chapter on Change and development (p. 228).

■ **Agree an order of priority between the various team objectives.**

■ **Establish what information needs to be collected in order to determine whether or not team objectives have been achieved.** For example, if one of the team's objectives is to minimize crisis situations through early identification and intervention it will need to ensure that it has access to information about referrals and referral patterns.

■ **Formalize the evaluation processes within the team.** Use team meetings to examine and discuss issues relating to the team's performance. Establish specific review sessions in order to examine and review the team plan and the range of objectives contained within it. Each major activity or initiative should be undertaken within a framework of written objectives and detailed plans. There should be a commitment to review these on a regular basis so that evaluation in terms of the stated objectives is an integral part of the activity.

■ **Examine the methods of evaluation developed in other teams and other local authorities and consider their relevance for your team.** These may include not only methods devised in other CSW teams but also those instituted in other contexts such as the Kent Community Care scheme (Challis and Davies 1985), the Bexley Community Care scheme (Chambers 1986), and the Program Analysis of Service Systems (Wolfensberger and Glenn 1975).

■ **Develop relationships with colleges, research institutes, etc.** Seek their help in devising and undertaking evaluative studies, especially in the more complex and time-consuming areas of assessment.

■ **Seek the views and opinions of others** – colleagues, other professionals, and most importantly the users themselves. Establish local forums involving a range of interested professionals, volunteers, and local residents in order to discuss and debate the work being undertaken in the community and to get feedback about the work of the team.

ORGANIZATIONAL GUIDELINES

D.1 *Evaluation and the wider organization*

■ **Evaluation needs to take place in the context of clear policies and defined directions.** Teams cannot be expected to perform well in organizational terms unless there has been clear agreement concerning their goals and priorities. There need to be processes, therefore, through which they can develop goals appropriate to the organization's policies and strategies.

■ **Organizations should seek to devise performance measures which are compatible with the goals of community social work.** Measures should be modified to emphasize preventive, not merely reactive, work and, where possible, output rather than input data.

● For example, where an elderly people's home is managed by a CSW team, instead of its performance being evaluated in terms of the beds occupied, its changing role may need to be recognized and judged in terms of the overall number of people being supported by the home, both residentially and in the community. There may have to be an adjustment of input measures, e.g. bed numbers, in order to reflect the reality of the reduced occupancy required by a flexible respite care policy and to allow staff to engage in various forms of outreach work.

● Evaluation strategies might include periodic inspections of key areas of service delivery, regular exercises focusing, for example, on the quality of care within residential establishments. Such quality-of-care exercises should be based on identified expectations concerning the standards which should apply, e.g. flexible meal times, residents' rights to retain their pension book, and residents' own views of the service.

● Strategies can also be developed on the basis of normalization principles and established processes such as PASS can be used to evaluate a range of services according to specific criteria (Wolfensberger and Glenn 1975).

D.2 *Team evaluation*

■ **CSW teams should be encouraged to document their work to facilitate evaluation.** The production of reports on community social work initiatives is as relevant an undertaking as case recording in respect of work with individual cases. Organizations should expect to see team plans, incorporating objectives and a review of performance. They should also expect to see reports on major initiatives and projects undertaken by the team.

■ **Teams should be encouraged to involve users and others in determining their impact on the community or the success of**

individual initiatives. Methods for encouraging such involvement might include:

● regular consultation with users in groups established by the team, for instance, mothers' groups, teenage groups, carers' groups;
● regular consultation with people in the care of the authority, e.g. residents in homes for the elderly or handicapped, children in foster care;
● the establishment of a team annual general meeting open to the local community where a report of the year's work is presented and plans for the coming year are discussed.

Change and development

ISSUES

A.1 *Education and training*

One of the most difficult challenges faced by CSW team managers in effecting change and developing new methods of working is the paucity of training in CSW, both in formal social work education courses and within local authorities through in-house training. There is little in the way of established models for CSW team managers to draw on and the task of equipping their staff to take on different roles and to work in different ways is one which places considerable demands upon them. While for the most part the contributing teams have achieved a great deal without significant support through education and training, it is unlikely that CSW can be developed on a wide scale without it. (See also: Chapter 4, p. 115; Chapter 5, p. 138.)

A.2 *Strategies for change and development*

Even when more training becomes available, much of the staff development and many of the new practices required in the change to CSW will have to be introduced 'in-house' as part of the day-to-day work of teams. A number of key operational activities can be identified which lie at the heart of effective team management and which any strategy for change towards CSW at team level would need to embody. These include setting objectives, developing a team approach, establishing systems to attain team objectives, joint working with individuals and agencies across organizational boundaries, and reviewing team performance. (See also: Chapter 4, p. 115; Chapter 5, p. 138.)

A.3 *The transition to CSW*

The combination of workload pressure within teams, the level of training resources in most local authorities, the limited relevance of training on most qualifying courses, and the varied nature of CSW itself presents a formidable challenge to the development of a decentralized approach to social services. It appears that the wide-scale adoption of CSW is inhibited by the difficulty which teams encounter in escaping the gravitational force of client-centred methods of working. It is often easier for workers to give priority to casework and to operate within established patterns of service delivery. In consequence, there is a real danger that CSW teams will remain in a transitional state where, although committed to a CSW approach, they will find themselves simply perpetuating previous models at a local level. (See also: Chapter 4, p. 97; Chapter 5, pp. 138, 164, 182.)

TEAM EXPERIENCE

B.1 *Education and training*

The picture conveyed by most of the contributors is one of very limited training support and overall strategy for training within the teams. The comment from Longbenton appears to be quite typical: 'The team has no policy for training and development beyond allowing . . . various members to undertake training courses.' For the most part the training resources available to the teams are limited and they have been forced to find their own mechanisms for training and support. These have included team days out, visits to other projects, use of outside consultants, links with colleges, and the use of any appropriate courses. Some of the teams found that while their training developments had no relevant expertise to offer them in the field of CSW, they were very willing to help them identify external sources of help and arrange *ad hoc* programmes involving these.

In general, however, the initiative had to be taken by the CSW teams and the resources available were very limited. The main exception to this picture is East Sussex where there has been a substantial investment in training and the change to decentralized working. Initially a training and development officer was allocated to each team, serving four or five patch teams, and two training centres were set up based on the campuses of a local polytechnic. In addition all managers were involved in a Local Government Training Board management skills course. The training and development officers aimed to help meet the range of training needs of staff at all levels and only a limited amount of their energies could be deployed in promoting training specifically related to CSW. It was possible, nevertheless, to engage in team-building exercises in several of the areas. A further initiative was a development programme in which teams worked on 'demonstration' projects designed to give them an early experience of community-orientated work and to make it possible for the learning to be shared between teams (Hadley, Dale, and Sills 1984).

B.2 *Strategies for change and development*

The contributing teams demonstrate some involvement in the key change activities outlined in A.2 above. The importance of a team approach and of joint working are widely acknowledged by the teams; team meetings, team days out and team discussion of issues are commonly employed techniques. 'The skill of making things happen through co-operation and interaction with the community requires the pulling together of many disparate pieces of information and the linking of people and groups who do not in the first place necessarily see any connection between themselves' (Longbenton). Joint working as the basis of developing a CSW approach is a priority activity for all the contributing teams.

B.3 *The transition to CSW*

Even for established teams the practice of CSW is in danger of remaining a marginal activity. Statutory work because of its immediacy assumes a high priority and cannot be ignored. If developing CSW is seen as additional work, then the issue of finding space for it has to be confronted. 'The single greatest bedevilling feature is the problem of not being able to see the developmental wood for the statutory trees, and not being in a position to breathe life into the magical 20 per cent margin within which to promote community development work' (Lochend). Other teams face the same problem and the creation of the space in which to develop fully a CSW approach appears to be a struggle.

PRACTICE GUIDELINES

C.1 *Education and training*

■ **Develop a strategy for training which reflects teams' plans and objectives.** Such a strategy might include:

- team discussions of specific issues relating to CSW.
- the use of regular team meetings to plan and review work;
- team days out to examine an issue in depth;
- the use of projects as a vehicle for learning (see, for example, Hadley, Dale, and Sills 1984);
- the use of outside 'change agents';
- contact with other CSW teams and practitioners;
- selective use of external courses;
- involvement of colleges and other higher education institutions.

C.2 *Strategies for change and development*

Teams, particularly those in the early stages of development, should focus on the following activities as key elements in the process of change and development:

■ **Teams should set themselves clear overall aims.** The first step in setting up a programme of change and development must be the identification of the main goals of the team. For a team in the early stages of adopting a CSW approach, certain aims are likely to be fundamental, including:

- developing a team approach;
- getting to know the community or neighbourhood;
- making links with others working in the community.

■ **Express these aims in terms of specific objectives.** For example, to get to know the community or neighbourhood is a broad undertaking comprising a wide range of subsidiary activities. In order to achieve this aim it will be necessary to identify and express these activities, through, for instance:

- talking to local people about needs, problems, etc.
- talking to other workers, volunteers, etc.
- collecting information about population characteristics, etc.

In stating these objectives a team will in effect be outlining a plan of action where time-scales can be established and responsibilities for specific tasks allocated. The plan of action can be monitored, reviewed, and if necessary modified. Setting specific objectives in this way need not be a complicated activity and can be accomplished in five key steps:

- Agree broad aims to be achieved within a specific time-scale.
- Establish the steps that need to be taken to achieve these aims. Express these steps in terms of objectives. Objectives are statements of intent. They should begin with 'to' and involve 'doing' something.
- Consider these objectives. What steps need to be taken to achieve them? Express these in terms of further objectives. Repeat the process until specific *tasks* are clear.
- Agree who does what by when. Write it down so that everyone is clear and progress can be reviewed.
- Review progress. Objectives should be measurable so that it is possible to determine whether or not they have been achieved.

Agreed aims and objectives, reflecting the most important activities the team wants to engage in, should be incorporated into a team plan. They should reflect the most important activities the team want to engage in over a specific time period. The team plan should be presented in an easily digestible form and should be reviewed regularly. Its development and implementation should be a shared process involving team members. A special meeting should be convened to ensure that sufficient time is allocated for the review; it should not be squeezed into other meetings.

■ **Promote the development of a team approach.** There are a number of simple ways in which a team approach can be promoted and developed:

● Establish regular contact points for all team members through team meetings. Where the team has bases in more than one setting, e.g. an old people's home, a day centre, a fieldwork office, rotate the venue to take in each workplace.
● Ensure a regular exchange of information, and hence understanding, about the jobs of each team member.
● Enable joint discussion of the problems of individuals and groups in the community to take place. Encourage 'new' solutions to established problems.
● Set up procedures within the team which enable information about the community to be collected and shared and to which all members can contribute.
● Establish a directory of skills, resources, interests, and needs of team members.
● Work collaboratively on specific tasks, e.g. establishing team objectives, compiling a community resources directory, initiating a community development project.
● Agree to spend time together at regular intervals in order to examine and develop the team's functioning. Meet away from the office and the telephone.

■ **Establish support systems which reflect the needs of the team and which are appropriate to a CSW approach.**

● Examine your work handling systems. Do they fit the philosophy of a CSW approach? Are you still operating a referral → allocation → caseload model? What could you change about this which would enable work to be shared and deprivatized and which would help you to develop more effective responses to needs?
● Establish systems for recording information about the neighbourhood, its needs and resources, and about your workloads. Use large-scale maps and coloured pins on acetate sheets to record types of problem, referrals, workers involved, resources, etc. This will give the team an overview of its work. Keep a list or card index of key resources and contacts.
● Establish good communication systems with the team – regular meetings, newsletters, wide distribution of minutes of meetings, plans, statements of objectives, organizational policies, etc.

■ **Seek to influence systems in the wider organization.** Crucial to the effective operation of CSW are systems which the team may not have the authority to establish on its own initiative. For example, the CSW team may need to lobby senior management to establish or obtain: local information systems on services and clients; local budgetary/financial control systems; access to flexible and responsive personnel systems for recruitment and employee relations.

■ **Teams should develop links with other people working locally and seek to collaborate with them in providing a range of services.**

● Use links with others to develop the team's knowledge and understanding of the community. Share information about needs and resources. The more successful the team is in getting to know its community and establishing a range of contacts, the more it will become known and trusted, and hence accessible.

● Engage key people in identifying which statutory and voluntary agencies it is most important for the team initially to link with. Work out the most appropriate strategies for developing links. These could include: visits to agency establishments, e.g. schools, clinics, police stations, sheltered housing, DHSS offices, housing offices, etc.; invitations to informal lunches or coffee mornings; liaison schemes, e.g. with GPs: offers of interviewing space in the team office for other agencies.

● Develop links made in respect of individual clients, e.g. at case conferences. Use these opportunities to talk informally about broader issues.

● Where larger agencies are involved with few local representatives, teams should work with colleagues in other teams to develop strategies of liaison.

● Recruit locally where possible and appropriate.

● Identify a specific activity which is time-limited and realistic in which you can involve other statutory and voluntary workers and local residents. Collective achievement in pursuit of a common task is an effective way of building links.

● Consolidate links in the neighbourhood by the development of more permanent liaison machinery, e.g. a volunteer forum, a local planning group, etc.

● Have something to offer – training for members of a tenants' association in how to run meetings, talks for volunteers, help to community groups in setting objectives or designing forms, photocopying facilities, etc.

■ **Establish a formal and regular review of team performance in relation to identified objectives.** Take a day out. Divide it into two parts: (a) review of performance over the last twelve months; (b) the preparation of plans for the coming year.

(a) Reviewing past performance. Consider the following:
 ● Have objectives been achieved? If not, why not?
 ● Were these objectives realistic or appropriate in the light of experience?
 ● Should different objectives be set?
 ● Were services being provided in a more preventive or community-orientated way?
 ● Has the team's knowledge of the community increased?
 ● Are working relationships within the team more effective? Is there more integration of roles and responsibilities?
 ● Have new links with other statutory and voluntary workers, and with users and other local residents, been established? Have existing ones been improved?

(b) Planning future performance. Reviewing performance will be easier if the team has a plan which focuses on the development of a CSW approach. Ensure, therefore, in the second part of the review day that the team develops a plan with clear and realistic objectives for the coming twelve months. Agree how to tackle the detailed work of preparing a team plan. Seek help if necessary from training or research staff, contacts in local polytechnics or universities, etc. The planning process will incorporate the following activities:

● bringing together overall policies and priorities of the wider organization, information from local needs and resources assessment exercises, local knowledge, and budgeting and resource information in order to establish team priorities for working in more locally focused ways;
● the identification of those areas which can realistically be tackled – these may be *problem based*, e.g. drug abuse, *geographically based*, e.g. high levels of deprivation in one

particular block of flats, or *team based*, e.g. the need to develop closer links with voluntary organizations.

C.3 *The transition to CSW*

■ **The transition from etablished patterns of work to a CSW approach requries the creation of significant space based on the management of work and workloads.**

● Plan to create space. Since it is not possible to impose a moratorium on existing work while the team develops other methods and approaches, the creation of space can only be achieved through a process of planned and gradual change in respect of established work patterns. There is little experience and few precedents on which to base such a process. The following steps are only a beginning but they will help.

● Use group supervision wherever possible. This will not only save time but will reinforce notions of 'team', help you to share information, learn from each other, and contribute to developing an overview of the community.

● Review all cases. Can you identify specific objectives for each? If not, consider whether they should remain open. Are other case objectives appropriate or realistic? Modify them as necessary.

● Agree a format for case recording to replace lengthy narrative accounts.

● Set aside time each week (minimum of half a day) for pursuing CSW objectives.

■ **Avoid developing CSW as a separate activity which is undertaken alongside or in addition to 'real' work.** If this approach is adopted CSW will always remain marginal as there will never be enough time to devote to its development. Seyd and her colleagues have developed a useful continuum for the development of CSW which emphasizes this point (Seyd *et al.* 1984: 41–5). This suggests that the traditional approach to social work is from *outside the community*. Social work which adds a certain amount of community work to an otherwise case work model can be defined as *social work alongside the community*. Only when individual and community approaches have become fully integrated can we properly talk about *social work from within the community* or *community social work*. (See also: Chapter 5, p. 147.)

■ **Aim to integrate established work patterns with CSW**. Rather than attempting to 'squeeze out' time from existing work in order to undertake CSW, teams need to convert these work patterns into new ways of responding. Simply to overlay one system on top of another will ensure that the creation of sufficient space to sustain both remains an insoluble problem. (See also: Chapter 5, p. 153.)

ORGANIZATIONAL GUIDELINES

D.1 *Education and training*

■ **Programmes for decentralization and the adoption of community-orientated methods of working should be backed by adequate training and development resources.**

■ **To ensure sufficient priority is given to training and development, ultimate responsibility for their implementation should be vested in line management.**

■ **Wherever possible training programmes should be integrated into the daily activities of the CSW teams rather than being treated as separate and discrete.** The project method is one well-proved way of achieving such integration.

■ **Encourage the exchange of learning within the department.** This can be achieved through such methods as common training programmes, seminars, inter-team visits, internal secondments of staff, information bulletins, and joint projects.

■ **Build links with other departments and agencies involved in community-orientated initiatives.** Back learning exchange beyond the boundaries of the department and authority, using similar methods to those for supporting exchanges within it.

■ **Support teams in initiating their own training and development programmes.**

D.2 *Change and development*

■ **Establishing the conditions for change:** it has been suggested from the experience of the management of change in a local authority which has pioneered decentralization in this country that there are a number of key components which are likely to determine the success of attempts to introduce major changes in methods of working (Hadley, Dale, and Sills 1984: 146–60). Any programme of change needs:

1. *Definition.* Define the nature of the aims of the change in a manner that is shared in and understood by all those involved.
2. *Legitimation.* Legitimate the new methods of working, with all the problems and risks they may involve.
3. *Facilitation.* Facilitate learning and development by providing wherever possible the necessary extra resources, whether these involve time, advice, and expertise, or additional expenditure.
4. *Motivation.* Motivate staff to carry through the changes by giving a high priority to their achievement, by gearing the programme to give individuals and groups opportunities to share in defining its aims and methods, and to undertake satisfying and rewarding activities as a part of it.
5. *Sharing.* Share the processes and experiences of change. It is important that both vertically – between different levels of management and staff – and horizontally – across teams and departments – the programme is experienced as a common challenge, rather than something imposed by 'them' on 'us'.
6. *Integration.* Integrate the activities involved into the ongoing work of the organization. Resist the tendency for special change programmes to be viewed as separate and distinct from day-to-day concerns and as having little relevance to long-term practice.

■ **Require all CSW teams to establish their own aims and objectives within the framework of organizational policies.** These should be written down and made available throughout the organization and to its users.

■ **Require all CSW teams to establish organizational systems and methods of evaluation related to their aims and objectives.** Set up procedures for regular review of team progress and for introducing changes in the light of these reviews.

■ **Seek to establish performance indicators within the**

organization which go beyond conventional input measures and reflect the attainment of CSW objectives. Wherever possible such indicators should be devised in close collaboration with the teams: if they are to contribute to the successful development of CSW they must make sense to the front-line workers as well as to senior management.

Concluding comment

Within the framework set out in the introduction, this chapter has attempted to provide an overview of some of the most important challenges facing management and teams in launching and developing CSW. It is not intended as a carefully programmed plan of action – taken as such it might induce either a nervous breakdown or instant retreat into the safety of old ways! Rather it offers a range of practices and initiatives which need to be considered. Managers and teams must decide their own starting-points and priorities and would be wise not to expect to be able to achieve too much too quickly. While CSW overlaps in many ways with more traditional forms of social work and social services, it involves some fundamental shifts in attitudes and practice which can only develop with time and experience.

7 Review and future directions

This final chapter has two main themes. First, we return to the critical questions raised about community social work (CSW) in Chapter 1. Secondly we consider the future development of CSW in terms both of the levels at which it may be initiated and of its evolution as a method of intervention.

In a sense this book as a whole can be taken as a commentary on the issues and criticisms discussed in Chapter 1. In particular, Chapters 3–6 have provided detailed discussion of most of the points raised. Here we seek only to review the argument on some of the more salient questions.

Community assumptions

CSW is not based on a rose-coloured vision of the nature of local social organization, or 'community'. Indeed, part of its very strength as an approach is the acknowledgement of the *variety* of communities and the kinds of relationships that exist within them, and the ability of CSW teams from their vantage-point at neighbourhood level to identify and respond to such differences. The experience of the contributing teams has illustrated how CSW teams can gain and up-date detailed knowledge of the particular communities they serve and how their methods of intervention have been shaped to take account of both their strengths and weaknesses.

Staffing

The recruitment and development of staff with appropriate commitment and skills are central issues for the future of CSW, particularly in the critical period of transition from more conventional methods of social work. The experience of practitioners suggests, not surprisingly, that the greatest problems are experienced with the staff who have the largest investment in traditional systems, namely the qualified social workers. Nevertheless, as the contributing teams have shown, with good support, time, and patience, new methods can be developed.

Once they have become established, they can create a momentum of their own. Experience in the authorities that have actively promoted change to CSW has illustrated how well-thought-out department training initiatives can aid the transition to new methods of working. There is also increasing evidence that the universities and colleges responsible for the training of social workers are beginning to give CSW a more central place in their teaching and that a growing number of newly qualified workers are actively seeking posts in CSW teams.

Relationships with users
Practice indicates that the issue of confidentiality is much less problematic than some critics have feared. It *can* cause special problems when teams are working closely with local communities but in the experience of the contributing teams it does not often do so. In particular, they point to the uselessness of blanket assumptions about what confidentiality involves and emphasize the need to negotiate the worker-user relationship afresh in each area served, in a way that reflects the culture of each different setting.

Team experience suggests the importance of facing up squarely to the care/control dilemma as it is encountered in the context of CSW and not trying to avoid the uncomfortable conflicts that may be involved by hiving off the controlling activities to specialists based outside the locality. It is also worth stressing two positive aspects of practical experience in this area. First, as more preventive methods take effect, intervention as controller becomes necessary less frequently. Second, people living in the local communities served by the teams often show themselves to be very aware of the need for team intervention and can frequently be supportive of the team in the action they take. More problems are reported in cases where the team feel that *no* intervention is justified but local opinion disagrees.

Participation
None of the teams contributing to this book is located in any of the authorities currently seeking to develop formal structures for sharing control of services with neighbourhood councils or forums. Nevertheless, their experience of working closely with a wide range of users and other people who have had little experience of collective action points to other ways in which

community empowerment can develop. The teams have helped in the establishment of numerous local groups, some focused on mutual aid (e.g. tenants' associations, single parents' and carers' groups), some with more general aims, such as neighbourhood associations. These have not only served the immediate purposes for which they were established but have often proved important in increasing people's awareness of wider issues and in giving them the confidence and strength to seek to influence them. In the broader context of local politics and service organizations, these are modest developments. Yet the development of such personal participation in community affairs may in the end be even more significant in affecting people's perceptions of themselves as proactive citizens with the potential to exert some influence on their local world, than the formal establishment of representative systems of neighbourhood democracy in which few can have direct involvement.

Equity
The diversity of local areas and differences in their capacities to cope with problems, as well as variations in the strengths of different social services teams, is well evidenced in practice. However, the CSW approach, if it is systematically applied, far from reinforcing these influences for inequitable treatment, should work to overcome them. The department deploying CSW teams, assuming an adequate information system, has a wealth of local data at its disposal on the relevant needs of different localities and on the capacities of its own teams. It is, therefore, well placed to adjust its inputs to compensate for the inequities revealed, and to continue to do so as further changes take place over time.

Skills
The experience of the contributing teams suggests that anxiety about the ability of workers to cope with the wide range of tasks involved in CSW is not generally justified. The scope of CSW *is* wide but, unlike specialist work, the different elements tend to be reinforcing because they are not compartmentalized. Further, the single-handed practitioner is a rarity in CSW. The approach is pre-eminently group- or team-based; consequently the strengths of all those involved are orchestrated. It should be emphasized that the worker in the CSW team is not expected to

deal with *everything*. Specialists, covering client groups which form small minorities of departmental caseloads, dealing with more esoteric methods of intervention, and with access to resources outside the usual scope of the team, continue to be required in a CSW strategy.

Management

Management in CSW is much more challenging than the limited administrative roles often involved in the leadership of traditional teams. Yet arguably the kinds of skills required are no more demanding than those needed to run any small business in the commercial world, an activity undertaken successfully by tens of thousands of people throughout the country. It is therefore not remarkable, perhaps, that competent people have been found to fill the posts of managers or team leaders in CSW and that most have apparently thrived in the work. This has been true not only of the limited number of bottom-up and pilot/priority-area initiatives, but also of the widespread developments involved when whole authorities have embarked on decentralization. It may be a defect of the traditional bureaucratic systems that we have relied on in the past that they have consistently underestimated the capacity of people at all levels to grow and develop in response to the challenge of more demanding jobs.

Future directions

We conclude with consideration of two aspects of future development: where it might take place, and the factors likely to affect its form and prevalence.

STARTING-POINTS

There may be a temptation to believe that CSW can only be initiated where the conditions for development are just right. For example, it must have the support of the local authority, the resources of a local office, adequate personnel, and the unanimous agreement of all the staff to be involved. Desirable though all these conditions may be, experience suggests that they are rarely, if ever, all available at one time and to insist on waiting for them may be an excuse for permanent inaction. In practice, significant change is seldom achieved in social organizations without elements of struggle and conflict. The examples of the pioneers in this field show that, where the innovators possess sufficient commitment and skill, major advances can sometimes be made towards the introduction of CSW in a wide range of settings and at different organizational levels, even in the face of indifference or hostility.

Those who want to embark on the development of CSW, therefore, should be opportunistic in the best sense of the word, making their first moves where and whenever the occasion allows. At one level this could be in individual practice. Or it could involve a team initiative, a pilot or priority area, or the adoption of new policies by the department or the local authority as a whole.

Individual practice

Even traditionally organized teams may provide some opportunity for community-related work. For example, a social worker dealing with a number of clients with similar problems on the same estate could adopt CSW methods in place of casework by, for instance, setting up groups and collaborating closely with locally based agencies and workers. The successful development of such practice may be the basis for persuading other members of the team to shift their own work more in the same direction and moving the team as a whole towards CSW.

Team-level initiatives

The examples of Longbenton, Normanton, and Huntly in this book have shown the very considerable scope that can exist at team level for the introduction of CSW methods within departments that are still generally organized on traditional lines. Commitment and political skill would appear to be the essential prerequisites for success in these circumstances.

Pilot- and priority-area teams

In some circumstances departments which are cautious about making any comprehensive commitment to CSW can be convinced of the value of limited involvement through pilot experiments or the application of the method to areas of special need. The Docklands, Honor Oak, and Lochend teams contributing to this book offer good examples and could be used to argue the value of this starting-point.

Departmental and inter-departmental schemes

Projects at these levels offer the widest scope for change. By the same token, as the experience of authorities who have attempted to move too fast at this level has shown, they are likely to require lengthy planning and negotiation if they are to succeed, including detailed discussion with staff and full political endorsement.

NEW DIRECTIONS

CSW as we understand the term means more than simply a set of skills or a particular method of delivering services to clients. It is founded on a fundamentally different conception of the relationship between public services and the people they serve from that traditionally associated with the post-war welfare state. Like the traditional model, it too is built on the assumption of collective responsibility for dealing with a range of social problems and their impact on individual citizens. But its exponents are critical of the limiting and compartmentalized features of the conventional bureaucratic and professional social services and believe that their interventions are often more disabling than helping in their end results.

In contrast, CSW seeks to develop services which respond sensitively to differences in local conditions, which interrelate flexibly with other services both formal and informal, and which are experienced by those receiving them as relevant and enabling.

In essence CSW is about *dialogue* in the sense that the educator Paulo Freire uses the term (Freire 1974). That is, dialogue between the social worker and the user, dialogue between the organizer and the neighbourhood, dialogue concerned with shaping and amending services in response to the needs and growth of the community. And it is also, of necessity, about the changes in the locus of power and decision making both within services and between them and their users. Understood in this context, CSW will be as much subject to change in the future as the services it currently provides.

The question remains, however, whether the conditions for

such developments are within the realms of possibility. Within the social services today CSW is still a minority activity. It fits uncomfortably with traditional bureaucratic and professional structures and processes and has mainly developed in spite of them, rather than with their support. Here and there, and in increasing numbers, more innovative local authorities are seeking to redesign their organizations so that they positively foster the development of community-orientated methods of working. But where traditional ideas and structures predominate, the development of CSW is likely to continue to be slow, piecemeal business exploiting gaps or quirks of the existing systems, but hampered by an overarching framework designed for the old orthodox methods, and always at risk of being curbed or discredited.

In the longer run, therefore, the future of CSW is likely to depend on the extent to which the traditional systems themselves are brought into question and alternative strategies are shown to be viable. The need for reassessment and change is increasingly recognized. The last decade in British politics has been marked by the end of the post-war consensus on the welfare state which, taken together with the economic crises of the same period, has provoked a greater readiness to re-examine the components of our welfare system than at any time since the 1940s. One major thrust in the ensuing debate has been to urge salvation by drastically reducing the scope of collective action and placing trust in free markets. But others have regarded such a response as illogical. The inefficiencies and wastefulness of the centralized welfare system do not of themselves invalidate the quest for human mastery of our social and economic environment in the attempt to build a more just and fulfilling society for everyone. The challenge is to learn from experience and to seek to create institutions which are more open, accessible, and responsive; to develop local policy-making processes and systems of service provision which encourage the involvement of workers and users, and act to create a culture of real social ownership – the ownership of decisions that matter.

A few years ago such words might have been dismissed as little more than sentimental rhetoric, so powerful was the grip of centralist ideology. Today, given the emergence of numerous community-orientated initiatives and their cumulative influence, the decentralist alternative can expect to be taken rather more seriously. In Britain, the development of locally focused services has not been confined to the personal social services but is strongly represented in housing (see e.g. Seabrook 1984; Power 1984; Boddy and Fudge 1984; Taylor 1986), policing (see e.g. Alderson 1979), and most recently community nursing (Cumberlege 1986). Some local authorities have aimed to move even further down the road towards local services and local control by integrating service management at the neighbour-hood level and seeking to set up neighbourhood forums which will share in their control (see e.g. Hambleton and Hoggett 1984; London Borough of Islington 1986). Nor can this movement towards decentralization be readily dismissed as some British quirk, a temporary deviation from the centralist road to be attributed to party-political power struggles. There is growing evidence that the trend is an international one (see e.g. Smith 1985; Hadley 1986), related to the contradictions emerging in the centralized welfare systems of many modern industrial states as disparate as Sweden and Poland, Israel and Quebec.

Community social work, therefore, should be seen not as some curious side-show in an otherwise bureaucratic world but as part of a much more widespread urge to find viable alter-natives to centralist, state-dominated systems. The challenge in the years ahead for practitioners who share this commitment will be to help shape and test such alternatives in a growing partnership with those they serve.

References

Alderson, J. (1979) *Policing Freedom*. London: Macdonald & Evans.

Audit Commission for Local Authorities in England and Wales (1985) *Managing Social Services for the Elderly More Effectively*. London: HMSO.

——— (1986) *Managing Social Work More Effectively*. London: HMSO.

Barclay, P. (Chairman) (1982) *Social Workers: Their Role and Tasks*. London: Bedford Square Press.

Barnes, M. (1984) The Aims of Decentralisation and Its Relationship with Planning. In *Policy Analysis and Evaluation*. London: PTRC Education and Research Services.

BASW (1985) *The Management of Child Abuse*. Report of a Project Group of the Professional Practice Division Committee of the Association. Birmingham: BASW Publications.

Bayley, M., Seyd, R., and Tennant, A. (1985) *Neighbourhood Services Project, Dinnington, Paper No. 12. The Final Report*. Sheffield: Department of Sociological Studies, University of Sheffield.

Beresford, P. (1984) *Patch in Perspective: Decentralising and Democratising Social Services*. London: Battersea Community Action.

Beresford, P. and Croft, S. (1986) *Whose Welfare: Private Care or Public Services?* Brighton: Lewis Cohen Urban Studies Centre, Brighton Polytechnic.

Blom-Cooper, L. (Chairman) (1986) *A Child in Trust: The Report of the Panel of Inquiry into the Circumstances Surrounding the Death of Jasmine Beckford*. London: The London Borough of Brent.

Boddy, M. and Fudge, C. (eds) (1984) *Local Socialism?* Hampshire: MacMillan.

Briar, S. (1976) The Current Crisis in Social Work. In G. Neil and H. Specht (eds) *The Emergence of Social Welfare and Social Work*. Itasca, Il.: Peacock.

Brown, G.W. and Harris, T. (1978) *Social Origins of Depression: A Study of Psychiatric Disorder in Women*. London: Tavistock Publications.

Brown, P., Hadley, R., and White, K. (1982) A Case for Neighbourhood-Based Social Work and Social Services. In P. Barclay, *Social Workers, Their Role and Tasks*. London: Bedford Square Press.

Butterworth, E. and Cole, I. (1985) 'The Scan Project: Final Report'. Unpublished report to the Home Office. York: Department of Social Policy, University of York.

Challis and Davies (1985) Long-Term Care for the Elderly: The Care Scheme. *British Journal of Social Work* 15:6.

Chambers, P. (1986) Paid Neighbours Improve Care for Frail Elderly.

Geriatric Medicine 16:11.
Cooper, M. (1980) Normanton: Interweaving Social Work and the Community. In R. Hadley and M. McGrath (eds) *Going Local: Neighbourhood Social Services*. London: Bedford Square Press.
Cumberlege, J. (1986) *Neighbourhood Nursing: A Focus For Care*. London: HMSO.
Currie, R. and Parrott, B. (1981) *A Unitary Approach to Social Work: Application in Practice*. Birmingham: BASW Publications.
Finch, J. (1984) Community Care: Developing Non-Sexist Alternatives. *Critical Social Policy* 9.
Fischer, J. (1976) *The Effectiveness of Social Casework*. Springfield, IL: Charles C. Thomas.
Freire, P. (1974) *Education: The Practice of Freedom*. London: Writers & Readers Publishing Cooperative.
Froland, C., Pancoast, D.L., Chapman, N.J., and Kimboko, P.J. (1981) *Helping Networks and Human Services*. Beverly Hills, Calif.: Sage.
Godbout, J. (1983) *La participation contre la démocratie*. Montréal: Editions Saint-Martin.
Goldstein, H. (1973) *Social Work Practice: A Unitary Approach*. Columbia, SC: University of South Carolina Press.
Guay, J. (1984) *L'Intervenant professionnel face à l'aide naturelle*. Chicoutini, Quebec: Gaetan Morin.
Guay, J. and Lapointe, Y. (1985) *Document d'initiation aux types d'intervention communautaire*. Quebec: Centre de Recherche sur les Services Communautaires, Université Laval.
Gyford, J. (1985) *The Politics of Local Socialism*. London: Allen & Unwin.
Hadley, R. (1986) Is Going Local Here to Stay? *Social Work Today*, 7 July, 1986.
Hadley, R. and Cooper, M. (eds) (1984) *Patch-Based Social Services Teams: Bulletin No. 3*. Lancaster: Department of Social Administration, University of Lancaster.
Hadley, R. and McGrath, M. (eds) (1980) *Going Local: Neighbourhood Social Services*. London: Bedford Square Press.
Hadley, R. and McGrath, M. (1984) *When Social Services Are Local: The Normanton Experience*. London: Allen & Unwin.
Hadley, R. and Scott, M. (1980) *Time to Give? Retired People as Volunteers*. Berkhamsted: The Volunteer Centre.
Hadley, R., Dale, P., and Sills, P. (1984) *Decentralising Social Services: A Model for Change*. London: Bedford Square Press.
Hambleton, R. and Hoggett, P. (eds) (1984) *The Politics of Decentralisation: Theory and Practice of a Radical Local Government Initiative*. Working Paper 46. Bristol: School of Advanced Urban Studies.
Handy, C.B. (1981) *Understanding Organisations*. 2nd edn. London: Penguin.
Henderson, P. and Thomas, D. (1980) *Skills in Neighbourhood Work*. London: Allen & Unwin.
Holman, R. (1983) *Resourceful Friends: Skills in Community Social Work*. London: The Children's Society.
Illich, I., Zola, I.K., McKnight, J., Caplan, J., and Shaiken, H. (1977) *Disabling Professions*. London: Marion Boyars.

Jenkin, P. (1983) Patch Systems and Social Services. In I. Sinclair and D. Thomas (eds) *Perspectives on Patch*. National Institute for Social Work, Paper No 14. London: National Institute for Social Work.

Kast, F.E. and Rosenzweig, J.E. (1981) *Organization and Management: A Systems and Contingency Approach*. Tokyo: McGraw Hill.

Kotter, J.P. (1982) *The General Manager*. New York: The Free Press.

Leat, D. (1983) *Getting to Know the Neighbours: a Pilot Study of the Elderly and Neighbourly Helping*. London: Policy Studies Institute.

Lee, T. (1971) Psychology and Architectural Determinism (Part 2). *The Architect's Journal*, 1 September, 1971.

Leissner, A. (1986) '. . . And what about the neighbours?' *Community Care*, 3 July, 1986.

Likert, R. (1967) *The Human Organization: Its Management and Value*. New York: McGraw Hill.

London Borough of Islington (1986) *Going Local: Decentralisation in Practice*. Papers for a public seminar, March, 1986. London: London Borough of Islington.

Miller, E.J. and Rice, A.K. (1967) *Systems of Organisation*. London: Tavistock Publications.

Mintzberg, H. (1973) *The Nature of Managerial Work*. New York: Harper & Row.

Mullen, D., Dumpson, J.R., and Associates (1972) *Evaluation of Social Intervention*. London: Jossey-Bass.

Mullender, A. and Ward, D. (1985) Towards an Alternative Model of Social Groupwork. *British Journal of Social Work* 15.

Payne, M. (1986) *Social Care in the Community*. London: MacMillan Education.

Peters, T.J. and Waterman, R.H. (1982) *In Search of Excellence: Lessons from America's Best-Run Companies*. New York: Harper & Row.

Phillips, D. (1981) *Do It Yourself Social Surveys: A Handbook For Beginners*. Polytechnic of North London Research Report No. 4. London: Polytechnic of North London.

Pincus, A. and Minahan, A. (1973) *Social Work Practice: Model and Method*. Itasca, Ill.: Peacock.

Pinker, R. (1982) An Alternative View, Appendix B. In P. Barclay, *Social Workers: Their Role and Tasks*. London: Bedford Square Press.

Power, A. (1984) *Local Housing Management: A Priority Estates Survey*. London: Department of the Environment.

Seabrook, J. (1984) *The Idea of Neighbourhood: What Local Politics Should Be About*. London: Pluto Press.

Seebohm, Sir Frederic (Chairman) (1968) *Report of the Committee on Local Authority and Allied Personal Social Services*, Cmnd 3703. London: HMSO.

Seed, P. (1973) *The Expansion of Social Work in Britain*. London: Routledge & Kegan Paul.

———— (1986) Caught in the Network. In *Community Care*, 23 January, 1986.

Seyd, R., Tennant, A., Bayley, M., and Parker, P. (1984) *Neighbourhood Services Project, Dinnington; Paper No. 8, Community Social Work*. Sheffield: Department of Sociological Studies, University of Sheffield.

Shields, R. and Webber, J. (1986) Hackney Lurches Local. *Community Development Journal*, 21 (2), April, 1986.

Simpson, D. (1980) Newham: The Docklands Project Team. In R. Hadley and M. McGrath (eds) *Going Local: Neighbourhood Social Services*. London: Bedford Square Press.

Sinclair, I. and Thomas, D. (eds) (1983) *Perspectives on Patch*. National Institute for Social Work Paper No. 14. London: National Institute for Social Work.

Smith, B.C. (1985) *Decentralisation: The Territorial Dimension of the State*. London: Allen & Unwin.

Specht, H. and Vickery, A. (1977) *Integrating Social Work Methods*. London: Allen & Unwin.

Taylor, M. (1986) For Whose Benefit? Decentralising Housing Services in Two Cities. *Community Development Journal*. 21:2.

Vickery, A. (1983) Going Patch: Implications for Practitioners and Trainers. In I. Sinclair and D.N. Thomas (eds) *Perspectives on Patch*. National Institute for Social Work Paper No. 14. London: National Institute for Social Work.

Warren, D.L. (1981) *Helping Networks: How People Cope with Problems in the Urban Community*. Notre Dame, Ind.: University of Notre Dame Press.

Whittaker, J.K. (1983) Mutual Helping in Human Service Practice. In J.K. Whittaker and J. Garbarino (eds) *Social Support Networks: Informal Helping in the Human Services*. New York: Aldine.

Willmott, P. (1986) *Social Networks, Informal Care and Public Policy*. London: Policy Studies Institute.

Wolfensberger, J. and Glenn, L. (1975) *PASS 3: Programme Analysis of Service Systems*, 3rd edn. Toronto: National Institute of Mental Retardation.

Yoder, J.A. (ed.) (1985) *Support Networks in a Caring Community*. Dordrecht: Martinus Nijhoff.

Young, K. (1985) The East Sussex Approach. In Hatch, S. (ed.) *Decentralisation and Care in the Community*. London: Policy Studies Institute.

Young, A.F. and Ashton, E.T. (1956) *British Social Work in the Nineteenth Century*. London: Routledge & Kegal Paul.

Younghusband, E. (1978) *Social Work in Britain 1950–75: A Follow-Up Study*. London: Allen & Unwin.

Name index

Subject index

Entries from Chapters 3–6 are prefixed, wherever relevant, by the letters A (Issue), B (Team Experience), C (Guideline), D (Departmental Guideline). See page 17 for an explanation of the use of these letters.

accessibility, 10, team boundaries, A 59, B 61, C 65; accepting referrals where they occur, B 77, C 80.

accountability: *see* evaluation.

administrative staff (*see also* staff in CSW teams): in contributing teams Huntly, 32; Normanton, 32; Longbenton, 35; Honor Oak, 37–8; Lochend, 41–2; Docklands, 45; Rye, 48; Whitehawk, 51; and referrals, B 77, C 79; involvement in CSW, 118, 141, 185–86; support for, C 81.

ancillary staff (*see also* staff in CSW teams): in contributing teams, 12, Huntly, 29; Normanton, 32; Longbenton, 35; Honor Oak, 37–8; Lochend, 41–2; Rye, 47–8; Whitehawk, 51;

women as, 21; taking referrals, B 76–7, C 79–80; delegated authority B 77–8; involvement in CSW, 118, 185–86; extending roles of, B 185–86; support for, C 81; conditions of service of, C 81;

approved social workers (ASWs) (*see also* mental illness): and CSW teams, B 169–70, D 178.

autonomy: identifying extent of team's, C 131–32; obtaining for integrative work, C 132; scope of team management's B 196, B 201, C 203, C 205; A 209; B 211–13; C 215–16; D 218–19.

Barclay Committee, 6
Barclay Report, 1, 7, 10, 115, 138.
Bexley Community Care Scheme, 226

examples in inter-agency work, B 126–31; 'safe' and 'unsafe' projects, B 201–02; management style and, B 198; in learning, C 231.

purposes of handbook: ix, 2, 22–3.

reception: facilities, A 72, B 73, C 75; open and closed methods of, A 72, B 74, C 77; speed and character of response, A 72, B 74, C 75–6; wider roles of receptionist, C 146.

records (*see also* referrals (formal)): importance of formal records, B 79; teams' own records systems, B 78–9, C 82; non-user related information, C 105; indirect work, C 133; on neighbourhood needs and resources, C 233.

referrals: who should take, A 76, B 76–7, C 79–80; where accepted, A 76, B 77, C 80; delegated authority for, A 76, B 77–8, C 80–1; informal (unrecorded) A 76, B 78–9, C 81–2; formal (recorded) A 76, B 79, C 81–2; speed of response to, B 74, C 75–6.

residential homes: client participation in, C 218.

residential staff: integration in teams, C 88; role as

community resource, B 141.

resource directories: C 233.

role flexibility: union attitudes to, 19; stretching traditional role in job descriptions, C 121; gaining union and professional support for, C 121–22; breaking down barriers between roles, C 174; authority policies and, A 182, B 183–84, C 188–89; social work roles and, A 182, B 184–85, C 180–91; non-social work roles and, A 182, B 185–86, C 191; staff feeling and, A 182, B 186–87, C 191–92; union reaction and, A 182, B 187–88, C 192.

schools: coterminous boundaries, B 62; liaison with, B 127, B 128, B 129, C 173.

Seebohm Report: 3, 31.

sheltered housing: B 129–31.

skills in CSW: developing in integrative activities, C 133; building out from traditional skills, A 139, B 139–41, C 145–51; informal style, A 139, B 141–42, C 151–53; integrating working methods, A 139, B 142–43, C 153–61; unitary approach, A 138, B 143,